Modern Library Chronicles

KAREN ARMSTRONG on Islam

DAVID BERLINSKI on mathematics

RICHARD BESSEL on Nazi Germany

ALAN BRINKLEY on the Great Depression

IAN BURUMA on modern Japan

PATRICK COLLINSON on the Reformation

JAMES DAVIDSON on the Golden Age of Athens

SEAMUS DEANE on the Irish

FELIPE FERNÁNDEZ-ARMESTO on the Americas

LAWRENCE M. FRIEDMAN on law in America

PAUL FUSSELL on World War II in Europe

JEFFREY GARTEN on globalization

MARTIN GILBERT on the Long War, 1914–1945

PETER GREEN on the Hellenistic Age

JAN T. GROSS on the fall of Communism

ALISTAIR HORNE on the age of Napoleon

PAUL JOHNSON on the Renaissance

FRANK KERMODE on the age of Shakespeare

JOEL KOTKIN on the city

HANS KÜNG on the Catholic Church

MARK KURLANSKY on nonviolence

EDWARD J. LARSON on the theory of evolution

BERNARD LEWIS on the Holy Land

FREDERIK LOGEVALL on the Vietnam War

MARK MAZOWER on the Balkans

JOHN MICKLETHWAIT and ADRIAN WOOLDRIDGE on the company

ROBERT MIDDLEKAUFF on the Gilded Age

PANKAJ MISHRA on the rise of modern India

PHILIP MORGAN on colonial America

ANTHONY PAGDEN on peoples and empires

RICHARD PIPES on Communism

COLIN RENFREW on prehistory

JOHN RUSSELL on the museum

CHRISTINE STANSELL on feminism

KEVIN STARR on California

ALEXANDER STILLE on Fascist Italy

CATHARINE R. STIMPSON on the university

NORMAN STONE on World War I

MICHAEL STÜRMER on the German Empire

MILTON VIORST on the Middle East

A. N. WILSON on London

ROBERT S. WISTRICH on the Holocaust

GORDON S. WOOD on the American Revolution

JAMES WOOD on the novel

THE CITY

JOEL KOTKIN

THE CITY

A GLOBAL HISTORY

A MODERN LIBRARY CHRONICLES BOOK

THE MODERN LIBRARY

NEW YORK

2005 Modern Library Edition

Copyright © 2005 by Joel Kotkin

Published in the United States by Modern Library,
an imprint of The Random House Publishing Group,
a division of Random House, Inc., New York.

MODERN LIBRARY and the TORCHBEARER Design are registered trademarks of
Random House, Inc.

LIBRARY OF CONGRESS CATALOGING-IN-PUBLICATION DATA
Kotkin, Joel.
The city: a global history / Joel Kotkin.
p. cm. — (Modern Library chronicles)
Includes bibliographical references and index.
ISBN 0-679-60336-0
1. Cities and towns—History.   2. Sociology, Urban.   3. Civilization.   I. Title.   II. Series.
HT111.K65 2005   307.76'09—dc22   2004058167

Printed in the United States of America on acid-free paper

Modern Library website address: www.modernlibrary.com

4 6 8 9 7 5

To my brother, Mark

ACKNOWLEDGMENTS

The writing of this book has been something like the intellectual equivalent of trench warfare. The scope has been so wide, and the need for information so pressing, that I have often felt overwhelmed by the work ahead and perturbed by the seemingly torturous pace of progress.

Such a grueling, albeit highly satisfying, experience would have been intolerable without the help and indulgence of many individuals. I first want to thank my agent, Melanie Jackson, and my publicist, Jackie Green, for their unwavering support. I also owe a great debt to my editors at Random House, first Scott Moyers and later Will Murphy, for their great editing and direction.

Editors at various newspapers and magazines have helped hone this effort. I am particularly grateful to editors of long acquaintance, especially Gary Spiecker at the *Los Angeles Times* and Steve Luxemburg and Zofia Smardz at *The Washington Post*. I also owe thanks to *The New York Times*'s Patrick J. Lyons; Barbara Phillips and Max Boot at *The Wall Street Journal;* and Ed Sussman at *Inc.* I would also like to express my special appreciation to Karl Zinsmeister at the *American Enterprise* for many wonderful opportunities, great conversations, and constant ecouragement.

I owe much to those who contributed most directly to this effort, my research assistants from the School of Public Policy at Pepperdine University, where I was a senior fellow until the summer of 2004. These include Heather Barbour, Joseph "Joe" Hummer, Mingjie "Carol" Li,

Cynthia Guerrero, and Sarah Priestnall, all of whom contributed significantly to this effort.

I am especially indebted to two assistants who, after graduation, continued to aid this effort. Erika Ozuna, now resident back home in McAllen, Texas, helped not only with general research, but mostly with that concerning her native Mexico. Reverend Karen Speicher not only did prodigious research, but also influenced the content, particularly in terms of the central role of religion. I also would like to extend my thanks to key Pepperdine personnel, especially former university president David Davenport, Sheryl Kelo, Brad Cheves, Britt Daino, Marie-Ann Thaler, and James Wilburn, as well as my colleague Michael Shires.

The research on cities also benefited from the support of the Milken Institute, notably Ross DeVol and Suzanne Trimbath, and most especially Perry Wong, who was kind enough to help me with the sections on Chinese history. I also feel a debt of gratitude to Ali Modarres, a professor at California State University at Los Angeles and an expert on Islamic cities. David Friedman, my good friend and intellectual partner, assisted with thinking on the book, most particularly in the sections dealing with Japan. In addition, I want to thank my colleague at the New America Foundation, Gregory Rodriguez, who offered his friendship as well as his understanding of Los Angeles and the impact of immigration. I should like to express my gratitude to Robert Carr, who cheerfully maintained and designed the electronic network without which this book could not have been written.

My understanding of Los Angeles was further enhanced by work I have conducted for the Economic Alliance of the San Fernando Valley with the assistance of Robert Scott, David Fleming, and Bruce Ackerman. In addition, I have been fortunate to work on projects with the Los Angeles Economic Development Corporation, particularly with Matt Toledo, Lee Harrington, and Jack Kyser. In the Inland Empire, I appreciate the opportunity to work with the La Jolla Institute and the Inland Empire Economic Partnership, in particular Steve PonTell and Terri Ooms. I have also learned a great deal about California and cities in general from Kevin Starr, now at the University of Southern California.

My understanding of other contemporary American cities was greatly assisted by my work in various locations. In many of these places, I have been assisted by my friend William Frey, a demographer working at the Brookings Institution and at the University of Michigan. John Kasarda at the Kenan Institute at the University of North Carolina also provided encouragement and timely comments as the manuscript was being prepared.

Speaking and work as a consultant has given me invaluable hands-on experience on the functioning of cities. I have been fortunate to learn much about the middle of America through my association with the Regional Chamber and Commerce Association of St. Louis, particularly in the persons of Dick Fleming, Robert Coy, and Debbie Frederick. Andrew Segal, David Wolff, and Mayor Bob Lanier of Houston also helped me to understand and appreciate the dynamics of that growing, vital Texas metropolis. My work with Delore Zimmerman, principal at CEO Praxis, has given me excellent insight into the dynamics of small cities in the Great Plains, while that with Leslie Parks has been invaluable in places such as San Jose and Portland, Oregon.

In New York, I have been fortunate to be a fellow at the Newman Institute at Baruch College, City University of New York, and to have many conversations with Henry Wollman, a prominent developer and director of the institute. Also in New York, I would like to extend my gratitude to the Center for an Urban Future, including Neil Kleiman, Jonathan Bowles, Kim Nauer, and Noemi Altman, colleagues on the center's 2004 study on the future of America's premier metropolis.

I was also helped in Europe, most particularly by Eduard Bomhoff and the city of Rotterdam, which sponsored a visit there to see and learn about that great port city. Geert Mak and Paul Brink in Amsterdam were essential guides to the essential precursor of the modern commercial metropolis. I further appreciate the assistance in understanding Montreal by my uncle (by marriage) Léon Graub and by numerous people in Paris, including my French in-laws.

In terms of Asia, I will always owe a debt to my Japanese sensei, the late Jiro Tokuyama, whose insights live with me even if he has gone into another realm. My friend Vincent Diau has been a constant source of information about new developments in China.

Perhaps no one was a greater aid in putting this book together than my friend and occasional coauthor Fred Siegel, professor of Urban History at Cooper Union in New York. Fred's knowledge of urban history, particularly in Europe and the United States, informed many of my reading decisions and, at times, challenged ideas that needed to be challenged.

It is to my family, who had to endure my endless complaining and occasional desk-pounding fits, that I owe the greatest debt. This includes my brother, Mark, to whom this book is dedicated, my sister-in-law, Pamela Putnam, and my remarkable mother, Loretta Kotkin. And most particularly to my greatest continuing inspiration, my beloved and ever patient wife, Mandy, my cherished daughters, the ever curious Ariel Shelley and the new addition to our California household, little Hannah Elisabeth. We expect to hear much more from those two young urbanites in the future.

CONTENTS

ACKNOWLEDGMENTS   IX

PREFACE   XV

INTRODUCTION: PLACES SACRED, SAFE, AND BUSY   XIX

CHRONOLOGY   XXIII

PART ONE

ORIGINS: THE RISE OF CITIES IN A GLOBAL CONTEXT

CHAPTER ONE: SACRED ORIGINS   3

CHAPTER TWO: PROJECTIONS OF POWER—THE RISE OF
   THE IMPERIAL CITY   9

CHAPTER THREE: THE FIRST COMMERCIAL CAPITALS   13

PART TWO

CLASSICAL CITIES IN EUROPE

CHAPTER FOUR: THE GREEK ACHIEVEMENT   19

CHAPTER FIVE: ROME—THE FIRST MEGACITY   27

CHAPTER SIX: THE ECLIPSE OF THE CLASSICAL CITY   35

PART THREE

THE ORIENTAL EPOCH

CHAPTER SEVEN: THE ISLAMIC ARCHIPELAGO   43

CHAPTER EIGHT: CITIES OF THE MIDDLE KINGDOM   52

CHAPTER NINE: OPPORTUNITY LOST   58

PART FOUR

WESTERN CITIES REASSERT THEIR PRIMACY

CHAPTER TEN: EUROPE'S URBAN RENAISSANCE   65

CHAPTER ELEVEN: CITIES OF MAMMON   75

PART FIVE

THE INDUSTRIAL CITY

CHAPTER TWELVE: THE ANGLO-AMERICAN URBAN REVOLUTION   85

CHAPTER THIRTEEN: INDUSTRIALISM AND ITS DISCONTENTS   97

PART SIX

THE MODERN METROPOLIS

CHAPTER FOURTEEN: THE SEARCH FOR A "BETTER CITY"   111

CHAPTER FIFTEEN: SUBURBIA TRIUMPHANT   117

CHAPTER SIXTEEN: THE POSTCOLONIAL DILEMMA   126

CHAPTER SEVENTEEN: "QUEENS OF THE FURTHER EAST"   137

CONCLUSION: THE URBAN FUTURE   147

NOTES   161

SUGGESTED READING   199

INDEX   207

PREFACE

The evolution of cities embodies the story of humanity as it rose from primitive origins to impose itself on the world. It also represents, as the French theologian Jacques Ellul once noted, man's fall from natural grace and the subsequent attempt to create a new, workable order.

"Cain has built a city," Ellul wrote. "For God's Eden he substitutes his own."[1] This striving to create a new kind of man-made environment occupied the original city builders from Mesoamerica to China, North Africa, India, and Mesopotamia. In the process, they forged a social and moral order transcending the old tribal and clan relationships that previously had shaped human relationships.

Two central themes have informed this history of cities. First is the universality of the urban experience, despite vast differences in race, climate, and location. This was true even before instant communication, global networks, and ease of transportation made the commonality among cities ever more obvious. As the French historian Fernand Braudel once noted, "A town is always a town, wherever it is located, in time as well as space."[2]

The sixteenth-century diary of Bernal Díaz, with which this book begins, reveals this in startling ways. A soldier with Cortés, Díaz encountered a totally alien urbanity—the great city of Tenochtitlán, now Mexico City—that still exhibited characteristics found in European cities such as Seville, Antwerp, or Constantinople.

Like a European metropolis, Tenochtitlán was anchored by a great religious center, a sacred space. It lay in a well-defended, secure location that allowed for an intense city life. The great Aztec capital also boasted large marketplaces that, while offering many strange and exotic goods, still functioned in much the same way as their counterparts in cities across the Atlantic.

These commonalities can be seen in cities across the world today. Police forces, commercial centers, and religious establishments in East Asia or East Anglia or the vast suburbs of Los Angeles often operate in similar ways, occupy the same critical places in the metropolis, and even share common architectural forms. Then there is the visceral "feel" of the city almost everywhere—the same quickening of pace on a busy street, an informal marketplace, or a freeway interchange, the need to create notable places, the sharing of a unique civic identity.

Many urban historians have identified this phenomenon with a particular kind of city—the densely settled, central urban area epitomized by New York, Chicago, London, Paris, or Tokyo. My definition is considerably broader and attempts to include as well many of the newer, sprawling metropolitan areas, such as my adopted hometown of Los Angeles, and also the many highly dispersed, multipolar metropolitan regions of the developing world. Although different in form from the "traditional" urban centers, these newer urban places all remain, in their essential characteristics, cities.

This leads to a second generalization about what characterizes successful cities. Since the earliest origins, urban areas have performed three separate critical functions—the creation of sacred space, the provision of basic security, and the host for a commercial market. Cities have possessed these characteristics to greater or lesser degrees. Generally speaking, a glaring weakness in these three aspects of urbanity has undermined life and led to their eventual decline.

Today, different cities in the world fulfill these functions with varying degrees of success. In the sprawling cities of the developing world, lack of a functioning economy and a stable political order loom as the most pressing problems. In many cases, people there still retain strong family ties and systems belief—whether ancient folk religions, Christianity, Islam, or Buddhism—but the basis of the material city has been undermined. This gives rise to a new historical phenomenon, the large city that grows without the familiar accrual of prosperity or power.

The essential problems facing urban regions in the West, and increasingly the developed parts of East and South Asia, are of a different nature. Cities in these regions are frequently relatively safe and, when their suburban rings are included, remarkably prosperous by historical standards. Yet these cities increasingly seem to lack a shared sense of sacred place, civic identity, or moral order.

Nothing better illustrates this than the rapid general decline in middle-class families in many of the world's most important urban cores. Today, elite cities often attract tourists, upper-class populations working in the highest end of business services, and those who can service their needs, as well as the nomadic young, many of whom later move on to other locales. This increasingly ephemeral city seems to place its highest values on such transient values as hipness, coolness, artfulness, and fashionability.

These characteristics, however appealing in their aspect, cannot substitute for the critical, longer-lasting bonds of family, faith, civic culture, and neighborhood. Nor can a narrow transactional or recreational economy play the same role as one based on a broad diversity of industries nurturing the ambitions of upwardly mobile families. Increasingly, these families seek refuge ever farther from the urban core, often in the periphery or in smaller towns outside the urban realm.

These phenomena do not represent as severe a challenge as the miserable poverty and instability common to the cities of the developing world. Yet the study of urban history also suggests that even affluent cities without moral cohesion or a sense of civic identity are doomed to decadence and decline. It is my hope that contemporary cities—wherever they are located—can still find ways to perform their historic functions and thus make this century, the first where a majority of people live in cities, an urban century not only in demographic terms but also in more transcendent values.

The reader may not fully agree with this analysis or many of my assertions. In some ways, that is not the critical issue. This book is designed primarily not as an analysis, but as a guide, luring the reader to explore further the fundamentals of the urban experience. Once introduced to this unfolding history, the reader will, I hope, more fully appreciate the complexity of the city experience that has so enriched my life and that of my family.

INTRODUCTION:

PLACES SACRED, SAFE, AND BUSY

On November 8, 1519, Bernal Díaz del Castillo saw a sight that would remain fixed in his memory for decades to come. The twenty-seven-year-old Spanish soldier[1] already had encountered signs of an ever intensifying urban civilization as he and his fewer than four hundred comrades marched from the humid lowlands of Mexico up into the volcanic highlands. And in a hint of what was to come, he noted "piles of human skulls," arranged in neat rows, atop the provincial temples.[2]

Then, suddenly, a city of almost unimaginable scale appeared, built high in the mountains on lakes crowned by a circle of volcanic peaks. He viewed broad causeways filled with canoes, and avenues upon which every kind of produce, fowl, and utensil was being sold. He saw elaborate flower-decked homes, large palaces, and temples rising bright in the Mexican sun:

> Gazing on such wonderful sights, we did not know what to do or say, or whether what appeared before us was real, for on one side, on the land, were great cities; and in the lake ever so many more, and the lake itself was crowded with canoes, and in the Causeway were many bridges at intervals, and in front of us stood the great City of Mexico. . . .[3]

The memory of "these sights"—penned forty years later by Bernal Díaz as an old man living in Guatemala—are like those that have inspired human beings ever since they began to construct great cities. Díaz's reaction could have been shared by a Semitic nomad first encountering the walls and pyramids of Sumer five thousand years earlier, a Chinese provincial official entering Loyang in the seventh century B.C., a Muslim pilgrim arriving by caravan to the gates of Baghdad in the ninth century, or an Italian peasant in the last century spying from a steamer the awesome towers of Manhattan island.

THE UNIVERSALITY OF THE URBAN EXPERIENCE

Humankind's greatest creation has always been its cities. They represent the ultimate handiwork of our imagination as a species, testifying to our ability to reshape the natural environment in the most profound and lasting ways. Indeed, today our cities can be seen from outer space.

Cities compress and unleash the creative urges of humanity. From the earliest beginnings, when only a tiny fraction of humans lived in cities, they have been the places that generated most of mankind's art, religion, culture, commerce, and technology. This evolution occurred most portentously in a handful of cities whose influence then spread to other centers through conquest, commerce, religion, and, more recently, mass telecommunications.

Over the five to seven millennia that humans have created cities, they have done so in myriad forms. Some started as little more than villages that, over time, grew together and developed mass. Others have reflected the conscious vision of a high priest, ruler, or business elite, following a general plan to fulfill some greater divine, political, or economic purpose.

Cities have been built in virtually every part of the world, from the highlands of Peru to the tip of southern Africa and the coasts of Australia. The oldest permanent urban footprints are believed to be in Mesopotamia, the land between the Tigris and Euphrates rivers. From those roots sprang a plethora of successive other metropolises that represent the founding experiences of the Western urban heritage—including Ur, Agade, Babylon, Nineveh, Memphis, Knossos, and Tyre.

Many other cities sprang up largely independent of these early Mesopotamian and Mediterranean settlements. Some of these, such as Mohenjo-daro and Harappa in India and Chang'an in China, achieved a scale and complexity equal to any of their Western contemporaries.[4] Indeed, for many centuries following the fall of Rome, these "Oriental" capitals were among the most advanced and complex urban systems on the planet. Rather than largely a Western phenomenon, with one set of roots, urbanism needs to be approached as having worn many different guises, though reflective of some greater universal human aspiration.

The primary locus of world-shaping cities in each region of the world has shifted over and over again. In the fifth century B.C., the Greek historian Herodotus noted the often rapid rise, and fall, of great places. As he traveled to cities both great and small, this incisive early observer noted:

> For most of those which were great once are small today; And those that used to be small were great in my own time. Knowing, therefore, that human prosperity never abides long in the same place, I shall pay attention to both alike.[5]

By Herodotus's time, some of the greatest and most populous cities of his past—Ur, Nineveh—had declined to insignificance, leaving little more than the dried bones of what had once been thriving urban organisms. Cities such as Babylon, Athens, and Syracuse were then in their glorious prime; within a few centuries, they would be supplanted by even greater cities, notably Alexandria and Rome.

The critical questions of Herodotus's time still remain: What makes cities great, and what leads to their gradual demise? As this book will argue, three critical factors have determined the overall health of cities— the sacredness of place, the ability to provide security and project power, and last, the animating role of commerce. Where these factors are present, urban culture flourishes. When these elements weaken, cities dissipate and eventually recede out of history.

THE SACREDNESS OF PLACE

Religious structures—temples, cathedrals, mosques, and pyramids— have long dominated the landscape and imagination of great cities. These buildings suggested that the city was also a sacred place, connected directly to divine forces controlling the world.

In our own, so much more secularly oriented times, cities seek to recreate the sense of sacred place through towering commercial buildings and evocative cultural structures. Such sights inspire a sense of civic patriotism or awe, albeit without the comforting suggestion of divine guidance. "A striking landscape," the historian Kevin Lynch suggested, "is the skeleton" in which city dwellers construct their "socially important myths."[6]

THE NEED FOR SECURITY

Defensive systems also have played a critical role in the ascendancy of cities. Cities must, first and foremost, be safe. Many cities, observed the historian Henri Pirenne, first arose as places of refuge from marauding nomads or from the general lawlessness that has characterized large portions of the globe throughout history. When a city's ability to guarantee safety has declined, as at the end of the western Roman Empire or during the crime-infested late twentieth century, urbanites have retreated to the hinterlands or migrated to another, safer urban bastion.[7]

THE ROLE OF COMMERCE

Yet sanctity and safety alone cannot create great cities. Priests, soldiers, and bureaucrats may provide the prerequisites for urban success, but they cannot themselves produce enough wealth to sustain large populations for a long period of time. This requires an active economy of artisans, merchants, working people, and, sadly, in many places throughout history until recent times, slaves. Such people, necessarily the vast majority of urbanites, have, since the advent of capitalism, emerged as the primary creators of the city itself.

CHRONOLOGY

B.C. ca. 25,000 *Homo sapiens* fully developed
      8000   Beginnings of animal husbandry and agriculture in Near
                  East
      7500–6800   Jericho settled
      7000   End of last Ice Age
      6000   Jericho builds walls and shows signs of administration
      4000   Food surpluses develop in Tigris-Euphrates Valley
      3500   First examples of writing found in Uruk, Mesopotamia
      3000   Start of Minoan civilization in Crete
      2600   Building of Great Pyramid at Cheops
      2500–2400   Regular trade develops between Sumer and Tilmun on
                  Persian Gulf
      ca. 2300   Sargon founds and rules Agade near Babylon, capital of
                  United Akkadian State
      2150   Emergence of Harappan cities in India
      2004   Fall of the last Sumerian dynasty
      2000   Opening of the Minoan age in Crete
      1960   Invasion of Semites shatters old Mesopotamian empires
      1900   Approximate date for birth of patriarch Abraham in
                  Mesopotamia
      1894   First Dynasty of Babylon under Samu-abum
      1792–1750   Hammurabi rules in Babylon
      1750   Emergence of Shang urban civilization in China
      1730   Hyskos invade and conquer Egypt
      1766   Approximate date for beginning of Shang dynasty
      1600   Rise of Mycenaean cities in Greece
      1400   Destruction of Knossos palace
      1400–1200   Golden age of Ugarit
      1200   Approximate time of Exodus of Israelites from Egypt
      1111   Approximate start of the Chou dynasty
      961–922   Solomon rules in Jerusalem
      814   Founding of Carthage

753	Legendary founding of Rome
600	Founding of Massilia, later Marseilles, by Greek colonists
592	Solon appointed to reconcile civil strife in Athens
587	Nebuchadnezzar re-captures Jerusalem
559–529	Reign of Cyrus the Great of Persia
515	Temple of Jerusalem restored
480–479	Persian invasion of Greece
475–221	"Warring States Period"
450	Establishment of the Law of Twelve Tables at Rome
431–404	Peloponnesian War undermines Greek city-states
338	Philip establishes hegemony over Greek city-states
332	Tyre falls to Alexander the Great
332	Founding of Alexandria
331	Alexander defeats Persian armies at Gaugamela
323	Death of Alexander
321	Chandragupta Maurya begins to build empire in India
221	Founding of Ch'in dynasty under Shih Huang-ti
168	Revolt of Jews against Seleucid Greeks
146	Carthage destroyed
100	Founding of Canton
63	Pompey conquers Jerusalem, defiles Temple
44	Assassination of Julius Caesar
31	Battle of Actium
A.D. 27	Founding date of Roman Empire under Augustus
54	Great fire of Rome under Nero
70	Destruction of Temple at Jerusalem
98	Trajan becomes first non-Italian emperor
161	Marcus Aurelius becomes emperor
220	Fall of Han dynasty
306	Constantine becomes emperor, makes Christianity state religion
324	Completion of original St. Peter's Basilica in Rome
326	Establishment of Constantinople as eastern capital of empire
395	Division of Roman Empire, as Byzantium emerges as center of the former Roman world
410	Alaric I the Visigoth sacks Rome
413	Augustine begins *The City of God*
421	Mythological founding date for Venice
476	Fall of Roman Empire in the West
500	Early construction of Japanese capital complexes

537	Completion of St. Sophia in Constantinople
570	Muhammad born in Mecca
581	Founding of Sui dynasty
618	Founding of Tang dynasty
622	Muhammad's *hijira* from Mecca to Medina
632	Death of Muhammad
635	Arabs occupy Damascus
637	Arabs capture Jerusalem
639–647	Arab conquest of Egypt; founding of Fustat, forerunner of Cairo
661	Caliphate moved to Damascus from Medina
690s	Arabic replaces Greek as primary language of administration
708	Founding of Nara
732	Charles Martel defeats Arabs at Poitiers
749	Caliphate moves to Baghdad
751	Arabs defeat Chinese army in Central Asia
794	New Japanese imperial capital at Heian (Kyoto)
800	Charlemagne crowned emperor in Rome
885–887	Paris successfully resists Norse invasion
960	Rise of Sung dynasty
968	Cairo founded
971	First customs house established in Canton
987	Hugh Capet elected king of France at Paris
1037	Building of St. Sophia in Kiev
1095	Beginning of First Crusade
1163	Beginning construction of Notre Dame Cathedral
1176	Beginning of wall and Citadel of Cairo under Saladin
1179	Philip Augustus becomes king of France, begins work on paving streets of Paris and building new walls
1192	Muslims, under King Muhammad, seize kingdom of Delhi
1204	Crusaders conquer Constantinople
1231	Genghis Khan seizes Peking
1250	Mamluks seize power in Egypt
1258	Notre Dame Cathedral completed in Paris
1258	Mongols capture Baghdad
1267–1293	Construction of Da Du, or Grand Capital, at the site of Beijing
1279	Mongol conquest of China completed
1291	End of the Crusades
1299	Mongols destroy Damascus

1300	Year for entrance into Inferno in Dante's *La divina commedia*
1303	Mongols defeated at Marj al-Saffrar
1325	Tenochtitlán founded
1325	Ibn Battuta starts his travels
1337	Start of Hundred Years' War between England and France
1347	Great plague wipes out half the population of Venice
1348	Great plague epidemic devastates Cairo
1368	Fall of Mongols and founding of Ming dynasty
1377	Ibn Khaldun finishes *The Muqaddimah*
1394	Seoul established as capital of Yi dynasty
1402–1424	Period of Yung Lo emperor, height of Ming foreign expansion
1421	Giovanni di Medici elected *gonfalonier* in Florence; first of his family to take power
1433–1434	Ming impose restrictions on foreign trade
1453	Constantinople falls to Ottoman Turks
1453	End of the Hundred Years' War between France and England
1486	Dante's *La divina commedia* published
1492	Columbus arrives in America
1492	Conquest of Granada; expulsion of Jews from Spain
1498	Vasco da Gama arrives in Calicut
1499	French seize Milan; the demise of Italian city-states
1506	Foundation stone for St. Peter's laid in Rome
1509	Portuguese fleet under Almeida defeats Muslim armada at Diu
1510	Portuguese seize Goa
1517	Mamluk dynasty falls; Ottomans seize Cairo
1519–1521	Conquest of Tenochtitlán
1520–1566	Reign of Süleyman
1522	Magellan's crew completes first circumnavigation of the globe
1533	Ivan the Terrible takes the Russian throne
1534	Portuguese take control of island of Bombay
1536	Britain imposes break with Rome
1561	Philip II moves court from Lisbon to Madrid
1563	Laying of foundation stone of Escorial
1571	Defeat of Turkish fleet at Lepanto
1572	Beginning of Great Revolt in the Netherlands against Spain
1576	The sack of Antwerp
1584	Toyotomi Hideyoshi moves into Osaka castle
1588	Defeat of Spanish Armada

1594	Henry IV of France converts to Catholicism
1600	Battle of Sekigahara ends in triumph of Tokugawa Ieyasu
1609	United Provinces sign treaty of peace with Spain
1615	Destruction of Osaka castle, last stronghold of Toyotomis
1624	Founding of New Amsterdam
1633	Tokugawa shoguns impose policy of "national seclusion" in Japan
1644	End of Ming dynasty
1664	British take over New Amsterdam; establish New York City
1665	British gain control of Bombay
1682	Louis XIV moves his court to Versailles
1689	Beginning of reign in Russia of Peter the Great
1690	Calcutta founded by Job Charnock, agent for British East India Company
1703	Founding of St. Petersburg
1764	Founding of St. Louis
1769	James Watt takes out patent for the steam engine
1772	Calcutta becomes capital of British India
1776	Publication of Adam Smith's *The Wealth of Nations*
1781	Founding of Los Angeles
1785	Tehran becomes capital of Persia
1788	Founding of Cincinnati
1789	French Revolution
1797	Napoleon destroys the Republic of Venice
1800	London passes the 1 million mark in population
1815	Defeat of Napoleon
1819	Founding of Singapore by Sir Stamford Raffles
1833	Founding of Chicago
1835	Passage of the Municipal Corporations Act in Britain
1841	Hong Kong ceded to Britain
1842	Treaty of Nanking opens Chinese ports and gives Hong Kong to Britain; first British concession opens in Shanghai
1844	Publication of *The Condition of the Working Class in England* by Friedrich Engels
1848	Passage of first Public Health Act by Parliament
1850	Beginning of Taiping rebellion
1851	British occupy Lagos
1851	Great Exhibition in London
1853	Commodore Perry enters Tokyo Bay
1853	Haussmann appointed prefect of Paris by Louis Napoleon
1854	Train service from Cairo to Alexandria opens

1857	Frederick Olmsted and Calvert Vaux win contest to design New York's Central Park
1860	Immediate suburbs incorporated into Paris
1861	British take over administration of Lagos to fight slave trade
1861	Czar Alexander II frees the serfs
1863	British take over customs collection in Shanghai
1867	Pullman Palace Car Company founded in Chicago
1867	Singapore becomes a colony of Britain
1868	Meiji Restoration in Japan
1869	Suez Canal opens
1871	Great Chicago fire
1871	Berlin proclaimed capital of German Empire
1872–1893	Founding of Chicago Public Library and University of Chicago, construction of Field Museum and Art Institute of Chicago
1876	Opening of Forest Park in St. Louis
1881	First appearance of word *downtown* in *Webster's Dictionary*
1883	Church of the Savior completed in Moscow
1888	Publishing of Edward Bellamy's *Looking Backward*
1895	Karl Lueger elected mayor of Vienna
1898	Consolidation of New York's five boroughs
1902	Publication of H. G. Wells's *Anticipations of the Reaction of Mechanical and Scientific Progress upon Human Life and Thought*
1902	Completion of Flatiron Building, New York City
1903	Construction of first "garden city" at Letchworth, England
1904	Opening of first part of New York subway
1905	First great Russian Revolution
1907	Publication of Dana Bartlett's *The Better City*
1908	Los Angeles enacts first comprehensive zoning ordinance in the United States
1910	Seoul occupied by Japan
1913	Los Angeles aqueduct completed
1917	Overthrow of czarist regime in St. Petersburg
1918	Russian capital moved to Moscow
1923	Great Kanto earthquake
1930	Publication of Sigmund Freud's *Civilization and Its Discontents*
1930	Presentation of Olmsted Plan for Los Angeles parks
1932	Construction begins on Moscow subway
1933	Church of the Savior demolished in Moscow
1935	Le Corbusier publishes *La Ville radieuse*

1936	Berlin Olympics
1939	Publication of Gottfried Feder's *Die nue Stadt*
1942	Opening of first large-scale public housing in Brooklyn, New York
1943	Abercrombie Plan announced for postwar London
1945	Division of Berlin
1946	Film *Tokyo in Twenty Years' Time* released
1947	Partition of India sparks mass urban migration
1947	Construction of Levittown, New York, begins
1949	Communist takeover of mainland China
1950–53	Korean War devastates Seoul
1951	Completion of Lerma aqueduct outside Mexico City
1953	Berlin riots
1960	Dedication of Brasília
1960	Nigeria gains independence
1961	Frantz Fanon publishes *The Wretched of the Earth*
1965	Singapore becomes independent
1965	Watts riots in Los Angeles
1966	Cultural Revolution begins, forcing urban dwellers out of China's cities
1968	Rioting in major American cities
1977	World Trade Center twin towers completed
1979	Islamic revolution in Iran
1979	Four Modernizations begin revitalization of China's urban economies
1988	Seoul Olympics
1990	Reunification of Berlin
1990	Pudong development outside Shanghai begins
1991	Leningrad renamed St. Petersburg
1991	Completion of Tokyo Metropolitan Government Building in Shinjuku, Japan's tallest
1992	Los Angeles riots
1993	Start of Santa Fe development outside Mexico City
1995	Bombay changes its name to Mumbai
2001	New York's twin towers destroyed by terrorists
2003	The majority of the world's population projected to be urban by 2007

PART ONE

ORIGINS:
THE RISE OF CITIES
IN A
GLOBAL CONTEXT

CHAPTER ONE

SACRED ORIGINS

Long before the first cities rose in Mexico, China, or Europe, the essential patterns of urban life evolved slowly in the Middle East. *Homo sapiens* is said to have achieved its present basic physical evolutionary form twenty-five thousand to forty thousand years ago and spread throughout virtually the entire habitable planet, including the Americas and Australia, by around 8000 B.C.[1]

With the end of the last Ice Age, stock breeding and agriculture spread and with them a more sedentary way of life. Small villages developed as centers of artisanal activities and trade. The most advanced, what might be called "proto-cities," appear to have developed most rapidly in a wide region that spread across the Syrian steppes, in Jericho, Iran, Egypt, and Turkey.[2]

MESOPOTAMIA

This region—extending from the west coast of Palestine to the Nile Valley in Egypt to the Tigris and Euphrates rivers—constitutes what is called the "Fertile Crescent." In the earliest period of recorded history, the farther one gets from this region, observed the German historian and archaeologist Werner Keller, "the deeper grows the darkness and signs of civilization and culture decrease. It is as if the people on the other continents were like children awaiting their awakening."[3]

The alluvial basin between the Tigris and Euphrates rivers, in contemporary Iraq, proved an ideal environment for a precipitous leap to urbanism. Here, in the area later known to the Greeks as Mesopotamia, the arid desert was broken by reedy swamps, with waters overflowing with fish, and banks teeming with wildlife. Here, too, sprouted native grains, wheat and barley, which could be cultivated into reliable crops, rewarding the Neolithic farmer with the critical surpluses upon which the beginnings of urban civilization depended.[4]

The early city builders also faced many critical challenges in this fecund environment.[5] Minerals, building stone, and timber were scarce. Rain was sporadic, and the rivers did not naturally, as in Egypt, inundate the large areas of dry land around them. As a result, the settlers in this region were forced to develop complex systems to irrigate their land.[6]

This huge effort required a moral and social order allowing for the intricate regulation of society and for a more dominating relationship toward nature, a major step away from the familial and clan relationships that had conditioned traditional village life for millennia. These earliest cities arose as the command posts for the carrying out of these functions. By modern or even classical standards, these urban agglomerations, the earliest of which can be traced as far back as 5000 B.C., were very small. Even by the third millennium, the powerful "metropolis" of Ur may have been no more than 150 acres and accommodated roughly twenty-four thousand people.[7]

The priestly class emerged as the primary organizers of the new urban order. It fell to them to articulate the divine principles placing man over nature, inculcate systems of worship, and regulate the activities of a large number of often unrelated people around complex communal tasks.

It is difficult, perhaps, to imagine in our current secular era the degree to which religion played a central role during most of urban history.[8] Like the Catholic Church, or Buddhist, Muslim, Aztec, and Hindu priesthoods later on, the Sumerian ecclesiastics provided these ancient urban centers with a critical sense of order and continuity. Priests set the calendars that determined times for work, worship, and feasting for the entire population.[9]

Given the primacy of the priestly class, it is not surprising that temples celebrating the gods dominated the earliest primitive "skyline." One of the earliest of these ziggurats, the shrine at Ur of Nannar, the Moon God, towered seventy feet over the flat Mesopotamian landscape.[10] The high temple, suggests Mircea Eliade, constituted a "cosmic mountain" connected directly to the cosmos.[11]

The temple dominated what might be called the "inner city" of early Sumerian urban civilization. Within this area's walls, the temple rose alongside the palace of the rulers and the homes of the principal citizens. These structures lent the whole district a sense of divine protection and security.[12]

The construction of these temples stimulated the commercial growth of early cities. In addition to slaves, ordinary workmen and skilled artisans participated in the construction of these first great structures, and many remained to service the needs of the priestly class. It was here as well, by roughly 3500 B.C., that the first recognizable systems of writing emerged, for both religious and commercial reasons.[13]

The priesthood held powerful sway over the material world. They controlled, on the gods' behalf, much of the land in the community. The "divine household" was in charge of maintaining the canals as well as the storage and distribution of the all-important agricultural surplus. *The Epic of Gilgamesh,* the origins of which go back to Sumerian times, speaks of the "sacred storehouse" that is the "seat of Ishtar, the Goddess."[14]

The temple also served as the first urban "shopping center," offering in an open setting a vast array of goods ranging from oils and fats to reeds, asphalt, mats, and stones. The temple even owned factories that manufactured garments and utensils.

Regimes and dynasties would come and go, but only catastrophic change would sweep away the religious institutions. The shrines of Ur, for example, were repeatedly restored by those who conquered the city. The hierarchy of gods or ways of worshipping might shift over time, but the centrality of the religious function remained for millennia.[15]

This pattern also persisted well past the heyday of the Sumerians. Virtually all the successor societies that emerged from the region—from the Babylonians and Assyrians to the Persians—envisioned their cities as essentially sacred places, with intimate ties to the divine. Babylon, the greatest of the Mesopotamian cities, was called Babi-ilani, or "the Gate of the Gods," the place from which the divinities were believed to have descended to earth.[16]

EGYPT

It is not clear whether or not Mesopotamia directly shaped the early Egyptian civilization, but the latter may well have been, as the historian Grahame Clark has noted, "fertilized from Sumerian seeds."[17] As in the early Mesopotamian cities, the first Egyptian conurbations rested economically on the critical agricultural surplus. The average Egpytian peasant produced, according to some estimates, three times as much food as he needed.[18]

But there were also many differences between these two early civilizations. In Egypt, control lay in the hands of the pharaoh, who claimed to be a god himself. The civil servants, rather than administering the irrigation and surplus economy for the benefit of the gods or a king, did so for an individual personifying both at the same time.[19] The intimate relationship between the civic identity and the priesthood, so critical in the evolution of Mesopotamian cities, was not nearly as pronounced.

For this, among other reasons, early Egypt does not serve us well as a primary focus on the origins of urbanism. Mesopotamian society revolved around city life and a permanent set of religious structures. Egyptian life centered around the royal court.[20] Administrators, priests, artisans, workmen, and their slaves identified themselves not with an urban place, but with the personage of the pharaoh. If the dynasty moved, as it sometimes did, so did the priesthood and the government.[21]

Of course, a civilization as great and as long-lasting as Egypt's still produced some significant cities. Thebes, for example, was praised in a hymn in the fifteenth century B.C.: "She is called city; all others are under her shadow, to magnify themselves through her."[22] In the world before the rise of cities such as Babylon, Egyptian cities had populations as large as, or even larger than, their Mesopotamian counterparts.[23]

Yet despite this, even great cities like Memphis or Thebes never assumed the independent identity, economic dynamism, and divine status associated with the various Sumerian urban centers. For one thing, Egypt's prolonged periods of universal order—in sharp contrast with unruly, fragmented Mesopotamia—did not promote the development of self-enclosed walled cities. Lack of competitive trade also slowed the development of a marketplace economy. Egypt would remain a civilization whose greatest achievement, the Pyramids, was constructed to house the dead, not provide an environment for the living. "Everything else in Egypt seemed to have found durable form," observed the urban historian Lewis Mumford, "except the city."[24]

INDIA AND CHINA

What Egypt did share with urban Mesopotamia was the religious focus of its civilization. Similarly, Harappa and Mohenjo-daro, constructed around 2500 B.C. in the present Pakistani provinces of Sind and Punjab, also placed monumental religious architecture at their core. As in Sumer, with which they maintained a trading relationship,[25] theocrats played a dominating role in the running of the city. Much of the worship seems to have been focused on the Mother Goddess, an important feature as well to the fertility cults of the Middle East.[26]

This religious orientation also applied to cities that had little or no direct connection with the Fertile Crescent. In China, around 1700 B.C., the Shang dynasty rulers placed temples at the center of their urban spaces. Priests or shamans played a critical role not only in divine matters, but in administration as well.

From the Shang as well we see the pattern of worship of ancestors that would play an important role[27] in the evolution of China's enduring and continuous model of urban civilization.[28] Religious devotion and practice was critical to the raising of mass conscriptions of peasant labor needed to build walls and city foundations. As an ancient Chinese poem has it:

> They set their plumb-lines vertical
> They lashed the boards to hold [the earth]
> And raised the Temple [of the Ancestors] on the cosmic pattern.[29]

Great cities throughout most of classical Chinese history would be dominated by adherence to the "cosmic pattern." Temples of the gods and ancestors, along with the palaces of the rulers, stood at the center of the city. Through propitiating these deities, the rulers hoped to regulate both the natural universe and the human one.[30]

THE AMERICAS

The primacy of the religious role was, if anything, even more striking in the earliest cities of the faraway Americas—places unlikely to have contact with either the Mesopotamian or the Chinese urban center. Like their counterparts in Mesopotamia and China, the first cities built in Mexico, Peru, and other early civilizations of the Americas also placed religious structures at the heart of their metropolitan centers.[31] Over a millennium before the rise of Tenochtitlán, Teotihuacán, a short drive from contemporary Mexico City, was home to over a hundred temples along its main avenue, the Street of the Dead.

To the south as well, among the Maya and in Peru, early cities center around temples, religious ceremonies, and regulations. On the northern highlands of Peru, the Chavin builders of the early first millennium B.C. constructed massive religious structures that represented both a major cultural advance and a foundation for future urban civilization on the west coast of South America.[32] Roughly two thousand years later, the Incas also built temples in the middle of their cities. Incan society rested on the notion that their rulers were gods and their capital, Cuzco, constituted "the navel of the world."[33]

Historians, amateur or otherwise, have tried to explain the similarities among the religious origins of ancient cities by insisting on some vague transmission of culture across vast distances. Perhaps a more fruitful approach would be to assume, as the American historian T. R. Fehrenbach notes, the existence of a "psychic unity" among early city builders in all parts of the world.[34]

CHAPTER TWO

PROJECTIONS OF POWER—
THE RISE OF THE IMPERIAL CITY

Without the notion of sacred space, it is doubtful cities could ever have developed anywhere in the world. Yet to grow beyond the city walls, urbanites needed to be able to settle, travel, and trade in territories beyond those controlled by a local lord, the gods, or their servants.

In Mesopotamia, a region that had long been dominated by a series of petty city-states, military conquest by one leader—and the shift of all power to one city—set the stage for the next critical phase of urban evolution. The earliest of these capital cities was established by Sargon, who around 2400 B.C. conquered the various city-states of Mesopotamia.

SARGON: THE CREATOR OF
THE IMPERIAL CITY

Sargon and other architects of the earliest imperial city were careful to build their legitimacy on the foundations and traditions of the earlier sacred places. Although the new rulers were Semites and not Sumerians, they maintained the old language for religious purposes, poetry, and mythological storytelling. In Mesopotamia, the tradition of respect for the old order by new conquerors persisted all the way through the Persian, Alexandrian, and Roman empires.[1]

As he bowed to the sacred past, Sargon initiated changes that would forever reshape the urban order. Wresting control of the economy from the priesthood, he allowed land now to pass into private ownership as opposed to merely the servants of the local god. The king was "chief entrepreneur" in charge of all the important irrigation canals, building construction, and commerce.[2]

Critically, Sargon broke with tradition by refusing to adopt one of the existing Sumerian cities as his capital. Instead he built a new imperial center at Agade, near the site that was to become Babylon. Unlike the original, physically constrained city-states, Sargon's new capital could draw on raw materials, finished goods, and masses of slaves from an empire that sprawled, at least briefly, to the shores of the Mediterranean.[3]

This first imperial capital, however, did not last long. Within four generations, the Sargonid Empire fell victim to nomadic invasions from the north. Eventually, venerable Ur was restored by a new dynasty as the principal city in the region. The new rulers did not return to the old temple-centered system, however, but instead retained many of the patterns of landownership and centralized control developed under Sargon and his successors.

BABYLON: THE FIRST URBAN COLOSSUS

By 1900 B.C., the focus of Mesopotamian power had shifted to a new capital at Babylon.[4] For the next 1,500 years, it would rank among the world's greatest cities, the incubator of an urban culture on a scale not before seen anywhere.[5]

Under the Babylonians, the stranglehold of religion over commerce was further weakened and trade encouraged over a wide array of cities.[6] This created a need for a system of laws that would be universally applicable to a wide variety of peoples from separate clans and different races.

The most famous laws, enacted by the Babylonian king Hammurabi, covered a wide range of criminal and civil situations. According to the prologue of his laws, Hammurabi had been ordered by the god Marduk to "make justice appear in the land, to destroy the evil and the wicked so that strong may not oppress the weak, to rise like the Sun-god over the black-headed one [humans] to give light to the land...."[7]

By Herodotus's time, Babylon had lost its place as the seat of empire but retained its status as a sacred place and center of learning; yet with a population estimated at 250,000, it remained a colossus, the world's largest urban area. Even under foreign rule, the city's great legacy inspired both respect and awe. With its vast population and stunning architecture, the Greek historian reported, the city still surpassed "in splendor any in the world."[8]

SECURITY AND URBAN COLLAPSE

The creation of empire, beginning with Sargon, allowed for the development of ever larger cities. The promise of security over a large expanse, even under such harsh rulers as the Assyrians, sparked an expansion of urban life and commerce. This occurred not only in the capital of Nineveh, the world's largest city in 650 B.C.,[9] but in many smaller urban settlements across the Assyrian Empire.[10]

This pattern repeated itself elsewhere in the ancient world. The Harappa urban civilization in India rested on the ability of cities to maintain order against invaders. Once nomadic raiders could penetrate the city walls, this early urban civilization collapsed. It would be many hundreds of years before large metropolitan centers would once again rise in the subcontinent.[11]

Similarly, the first great cities of the Americas—from the Olmecs and Maya in Central America to the pre-Incan civilizations in the Andes— flourished as centers of empires that provided the security critical to large-scale urban growth.[12] Under such a protective regime, Teotihuacán, in central Mexico, grew to a population of between fifty and eighty-five thousand from the fourth to the sixth centuries A.D. Yet an invasion by less civilized people from the north in 750 A.D. had left it largely deserted.[13]

CHINA: THE ENDURING URBAN ORDER

China arguably supplies the most enduring example of the imperial role in city building. A unique, indigenous urbanism in China had begun in the second millennium B.C., but for the most part, the early cities stood as relatively small ritual centers, with surrounding workshops for artisans servicing the court. The creation of the united empire under the Zhou around 1110 B.C. sparked the first development of large walled towns; indeed, the character for wall and city was identical.[14]

The Zhou dynasty and its successors the Han and the Tang devised a pattern of centralized control unparalleled in its duration and thoroughness.[15] For over a millennium, the capital cities of Loyang, Chang'an, and Kaifeng consistently ranked among the world's largest. Shifts in relative importance depended largely on the location of the ruling dynasts.[16] "It is the sovereign alone who establishes the capital," states the Confucian classic *Zhou Li.* Other cities, whether large administrative centers or the local government unit, or *hsien,* derived their importance largely from their role as administrative centers for a portion of the empire.[17]

In ensuing centuries, other neighboring Asian countries adopted the Chinese model of urbanism. Japan's first major centers—Naniwa, Fujiwara, and Nara—consciously borrowed from the Chinese city-empire of Chang'an.[18] In A.D. 794, the Japanese constructed a new, and more permanent, capital city at Heian, or Kyoto, which grew to be home to over one hundred thousand residents and served for over a millennium as essentially a ceremonial capital centered around the household of the emperor.[19]

Similarly, Seoul, established as the capital of the Yi dynasty in A.D. 1394, served, in the words of two Korean historians, as a "pastoral mandarin capital" for roughly five hundred years. Following the classical Chinese model, the city was laid out as an administrative center, surrounded by walls and dominated by the royal bureaucracy.

CHAPTER THREE

THE FIRST COMMERCIAL CAPITALS

The development of imperial cities with control over large areas allowed for the rapid growth of trade in all areas of early urban growth, from China to Egypt, Mesopotamia, and eventually the Americas. Despite this, the overall role of merchants and artisans in urban society remained sharply circumscribed.

Today, the entrepreneurial class is often assumed to be the critical, if not the dominant, shaper of a vital urban area. Yet in the ancient world, even when merchants and artisans accumulated considerable wealth, power remained concentrated in the hands of priests, soldiers, and bureaucrats. Often merchants served simply as middlemen, implementing the trade initiatives of the state or the priesthood. In Egypt, one historian notes, the pharaoh stood as "the only wholesale merchant."[1]

In China, urban merchants used their wealth to scale the rigid barriers of class, seeking ways for themselves or their children to enter the government class or the aristocracy. Even the layout of the Chinese city reflected the priorities of the society: The ruler's palace lay in the middle of the metropolis, while the markets were placed in far less auspicious and peripheral locations.[2]

THE RISE OF PHOENICIA

The search for the origins of the commercial metropolis—so important to the later development of urbanism—leads us away from the great city-empires and instead to a narrow strip of land between the coastal mountains and the Mediterranean.

The climate in the area that would later become known as Phoenicia was particularly amenable to human settlement. As an Arab poet would write, it "carried winter on its head, spring on its shoulders whilst summer slumbers at its feet."[3] Early port cities, such as Ugarit north along the Syrian coast, developed as trade centers for empires of the Hittites and Egyptians as early as the middle centuries of the second millennium B.C.[4]

At a time when almost all other city dwellers feared the open sea, Phoenician traders scoured a vast extent of the known world. Their black ships explored everywhere from the far western coast of Africa to Sardinia, Cyprus, Spain, and even Great Britain.[5] Although the main Phoenician cities such as Tyre or Sidon never grew much larger than forty thousand people—a fraction of the size of Babylon[6]—they arguably spread their influence over a wider array of places than any civilization up to that time.

Unlike the great empires, the Phoenicians never expanded deeply into the interior. Clinging to the coastline, they instead developed an urban life based predominantly on trading goods, and sometimes services, to their more powerful neighbors.[7] The Phoenicians' genius lay in making themselves indispensable, preferably at a healthy profit.

"WHOSE MERCHANTS ARE PRINCES"

By the ninth and eighth centuries B.C., Phoenician cities such as Bylbos (a key port for the Lebanese cedar trade), Tyre, and Sidon had become wealthy and powerful in their own right. Here, for the first time, we see the emergence of an influential, even dominant, merchant class. Tyre, wrote Isaiah, was "the crowning city, whose merchants are princes and whose traffickers are the honorable of the earth."[8]

Phoenician contributions extended well beyond their role as traders in goods. In a way later seen in such cities as Venice, Amsterdam, and Osaka, they also developed skills as artisans and craftsmen. Phoenicians fashioned glass, jewelry, garments, and other adornments worn from the wilds of Spain to the already ancient cities of Sumeria. Homer, in *The Iliad*, speaks of Paris clothing Helen in "the bright robes woven by the women of Sidon."[9] One particularly important industry grew from their mastery of the complex formula for extracting purple dye from the glands of a sea snail found on their beaches. It was from this dye, *phonikes* ("red" or "purple" in Greek) that the region derived its name.[10]

Phoenician cities also exported their expertise. They were the designers of beautiful urban places, palaces, and temples around the ancient world, including Solomon's Temple at Jerusalem.[11]

The Phoenicians' greatest cultural contribution—the alphabet—also derived from the demands of commerce. Phoenician merchants and artisans learned from the Mesopotamians and Egyptians the value of writing as a way to keep accounts and lay down laws. Starting around 1100 B.C., these practical urbanites devised a system that was both simpler and more accessible than the old hieroglyphs. This system of writing became the basis for the Greek and then the Latin alphabets.[12]

As befitted talented entrepreneurs, the Phoenicians appreciated their own value. They were quick to remind their customers that they would do their bidding for profit, not out of compulsion. When the pharaoh sent a mission to procure wood for a sacred vessel for the god Amon, the king of Bylbos rudely reminded the Egyptian representative: "Nor am I the servant of him that sent thee."[13]

THE ROOTS OF PHOENICIAN DECLINE

Like the Greek city-states that would inherit their commercial empire, or the Italian cities of the Renaissance two millennia later, each Phoenician city was covetous of its own independence. Cities were run, for the most part, by mercantile interests whose primary concern was expanding trade.

The civic parochialism of the mercantile elite served to limit the Phoenicians as empire builders. When their traders founded permanent outposts far from their native land, their tendency was to build a new, independent city.

Carthage in North Africa was the greatest of these colonies. Tradition has it that Carthage was founded in 814 B.C. by natives of Tyre. Known as Quat-Hadasht, or "New Town," it served as a base for the expanding Phoenician trade with the lands rimming the western Mediterranean. Gradually, the burgeoning trade center's influence was felt from the Atlantic coast of Spain all the way north to Cornwall and, by some accounts, the coast of Guinea.[14]

By the fifth century B.C., Carthage's population surpassed that of Tyre and Sidon combined. It was now among the powerful states in the Mediterranean, with an impressive fleet and a series of alliances with various regional powers, including the Etruscans in Italy. Other Phoenician outposts in the west looked to Carthage for leadership and protection against opposing city-states, largely those established by the Greeks.[15]

This shift in allegiances away from the home cities undermined Phoenicia itself. Without the help of their progeny, the old cities could no longer stave off assaults from the increasingly aggressive Assyrian, Babylonian, and Persian empires. Eventually, the cities lost both their independence and their place as the primary trading hubs of the ancient Mediterranean. The Phoenician "golden age" was coming to an end.[16]

In time Carthage, too, would succumb to the limitations inherent in a purely commercial city in ancient times. Proud bearers of Phoenician cultural and political values, the Carthaginians—whose number reached a peak of between 150,000 and 400,000[17]—operated a system of government scaled for a city-state, with elected consuls, or *suffetes,* a senate, and a general assembly. This constitutional format was usually dominated by the commercial aristocracy. Slaves and servants did the dirty work, soldiers and sailors fought, priests propitiated, but the wealthy ruled.[18]

As was true with their Phoenician forebears, Carthage's stubbornly commercial character contributed to its fall. It lacked any broader sense of mission or rationale for expansion other than profit. Even as they maintained ties to other colonies, the Carthaginians did not seek to incorporate into a coherent empire. They remained, first and foremost, a nation run by business interests.[19]

In the world of antiquity, a metropolis designed for business was no match ultimately for a city built for conquest. An ideology based on profit and narrow self-interest could not stand up to the imperial vision that would dominate urban history until the dawn of the modern era.

PART TWO

CLASSICAL CITIES
IN EUROPE

CHAPTER FOUR

THE GREEK ACHIEVEMENT

During the earliest period of urban history, Europe was a backwater, home to primitive, fiercely contentious people. The earliest evidence of cities close to Europe was in Crete, an island off the Greek mainland. Here the long-oared ship served to bring critical trade goods, notably olive oil and tin, the latter needed to make bronze implements and weapons. Enriched by this commerce and by ideas brought from Egypt and Mesopotamia, a distinct urban culture emerged here.[1]

CRETE

Like many Near Eastern civilizations, the Cretans worshipped the Earth Mother as a principal deity, but their cities expressed a new kind of spirit, one that later would help define the classical urbanity of Europe. The island's principal city, Knossos, was home to both a vibrant commercial culture and a highly naturalistic art. Secure in their island redoubt, the city's light, airy houses stood in stark contrast with the darker, more somber domiciles common in the Near East.[2]

Crete awakened the Greek mainland to the possibilities of urban civilization. The rough adventurers of archaic Greece now experienced the comfort and affluence of a successful trading city.[3] By the sixteenth century B.C., Crete's power was fading, likely the result of natural disasters and invasions from hardier, more warlike people from the Greek main-land.[4]

MYCENAE: GREEK PRECURSOR

Building on the accomplishments of Crete, the first builders of major cities in Europe, the Mycenaeans, displayed many of the basic patterns that would characterize Hellenic urbanism for the next millennium. War-like and contentious, they fought with one another and with foreign peoples throughout the eastern Mediterranean; the most celebrated conflict of this time stemmed from the war with Troy, as described by Homer in *The Iliad.*

Their contentious spirit also was a reflection of the country's environment. The rocky country of Greece, with its chains of mountains and compact valleys, promoted political fragmentation and discouraged the creation of sprawling city-empires. Generally the sea provided the only convenient avenue of expansion. Early cities such as Athens and Thebes began to colonize surrounding islands, including Cyprus, Melos, and Rhodes. Trade took them even farther out, as suggested by the tale of Jason and the Argonauts, to the forbidding reaches of Europe, all the way to Jutland, in present-day Denmark, where precious amber was pro-cured.[5]

THE CLASSICAL POLIS

In the twelfth century B.C., barbarous, warlike nomadic invaders de-stroyed most major Greek settlements, including Mycenae itself. Trade collapsed, cities were abandoned, and a dark age ensued. It took four cen-turies for Greek urbanism once again to flourish. True to the past pat-terns, Greece remained an archipelago of small city-states, tiny countries anchored around an urban core and its surrounding hinterland. Compe-tition between each city, or polis, was intense, expressed not only in con-ventional warfare, but in vying over foreign markets, skilled labor, the arts, and even in athletic contests. As Plato would later observe: "Every city is in a natural state of war with every other, not indeed proclaimed by heralds, but everlasting."[6]

Driven by this competitive spirit, the Greeks created a highly indi-vidualistic intellectual culture encompassing art, sculpture, and drama that to this day defines much of the Western urban ideal. They incubated an aggressively urban consciousness that would resonate with city dwellers for centuries to come. Socrates expressed this new sensibility when he remarked: "The country places and the trees don't teach me anything, and the people in the city do."[7]

Unlike philosophers elsewhere, focused on divinity and the natural world, Greek thinkers pondered the role of citizens in guaranteeing the health of the *koinonia*, or community.[8] Citizens, Aristotle noted, were like hands on the deck of a ship. Their duty was to assure "the preservation of the ship in its voyage. . . ."[9] In Athens, this led to an even more radical notion—that, as the Athenian legislator Solon would remark, citizens should, by right, be "the masters of the state."[10]

This ideal was made practicable by the relatively small size of Greek cities. In the fifth century B.C., no Greek city, with the exception of Athens, was home to more than 150,000 inhabitants. And only a fraction of the residents in any city were citizens. Even Athens, the largest, never had more than 45,000 citizens[11] out of a total population of 275,000.[12]

Unlike the Phoenicians, the Greeks traditionally had little respect for commerce. Hermes, the god of thieves, performed simultaneously as the god of merchants. Craftsmen, whose works we still admire today, fared little better. Their minds, Plato complained, were "as cramped and crushed by their mechanical lives as their bodies are crushed by the manual crafts."[13] Nor was the status of women particularly elevated. Greek romantic idealism worshipped (if anything) not love between men and women, but friendship as well as homosexual relationships between men.[14]

Everyday life in cities such as Athens must have been, even for most citizens, mean, dirty, and uncomfortable. In the shadow of great buildings like the Parthenon, houses were small, alleys narrow and filled with every kind of vermin. "The city is dry and ill-supplied with water. The streets are nothing but old lanes," wrote one shocked visitor. "The houses [are] mean with few better ones among them." Not surprisingly, pestilence was a constant fear. Intermittently, plagues would sweep through the city, killing far more Athenians than armed conflict; one epidemic in 430–428 B.C., according to Thucydides, carried off a quarter of the Athenian armed forces.[15]

THE GREEK DIASPORA

Given the harsh conditions at home, it was natural for Greeks to seek a better life elsewhere. In contrast with the environs around Babylon or even the Phoenician city-states, the country surrounding the Greek city-states was generally unproductive; the overgrazed and depleted Greek countryside was increasingly incapable of supporting the growing population. To bring in new sources of food and raw materials, Greek cities planted colonies from the west coast of Asia Minor (present-day Turkey) to Sicily and southern Italy. By 600 B.C., the Greek influence had reached the Gallic coast at Massilia, modern-day Marseilles, and as far as the Catalonian coast.[16]

At one time the Greeks had looked down on the mercantile-minded Phoenicians, but necessity forced them to outdo them as traders. The change could be felt in the heart of the Greek cities. The agora, once simply a place of assembly, had evolved by the fifth century B.C.—to the dismay of some philosophers and aristocrats—into a large, boisterous, and increasingly complex marketplace.[17] The great Persian king Cyrus, Herodotus tells us, described the typical Greek agora as "a meeting place in the middle of their city where they gather together, swear oaths, and deceive each other."[18]

Greek expansion depended not so much on market savvy as on brute force, particularly naval power.[19] For a moment, Athens under Pericles possessed the military might to siphon off foreign wealth to initiate massive building programs and still subsidize the incomes of much of the citizenry. "Because of the greatness of our city," Pericles boasted, "the fruits of the entire earth flow to us."[20]

In the process, the Greeks promoted a rapid expansion of the urban frontier from present-day Messina in Sicily to Marseilles, Nice, Monaco, and Byzantium on the Bosporus, later to grow into the great capital Constantinople. Greek city-states provided a model for these new towns, each of which developed its own agora, theater, and temple.

Some colonies grew to be large cities themselves. Syracuse, initially a colony of Corinth, eventually became many times larger and far more powerful than its early founding polis. Under the rule of Dionysius I, it emerged the largest city in Europe, controlling most of Sicily and parts of southern Italy. Another important new city, Rhodes, founded in 408 B.C., was a model of classical planning, with broad avenues, drains, and a well-placed harbor.[21]

THE TWILIGHT OF THE CITY-STATES

These achievements ultimately could not protect the Greek city-states from the threat posed by larger, well-organized empires. Like the Phoenicians, they never developed an overarching ideology or governmental structure allowing for a stable confederation among themselves. Dismissive of other races as inherently inferior, they evidenced a profound difficulty relating to people of different cultures.

No matter how fearsome in war, these parochial cities were not well suited to fend off empires that had evolved more tolerant and expansive governing systems. The founder of the Persian Empire, Cyrus the Great, possessed a remarkably cosmopolitan vision. Rather than annihilate or enslave his opponents, Cyrus envisioned a multinational empire where foreign cultures were to be respected and preserved, albeit under Persian supervision.

This policy worked remarkably well, even among those Greek city-states conquered by the Persians. Many, particularly the merchants along the Ionian coast, welcomed the security and greater access to markets created by an alliance with a wider empire.[22] The expansion failed only when Persia tried to assault Greece itself. Threatened with the loss of their traditional independence, the Greek city-states under Athenian leadership expelled the multinational Asian foe in 480 B.C. in Salamis, one of the landmark battles of European history.

But even such a heroic victory could not unite the quarrelsome city-states. Shortly after defeating the Persians, they returned to fighting among themselves, sometimes spurred on by the subtle diplomacy and gold of the Persians. By the end of the Peloponnesian War in the later part of the fifth century B.C., Athens was defeated by a Sparta-led coalition of cities. Thousands of slaves and many *metics,* foreign residents critical in several of the trades, fled the city. Reeling from the disaster, Athens became increasingly repressive, executing or exiling many of its greatest minds and persecuting the economically critical *metics.* Although democracy was restored by the end of the century, the era of leadership by the Greek city-states in the ancient world was over.[23]

ALEXANDER AND THE HELLENISTIC CITY

The final blow fell not from the Asiatic east, but from the rough-hewn north. In 338 B.C., armies of the obscure northern kingdom of Macedonia, under King Philip, overwhelmed the last resistance of the city-states.

The Greeks could take solace in the fact that Philip's son and successor, Alexander, was a student of Aristotle and an avid admirer of Greek culture. But Alexander was hardly an uncritical follower of Greek practices. Having seen the failures of the Greek cities, Alexander fostered an imperial vision closer to that of the Persian Cyrus. In a way irritating to both Macedonians and Greeks, Alexander sought to create not an empire of conquered peoples, but a commonwealth of races. Once he decisively defeated the Persians, he quickly co-opted their officials and integrated a large part of their infantry into his expanding army.

Alexander's vision of a cosmopolitan world empire posed a lethal threat to the independence of the city-states. When the ancient city of Thebes rebelled against the Macedonians, this normally enlightened conqueror burned it to the ground and sold the inhabitants into slavery.[24] The remaining Greek city-states, including Athens, never again emerged as powerful independent entities.[25]

ALEXANDRIA: THE FIRST GREAT COSMOPOLIS

Alexander exported Hellenic urban and commercial culture beyond its previous spheres of influence, even into India itself. The economic impacts were dramatic. The widespread diffusion of coinage minted by Alexander and his successors provoked an explosion in transnational trade,[26] among whose primary beneficiaries were former Greek colonies such as Rhodes and Syracuse.[27]

Alexander's greatest urban legacy, however, lay in the new cities he and his successors founded. Antioch, Seleucia, and most notably Alexandria employed rational planning principles on a scale rarely seen in older Greek cities. Starting from scratch, each city was designed with a proper agora, temple, and government buildings. Here we see the systematic, planned development of large-scale public works.[28]

Alexandria in Egypt was the greatest of these new cities. Built around the site of the tiny fishing village of Rhacotis, Alexandria was designed as

an entrepôt for trade between Africa, the Near East, and the Mediterranean world. Its construction reflected a conscious plan to replace
Phoenician Tyre, which Alexander himself had destroyed after a long
siege, as the trading center of the eastern Mediterranean.

This ambitious vision required first the construction of a huge new
harbor. Later, the Ptolemies, the Macedonian Greek family that took over
Egypt after Alexander's death in 323 B.C., constructed a massive light-
house on Pharos island to guide ships safely into the harbor. Alexandria
was graced with elegant parks and contained buildings—notably the museum and library—that also made it the intellectual center of the Mediterranean world. The more practical aspects of city planning were also
not ignored; the avenues were wide, the streets cleaner, and the sanitation
systems more reliable. Unusual for the time, much of the city was built of
stone to protect it from fire.[29]

Alexandria quickly fulfilled its founder's purpose. Fleets based in the
city traded with customers as far away as India and the horn of Africa.
Ptolemaic bureaucrats supervised a complex command economy that
took censuses, registered cargo holds, and restricted imports to spur domestic industry. The regime also pushed the productivity of Egypt's famous fertile agriculture—barley, wheat, and papyrus—to unprecedented
levels.[30]

These cities also represented a critical breakthrough in terms of gender. Women gained new property rights. Some even achieved political
power, as evidenced by the careers of several queens, including the famous Cleopatra VII, who would also be Egypt's last Greek ruler. In Hellenistic cities, notably Alexandria, and in Greek-dominated southern
Italy, female poets, architects, and even students of philosophy rose to
prominence.

In the new urban milieu, large colonies of Jews, Greeks, Egyptians,
and Babylonians coexisted, if not always cordially. Alexandria was particularly notable in this sense, becoming, in the words of the historian
Michael Grant, "the first and greatest universal city, the supreme Hellenistic melting pot."[31]

The cosmopolitan atmosphere spurred rapid cultural and scientific
development. Egyptian, Jewish, Persian, Babylonian, and other cultures
benefited from exposure to the Greeks; the Greeks, meanwhile, acquired
the Babylonian knowledge of the planets, the literature of pharaonic

Egypt, and from the Septuagint, the translation into Greek of the He-brew Bible, exposure to the ancient Mosaic texts.

UNRAVELING OF ALEXANDER'S VISION

This great cosmopolitan experiment began to unravel barely a century after Alexander's death. Increasingly, Greek rulers and settlers, who ac-counted for no more than 10 percent of the total population in the new Hellenistic kingdoms, refused to share power and prestige with the races among whom they had settled.

By the second century, many Egyptians and Persians chafed against their growing marginalization, sometimes taking the form of insurrection against Greek rule.[32] In Judea, local religious partisans revolted against at-tempts by the Seleucid Greeks to impose pagan worship on the small but stubbornly independent-minded populace. In 168 B.C., the Jews success-fully broke away from Greek rule, reestablishing their own independent state.[33]

Even in Alexandria, conflicts among Greeks, Jews, and native Egyp-tians worsened. Corruption and palace intrigue increasingly undercut economic progress and weakened the authority of the rulers. Less than two centuries after Alexander's conquest, his Mesopotamian possessions fell to the Parthians. The Greek Indian colonies dropped even more quickly outside the orbit of the Hellenistic world.[34]

CHAPTER FIVE

ROME—THE FIRST MEGACITY

Titus Petronius, the son of wealthy Romans and courtier to Emperor Nero, spent his time carousing through the back alleys of the city's streets, dallying with the prostitutes and loose aristocratic ladies with equal enthusiasm. Later forced to commit suicide because of his alleged complicity in a palace intrigue, Petronius left behind remarkable descriptions and insights into this city and the empire that it had created.[1]

By his time, Rome had grown to a scale not to be seen again till modern times—a massive, sprawling capital city, a warren of marketplaces, drinking places, temples, crowded tenements, and aristocratic villas. In Petronius's Rome, we transcend the bounds of antiquity and move closer to contemporary New York City, Tokyo, London, Los Angeles, Shanghai, or Mexico City. With a population of more than 1 million, Rome was two to three times larger than early giant cities such as Babylon.[2] Like later urban leviathans, noted Lewis Mumford, Rome suffered from what he called "megalopolitan elephantiasis," a total loss of human scale.[3]

Yet to their everlasting credit, the Romans created the legal, economic, and engineering structures that allowed this leviathan to function as the nerve center of the world for roughly half a millennium. At its height, this greatest of city-empires ruled an expanse stretching from Britain to Mesopotamia and contained as many as 50 million people.[4]

"THE VICTORIOUS ROMANS"

How had the Romans managed this bold step into the urban future? In many ways, they did so by fusing the two great building blocks of ancient cities, religious conviction and organized military power. The Romans were unshakable in their presumption of greatness and relentless in their pursuit of empire. As Petronius noted:

> The entire world was in the hands of the victorious Romans.
> They possessed the earth and the seas and the double field
> of stars, and were not satisfied.[5]

Rome's great power did not lie with its geography or natural endowment. The Tiber, which flows through the city, does not rank as a great river alongside the Tigris, the Euphrates, or the Nile. True, the city's heart enjoyed the protection of its seven hills, and its inland location provided a shield from sea invasion. But certainly these presented only a modest barrier to a determined and accomplished conqueror.

Rome enjoyed some basic economic assets, but nothing more than many other towns. The mild climate and decent soil supported a small community of shepherds and farmers. The city lay close to a point where the Tiber is most easily crossed, making early Rome a natural trade route for the surrounding peoples, notably the Etruscans, possessors at the time of a more advanced culture. Deposits of salt provided a significant item for the Romans to trade.[6]

The source of Roman greatness lay instead in their peculiar civic mythology and sense of divine mission. The city was said to be founded in the year 753 B.C. by two brothers, Romulus and Remus, abandoned by the Tiber and raised by a she-wolf. They were bloody-minded from the start, turning murderously on each other. Mars, the god of war and agriculture, developed early a strong following among these rough villagers.[7]

Initially, toughness alone was not sufficient to resist the Etruscans, who seized control of the little settlement in the seventh and sixth centuries B.C. and established a kingship there. In many ways, the Romans benefited from this defeat, which exposed them to a more sophisticated culture and linked both the Greek and the Phoenician worlds.[8]

Once freed of foreign domination, the Romans quickly reformed their fledgling city-state, which in the fifth century B.C. accommodated barely forty thousand people. By 450 B.C., they codified their government with the Law of the Twelve Tables. The codes covered everything from market days, the relationship between patrons and clients, the rights of aristocrats, and protections for plebeians.

Roman law was designed to shape the behavior of the citizen, preferably through self-regulation, into conformity with deeply held notions of personal and civic virtue. Even the Latin word *religio* itself, suggested the historian F. E. Adcock, was meant to convey the citizen's obligation to family, civic duty, and the gods.[9]

The Romans were deeply attached to their place and exhibited a powerful sense of continuity with their past. The household was at the center of everything; each family maintained an altar to honor both their ancestors and the gods.[10] Rome's historic core, noted Livy, was "impregnated by religion. . . . The Gods inhabit it."[11]

Identification with tradition remained keen throughout most of their long history. Laws might be amended, but connection to the past lent them inestimable credibility. Something great, in their eyes, also meant something ancient.[12] "Here is my religion, here is my race, here are the traces of the forefathers," wrote the Roman statesman Cicero in the century before Petronius. "I cannot express the charm I feel here, and which penetrates my mind and my senses."[13]

The Romans' commitment to their res publica, or "public thing," survived even after repeated disasters. Roman armies could be defeated— the city was even briefly occupied by Gallic invaders in 390 B.C.—and the city could suffer numerous fires but was always rebuilt around its ancient site. These attachments helped the Romans nurture their independent identity at a time when Greek culture dominated many other Italian cities.[14]

What Cicero felt in his "mind" and "senses"—this peculiar identification with the idea and place of Rome—also drove the city's relentless expansion. Over the third and second centuries B.C., the Romans fought and eventually overcame the Etruscans and the Greeks. Arguably the most critical triumph took place in 146 B.C., with the destruction of Carthage, the city-state that presented the most potent threat to Roman hegemony in the Mediterranean world.

THE MAKING OF THE IMPERIAL CITY

By the second century B.C., Rome already was taking on the trappings of a major city-empire. New arches and temples rose, along with massive port facilities, aqueducts, and an ever expanding Forum in the center of the city. Around the impressive public façades, thousands of crowded tenements, small marketplaces, and shops grew to service the needs of the ever expanding population.[15]

Over the next hundred years, the successes of the empire would undermine the old republican institutions. Newcomers, including slaves, now accounted for as much as a third of the population. Long-standing conflicts between wealthy patricians and hard-pressed plebeians intensified. The popular leader Tiberius Gracchus pointed out that old soldiers returning to Italy from triumphant wars found themselves landless and forced to live "homeless and houseless ... with their wives and children. ... Lacking a family altar or burial plot, they fight and die so that others could enjoy wealth and luxury."[16]

A century of political instability and rebellions, including the famous slave uprising under Spartacus, set the stage for imperium. Proclaimed dictator in 49 B.C., Julius Caesar imposed order on the increasingly fractious republic. Caesar was also an urban innovator, determined to make Rome a fit capital for the vastly expanded empire. He legislated height limits for the city's ubiquitous and often creaky tenements, enforced the use of tiles and open space between buildings to prevent fire, and initiated an ambitious expansion of the Forum.

Caesar's assassination in 44 B.C. prevented him from carrying out his grand designs. This would be left to his successor Augustus.[17] During Augustus's reign, Rome emerged as a city of grand palaces, temples, and other public buildings. As Augustus himself is said to have remarked: "I found the city made of brick and left it made of marble."[18]

ROME: THE ARCHETYPAL MEGACITY

Augustus's triumph at Actium in 31 B.C. over the armies of the last Ptolemaic monarch, Cleopatra VII, and her ally Mark Antony marked the close of the Hellenistic era. The Romans already had subdued virtually all the Greek city-states, the larger part of the old Seleucid Empire, and much else beyond. For the next four centuries, the history of urbanism in the West would be written largely by the Romans and those who submitted to their will.

Some have maintained that the Romans lacked the Greek flair for originality as philosophers, city builders, or architects. This is unfair. Of course, the Romans took what they found in the Hellenized world and built upon it. But they also transformed or rebuilt cities, such as Carthage, and helped restore others, including venerable Athens.[19]

Rome pushed the frontiers of urbanity to new levels, first of all in Rome itself. The city undertook an unprecedented program of public works—roads, aqueducts, sewers—that made it capable of sustaining its ever growing population. The Greeks, one Roman writer asked, boasted of their "useless" art, and Egypt's legacy lay in "idle Pyramids," but what were these compared with the fourteen aqueducts that brought water to Rome?[20]

Yet beneath these achievements lurked a deplorable reality. Elegant marble work may have covered the great buildings of the new Forum Augustum and its Temple of Mars, but most Romans lived in slumlike dwellings. There were twenty-six blocks of *insulae,* or apartment houses, for each private *domus.* Despite the legislation of the Caesars, many apartment buildings still creaked, sometimes collapsed, and all too often caught fire.[21]

Day-to-day life was often chaotic. The streets rarely ran in a straight line, but curved, crowded with both people and refuse. In the daytime, the human stampede dominated; an order of Julius Caesar restricted the flow of carts to the evening. When evening fell, the noise and commotion actually worsened. As the satirist Juvenal asked:

> What sleep is possible in a lodging? The crossing of the wagons in the narrow, winding streets, the swearing of the drovers brought to a standstill, would snatch sleep from a sea-calf or the Emperor Claudius himself.[22]

Despite its blemishes, however, Rome represents something new in urban history. The very need to feed, clothe, and bring water to the megacity's population forced many innovations in economic organization. The purpose of empire, suggested the world-wise Petronius, was to secure the resources to sustain the city's swelling numbers of households, no matter what the cost in human lives. "The Fates are bent on war," the courtier observed. "The search for wealth continues."[23]

The very task of absorbing these resources presented monumental challenges. The city was served by three ports, bringing in the grain that sustained its population, the luxuries demanded by its wealthy, and the slaves who served them. There were massive warehouses and highly specialized markets for everything from vegetables and pigs to wine, cattle, and fish. Roman commerce was so robust that even ambitious freedmen, like Trimalchio in Petronius's *Satyricon,* could amass the enormous wealth that allowed them to acquire considerable social status.

Urban retail on a modern scale here makes its first sustained appearance. Dealers in books, precious stones, furniture, and clothing concentrated in specialized districts. There were both the *horrea,* which served as supermarkets, and a vast number of smaller shops, located mostly on the ground floors of the *insulae.* At its most sophisticated, Rome presaged the contemporary shopping center; the Mercatus Traini offered a vast array of products in its five stories of shops.[24]

Rome's economy has widely been described as parasitic, feeding off the riches of conquered nations. Dried fish from Spain, walnuts from Persia, wine from Gaul, and, of course, slaves from many countries poured into a city; the world received relatively few Roman goods in exchange.[25] Yet if Rome drained the world for its commerce, its genius for the administration of government provided an unprecedented level of security— sparking a new golden age of city building across vast regions of the settled world.

"A CONFEDERATION OF URBAN CELLS"

York, London, Trier, Paris, Vienna, and Budapest, important cities of the European future, owe their birthright to the urban genius born on the banks of the Tiber.[26] Romanization, in many senses, stood synonymous with the advance of urbanization.

Unprecedented security allowed for these developments. "The Romans," observed Edward Gibbon, "preserved peace by constant preparation for war."[27] Legions placed near border areas, walls, and roads protected the cities, from the Saharan wastes to the edges of frigid Scotland. Walls and other defensive fortifications were critical to the survival of cities in such remote locations. Yet these places, such as Trier in Germany and Verulamium (St. Albans), were more than military outposts. By the first and second centuries A.D., even British towns boasted street grids, sophisticated drainage systems, bathhouses, and piped water.

Most impressive, this flowering of urban civilization was not simply the result of imperial edict; it had a grassroots energy as well. A spirited competition among the various cities sparked lavish new building projects, theaters, and stadia. Rome allowed considerable self-government to individual cities; the empire itself, notes the historian Robert Lopez, functioned as "a confederation of urban cells."[28]

Europe would not again see such a proliferation of secure, and well-peopled, cities until well into the nineteenth century. People, products, and ideas traveled quickly through the vast archipelago of "urban cells," over secure sea-lanes and fifty-one thousand miles of paved roads stretching from Jerusalem to Boulogne.[29] Wealthy and highly mobile young Romans thought nothing of going abroad for their education, to Athens, Alexandria, Massilia (Marseilles), or Rhodes.[30]

Commerce and technology also spread to the frontiers. Craftsmen from the Mediterranean brought with them the techniques for the manufacture of glass, pottery, and farm utensils. By the third century A.D., the Rhineland had emerged, for the first time, as a major industrial zone. The frontiers of trade, through both sea and land routes, expanded to the previously untapped markets of India and even China.[31]

At its height, Rome turned the ideal of a cosmopolitan world empire earlier conceived by Cyrus and Alexander into a living reality. Emperor Claudius himself, Tacitus tells us, observed that the gradual extension of citizenship constituted one of Rome's greatest advantages over the more restrictive Athenian state. "The grandsons of Gauls" who had battled Julius Caesar, Gibbon comments, now "commanded legions, governed provinces and were admitted to the Senate."[32] By the third century A.D., Roman citizenship was made available to free men throughout the known world; less than half the Senate now came from Italy.[33]

Foreigners, starting with the Spaniard Trajan in A.D. 98, now rose to the supreme post of emperor. Over the ensuing centuries, the heads of state came from such varied places as Gaul, Syria, North Africa, and Thrace. All these diverse men stayed and ruled from Rome, the sacred capital of all other cities. "Rome," declared Aristeides, a Greek writer in the second century, "is a citadel which has all the peoples of the earth as its villagers."[34]

This universalist notion was perhaps best expressed by Marcus Aurelius, the emperor and philosopher, who assumed the principate in A.D. 161 at the death of Antoninus Pius. Aurelius, like a classical Roman, considered his "city and fatherland" to be Rome. But as emperor, he saw Rome's mission in the broader sense to "do the work of man" across the entire breadth of the known world.[35]

CHAPTER SIX

THE ECLIPSE OF THE CLASSICAL CITY

By the time of Marcus Aurelius, Rome's imperium was already under assault. One primary cause lay in Rome's increasing dependence on slavery. Although always an important part of the classical world, slaves now increasingly replaced the artisans and shopkeepers who had made up an important middle element of Roman society. Many of these then became debtors and dependents on the state; eventually as many as one in three residents of the capital lived on the dole.[1]

In the past, conquest had provided opportunities for displaced Romans. Now the empire, no longer capable of acquiring new territories, was on the defensive, struggling mightily, and at great expense, to protect its vast network of cities. With the breakdown of security and easy communication, long-distance trade declined. Over the ensuing centuries, the currency, the denarius, was consistently debased.

Perhaps even worse, Romans of all classes seemed to be losing a sense of moral purpose. Cynicism and escapist ideas infected the culture. Many in the elites openly despised Rome's harried urban life, choosing instead to escape to their villas in the rustic countryside or along the Bay of Naples. "There is in the city," noted one observer from the eastern part of the empire in the late 300s A.D., "a Senate of wealthy men. . . . Every one of them is fit to hold high office. But they stand aloof, preferring to enjoy their property at leisure."[2]

The Roman middle and working classes increasingly lost themselves in the ever more lavish entertainments put on by the state. Many Romans filled their idle hours with the spectacle of exotic animals, brutal gladiatorial displays, and theatrical performances. "The Roman people," the moralist Salvian complained, "are dying and laughing."[3]

A series of epidemics, some contracted from troops returning from Mesopotamia, increased the sense of gloom. One particularly bad outbreak in the third century A.D. reportedly carried off five thousand Romans a day for several months.[4]

THE CITY OF MAN VERSUS THE CITY OF GOD

Amid these woes, some found solace in religion. Many attached themselves to exotic cults from Egypt, Mesopotamia, and other centers of the ancient world. One new import from the East, Christianity, proved more enduring than any of the others. Over time, it would take over the empire itself.

To the remaining contemporary pagans, and later to Gibbon, the growing influence of these new belief systems fatally wounded the classical urban civilization. The fall of the empire, Gibbon would write acidly, represented "the triumph of barbarism and religion."[5] In this Gibbon is correct, but only to a point. The new ideas themselves—most particularly Christianity—did not destroy Rome. Without a collapse first of the old values, the ascendancy of the newer ones would have been unthinkable.

Ironically, Christianity's rapid growth could not have taken place without the empire's expansive urban infrastructure. Paul, the primary architect of the faith, was himself a quintessential product of the Roman urban world. A Hellenized Jew and Roman citizen from Tarsus, a major trade crossroads, Paul traveled the sea-lanes and roads connecting various cities of the empire—Antioch, Ephesus, Corinth, Damascus, Athens, and Rome itself.[6]

Christianity utilized Roman means for its evangelical ends, but the faith itself rejected many of the city-empire's core values. Borrowing its theology largely from the Jews, the Christians rejected the old place-based notion of *religio* for faith in a single, transcendent god. "When they persecute you in one town," Christ is quoted in Matthew, "flee to the next. . . . You will not have gone through all the towns of Israel, before the Son of Man comes."[7]

Such a notion clashed directly with the culture of classical paganism. The concept of civic patriotism so passionately expressed by Cicero meant little to Christians, whose own God, while on earth, wandered homeless and died like a common criminal.[8] "Nothing is more foreign to us than the state," the Christian writer Tertullian insisted.[9]

The Christians were further alienated by long periods of Roman persecution. Rome was, as one Christian writer put it, "a city created for corruption of the human race, for the sake of whose rule the entire world has undeservedly been subjugated." Cyprian, the bishop of Carthage in the third century A.D., celebrated the plagues visiting Rome and other principal cities of the empire as just retributions for its crimes and infidelity.[10]

This antiurban perspective was most famously expressed by Saint Augustine in his *The City of God*. Like Cyprian, a Carthaginian, Augustine portrayed Rome as the "earthly city," or *civitas terrena*, that "glories in itself" and whose own wickedness deserved punishment. Rather than propose a program to reform the dying metropolis, Augustine urged Romans to seek entrance into another kind of metropolis, "the City of God," where "there is no human wisdom, but only godliness."[11]

"ALL IS NEGLECT"

By the fifth century A.D., when Augustine wrote his great treatise, neither the flock of Christians nor the church, now headquartered at Rome, could have prevented the collapse of the empire. Birthrates were falling and cities emptying, particularly in the more exposed cities closer to the frontiers.[12] Rome itself was increasingly isolated from the major centers of imperial power.[13] Even in Italy, commercial and political focus shifted to other cities, notably Ravenna and Mediolanum (Milan).

Deprived of its imperial role, Rome saw its population plummet. New building stopped and older structures collapsed. In 410, the city was sacked by the Visigoths. The city retained a ragged independence for a bit longer, until it was seized by the German king Odoacer in 476.

Worse indignities were to follow. Racetracks turned to grain fields; aqueducts were abandoned; the baths closed permanently. By the seventh century, Rome was reduced to a city of thirty thousand. "Once the whole world gathered here to climb high," observed Pope Gregory, surveying the devastation. "Now loneliness, desolation and mourning reign."[14]

Following the fall of Rome, city life in Western Europe began slowly to fade. For centuries there developed what one historian calls a "simplification" of culture, a moving inward, "a time of narrowing horizons, of the strengthening of local roots, and the consolidating of old loyalties."[15]

Deurbanization did not happen at once and everywhere. Pockets of Roman city life persisted in some areas for centuries. Sporadic attempts were made to restore the empire. But by the seventh century A.D., the old trade links between the old imperial cities were severed. The great port of Marseilles, thriving for centuries after the empire's collapse, fell into disrepair.

Western Europe and nearby parts of North Africa now devolved into a mosaic of warring barbarian fiefdoms. Virtually all the West's great cities, from Carthage to Rome and Milan, experienced deep population declines.[16] In the periphery of the empire, the losses were, if anything, more catastrophic and lasting. Trier, a bustling German provincial capital with a population of roughly sixty thousand in the early fourth century A.D., devolved into a set of rural villages clustered around a cathedral. As late as 1300, after the restoration of walls and an improvement in the economy, the city still was home to barely eight thousand people.[17]

In most places, the older urban civilization all but evaporated. Less than 5 percent of all the people in Catholic Europe during the seventh and eighth centuries A.D. lived in towns of any size. One French bishop, wandering the increasingly deserted villages of his diocese, noted that "everywhere we find churches whose roofs have fallen in and whose doors are broken and come off their hinges." Animals wandered the aisles up to the altars. Grass grew through the floors. "All," the churchman noted, "is neglect."[18]

CONSTANTINOPLE: URBAN SURVIVOR

Constantinople, the former Greek Byzantium, now stood as the last great redoubt of classical urbanism. Declared the imperial capital by Constantine around A.D. 326, the city stood astride the Bosporus, separating Europe from Asia. Secure behind its walls and with its magnificent harbor, Constantinople survived the barbarian onslaught. Within a century, its population expanded from roughly fifty thousand residents to over three hundred thousand, easily exceeding that of decaying Rome, Antioch, or Alexandria.[19] At its peak in the sixth century A.D., it stood as Europe's dominant city, approaching half a million people, and controlled a huge empire ranging from the Adriatic to Mesopotamia and from the Black Sea to the horn of Africa.

Unlike Rome, which cultivated older cities and founded new ones, Constantinople flourished at a time when other cities in Europe and the Near East were in decline. "Oh, to be in the city!" was a refrain heard often by Byzantines when forced, by necessities of business or government, to travel to the far-flung, dispirited, and often depopulated provincial towns.[20]

Constantinople proclaimed itself the new Rome, yet it was never to achieve the scale and imperial breadth of its predecessor. In his *Chronographica,* the eleventh-century historian Michael Psellus compared Constantinople to "a baser metal" devolved from "the golden streams of the past."[21] Cut off from the West, the city experienced, in the words of Henri Pirenne, a "progressive orientalization." Indeed, visitors from the West noted all the signs: powerful court eunuchs, elaborate court rituals, an increasing despotic centralization of power.[22]

Perhaps even worse, Constantinople turned away from the classical world's cosmopolitan notions, particularly on issues of religion. The imperial regime increasingly persecuted Jews, Christian "heretics," and pagans. The historian Procopius observed of Emperor Justinian: "He did not think that the slaying of men was murder unless they happened to share his own religious opinions."[23]

Many potential allies who might have rallied to the old inclusive empire now turned against the regime. Some groups, including the Jews and even some Christian sects, actively assisted first the Persians and later the Muslims in hacking away pieces of the empire.

Other forces also worked to undermine the city and its dwindling empire. Natural disasters, such as earthquakes, followed by the great plagues of the late sixth century A.D., wiped out one-third to one-half of Constantinople's population and many of the smaller cities entirely.[24] Debilitated from disease and internal dissension, its population in decline, the empire was ill prepared to counter the rise of Islam in the seventh and eighth centuries.

Despite its many problems, the empire persisted—its greatest virtue, noted the historian Jacob Burckhardt, was its "tenacity"—but devolved increasingly into an archipelago of relatively small, perennially threatened armed fortresses. Byzantine defensive prowess, diplomacy, outright bribery, and dissension within the Muslim world all conspired to keep Constantinople safe from final conquest until it fell to the onslaught of Turkish cannons in A.D. 1453.[25]

PART THREE

PART THREE

THE
ORIENTAL
EPOCH

CHAPTER SEVEN

THE ISLAMIC ARCHIPELAGO

In 1325, Abu Abdullah Muhammad ibn Battuta left his native city of Tangier and headed east, to begin his sacred hajj, or pilgrimage, to Mecca. Later, having performed his religious duty in Arabia, he traveled on for almost the next quarter century, sojourning at trading posts along the coast of East Africa, across the caravan towns of the Central Asian steppe, and to the gilded cities of India and the Silk Road.

For most of the journey, covering thousands of miles and scores of cultures, ibn Battuta felt at home almost everywhere. He encountered many different races, languages, and cultures, but most cities lived within the familiar bounds of Dar al-Islam, the house of Islam, a world embracing one God and the revelations of one man, the prophet Muhammad.

It had been nearly a millennium since Rome, and its vast urban network had suffered its final agonies of decline. The Eternal City's successor, Constantinople, still survived behind its walls but was fatally weakened and surrounded by enemies. It now stood as the only European city among the twenty largest in the world; almost all the rest were part of the Oriental world, either in China or within Dar al-Islam.[1]

Muslim primacy had contributed much to the weakening of European urbanism. By taking control of both the Mediterranean and the trade routes to the East, Muslims had cut off European commerce from critical sources of both wealth and knowledge.[2] "The Christians," observed the Arab historian ibn Khaldun, "could no longer float a plank on the sea."[3]

Products like papyrus disappeared from European monasteries; wine long purchased from the Mediterranean now had to be grown locally. Only a trickle of luxury products, usually sold by Syrian and Jewish traders, appeared in Europe's marketplaces and aristocratic courts.[4]

In contrast, such goods crowded the bazaars in the often dazzling Muslim cities, from Toledo and Córdoba in Spain to Delhi in distant India. Muslim traders and missionaries now extended their influence to the islands of Southeast Asia and established colonies in the thriving coastal cities of China itself.

MUHAMMAD'S URBAN VISION

Islamic civilization rested upon a powerful vision of human purpose. Like the classical civilization it supplanted, it was at its core a profoundly urban faith. The need to gather the community of believers was a critical aspect of Islam. Muhammad did not want his people to return to the desert and its clan-oriented value system; Islam virtually demanded cities to serve as "the places where men pray together."[5]

The history of early Islam is one of urban dwellers. Muhammad was a successful merchant in Mecca, a long-established trading and religious center on the barren Arabian peninsula. This city long had been influenced by first Hellenistic and then Roman rulers; its varied population included pagans, Jews, and, after the second century, Christians.[6]

Mecca and the other trading cities of the Hijaz, in the northwest corner of the peninsula, lacked the strong agricultural roots common to many early cities. Its dry, unforgiving climate—one tenth-century Arab topographer described the city as being afflicted with "suffocating heat, a pestilential wind, and clouds of flies"[7]—left only commerce as the basis for its economy.

Most Meccans were descended from bedouins, who wandered the vast expanse of the Hijaz in search of grazing land and water for their flocks. Organized into clans, bedouins supplemented their meager incomes by protecting or raiding caravans. These clans were frequently contentious, respecting only basic family-based loyalties. Ibn Khaldun noted that such strong links were natural outgrowths given the harsh environment of bedouin life. "Only tribes held together by a group feeling," he observed, "can live in the desert."[8]

By the early decades of the new millennium, some of these clans settled in cities such as Mecca and started their own caravans, profiting from the growth in trade between the Levant and Yemen. Mecca slowly grew into a settlement of as many as five thousand.

The old clan loyalties of the desert culture posed a distinct threat to this nascent urban community. Meccans lacked the common ethos and rule of law applicable to unrelated people that had held cities together since Mesopotamian times.

Muhammad, a member of the Qurayshi, one of the more powerful clans at Mecca, grasped the need for such an order, a higher purpose that would replace the chaos of the blood feuds inherent in the old clan society. His system of belief, Islam, was both a religious program and a call for social justice and order.

Muhammad's ideas, revealed in the Koran, concerned themselves with the traditionally weaker members of society. He demanded that women, long subject to abuse of all kinds, be protected from harsh treatment. Men were limited to four wives, unlike in the past, where wealth was the only limiting factor, and commanded to treat them with proper respect.

The poor, too, were to be protected. Alms giving became a necessary expression of faith. Among the wealthy, instructed the Koran, "there is a recognized right for the beggar and deprived."[9]

Perhaps the most far-reaching aspect of Muhammad's message was his notion of greater *ummah,* or community, bound by a single faith. This concept overturned both traditional pagan worship and the ancient primacy of clan affiliations. The traditional leaders of the clans seem to have understood this. In 622, they forced the Prophet and a handful of followers to flight, or *hijira,* to the rival city of Medina, two hundred miles to the north. That city, with its large Jewish colony, proved more receptive to the Prophet's monotheistic message.[10]

Swelled with new converts, Muhammad's forces occupied Mecca in 630. Soon the *ummah* was spreading rapidly across Arabia. The Arabs, once a feuding group of clans, now became a single, highly motivated people. "Had you given them away all the riches of the earth," the Koran says, "you could not have so united them. But God has united them."[11]

THE NATURE OF THE ISLAMIC CITY

After Muhammad's death in 632, his successors, the caliphs, determined to implement the Prophet's vision. The Muslim epoch represented a new beginning in urban history. Spreading through the Near East and North Africa and into Spain with remarkable energy between the seventh and ninth centuries, Islam broke dramatically with the long-standing traditions of classical urbanism, which, as Socrates saw it, found "people in the city" as a primary source of knowledge.[12] Islam would foster a sophisticated urban culture but did not worship the city for its own sake; religious concerns, the integration of the daily lives of men with a transcendent God, overshadowed those of municipal affairs.

The primacy of faith was evident in the layout of Islamic cities. Instead of the classical emphasis on public buildings and spaces, mosques now arose at the center of urban life.[13]

This religious orientation, and the attendant laws governing day to day, differentiated the Muslim conquest from those of the other nomadic invaders who also preyed on the decaying classical civilization. When the Germans, Huns, and others seized the great cities of Rome, Persia, and Byzantium, they generally left little more than ruins and ashes. The Muslims, in contrast, sought to incorporate newly acquired cities— Damascus, Jerusalem, and Carthage—into what they believed to be a spiritually superior, urban civilization.

DAMASCUS: PARADISE ON EARTH

In 661, the caliphate abandoned Medina as their political capital and moved to Damascus, a city more suited to handling the administration, communication, and commercial needs of the expanding empire. In contrast with Mecca or Medina, Damascus lay in a fertile region, nourished by the Baradá River, which flows from the mountains of Lebanon. As the Arab poet ibn Jubayr wrote:

> If Paradise be on earth, Damascus must be it; if it is in heaven, Damascus can parallel and match it.[14]

Damascus broadened the exposure of the Arabs to other cultures. Damascus was a great cosmopolitan city, home to various Christian sects and Jews. Under Islam, these "peoples of the book" were allowed to practice their faiths, often far more freely than under the former Byzantine rulers. The Koran suggested that the *dhimmis* (protected persons) be made "tributaries" to the new regime and thus "humbled," but otherwise their rights were assured. This relative toleration led the Jews and even some Christians to welcome, and even assist, in the Muslim takeover of their cities.[15]

The cosmopolitan character of Islamic urban life also spurred the growth of trade, the elevation of the arts and sciences.[16] In the newly conquered cities, the Arab souk often improved on the Greco-Roman agora. Rulers developed elaborate commercial districts, with large buildings shaded from the hot desert sun, with storerooms and hostels for visiting merchants. The new rulers built large libraries, universities, and hospitals at a pace not seen since Roman times.[17]

The new urban spirit extended well beyond the walls of Damascus. Basra in Iraq, Fez and Marrakesh in North Africa, Shiraz in Iran, and Córdoba in Spain all testified to the civic imagination of the new order.[18] Córdoba, wrote one German nun, was "the jewel of the world, young and exquisite, proud in its might." So great was the cultural pull that in Córdoba, complained one ninth-century Christian scholar, few of his brethren could write Latin adequately but many could "express themselves in Arabic with elegance and write better poems in this language than the Arabs themselves."[19]

BAGHDAD: "CROSSROADS OF THE WORLD"

Baghdad, the new capital founded by the Abbasid caliphate in the late eighth century, emerged as the greatest of these early Muslim cities. Located between the Tigris and Euphrates rivers, close to the site of both ancient Babylon and Ctesiphon, the former capital of the Sassanid Persian Empire, the city was described by one contemporary observer, Abu Yousuf Yaqub ibn Ishaq, as the "crossroads of the world."

Designed to be a great capital, Baghdad was constructed with a circular plan: wall, moat, and inner wall surrounding the palace.[20] Its population, at least a quarter million inhabitants, dwarfed those of contemporary Venice, Paris, and Milan, then the leading cities of Europe, and equaled the last great redoubt of Greco-Roman civilization, Constantinople. By 900, it was likely the largest city in the world.[21]

In the ensuing centuries, the caliphate would shatter and Baghdad would lose its exclusive hold on political power. But still the city retained a notable intellectual productivity. Libraries and academies flourished, helped by the introduction of paper and the circulation of books, including translations of Western and Persian classics. Over time, Arab scholars developed thinner paper, making books more portable and easier to write.[22]

CAIRO'S GOLDEN AGE

The establishment of multiple Islamic capitals helped foster the creation of new centers in Spain, Persia, and especially Egypt. Founded in the tenth century, Cairo expanded over the ensuing three centuries from a courtly center of caliphal administration to a full-fledged cosmopolitan city. It became, as the historian Janet Abu-Lughod noted, "a metropolis inhabited by masters and masses alike."[23]

By the time of ibn Battuta's arrival, the city was under the rule of the Mamluks, a group of Turkish warrior-slaves who had seized it a century earlier. Grown to nearly five times its original walled area, Cairo had become an unsurpassed center of learning, with colleges, a library boasting more than 1.6 million books, and a major hospital. Its famous Citadel now towered over a sprawling giant of a city.[24]

Cairo controlled transcontinental markets as perhaps no city had done since the days of Rome. The Egyptian metropolis, ibn Battuta wrote, served as

> mistress of broad provinces and fruitful lands, boundless in the profusions of its peoples, peerless in its beauty and splendor, she is the crossroads of travelers, the sojourn of the weak and powerful.[25]

The Qasaba of Cairo, with its hundreds of stores, its upper stories home to some 360 apartments, and a permanent population of roughly four thousand, formed the greatest of these bazaars. One contemporary Egyptian writer noted the astonishing "abundance and diversity of goods" and a deafening hubbub punctuated by "the cries of porters carrying merchandise and delivering it to river barges."[26]

The Qasaba served as a critical terminus for Arab merchants who now dominated the great trade routes linking Africa, China, and India with the Mediterranean world. Porcelain, textiles, spices, and slaves flowed into ports such as Alexandria and down to Cairo. Many of the luxury items most coveted in Italy and the rest of Europe filtered through traders—Muslim, Jewish, or Christian—operating out of the city on the Nile.

In a manner seen under Sargon in ancient Mesopotamia and, later, Rome, this commercial vitality rested on a strong security regime. At a time when travel in Europe was exceedingly difficult and dangerous, a visitor like ibn Battuta to fourteenth-century Egypt could travel in safety, through a thoroughly urbanized, interconnected world:

> There is no need for a traveler on the Nile to take any provisions with him, because whenever he wishes to descend on the bank he may do so, for ablutions, prayers, purchasing provisions, or any other purpose. There is a continuous series of bazaars from the city of Alexandria to Cairo. . . .[27]

FROM NORTH AFRICA TO THE BORDERS OF CHINA

Islam's rise also created the conditions for a widening archipelago of major trading centers dominated largely by Muslim merchants.[28] Never before had one faith, or urban system, held such a wide sway. Dar al-Islam provided a common set of rules, modes of behavior, and cultural norms across myriad cities. Islamic regimes, for example, instituted a special office, known as a *wakil al-tujjar,* to supply legal representation and lodging to foreign merchants.[29]

These institutions spread well beyond Islam's traditional heartland. By the thirteenth century, over thirty independent Islamic trading states, including Mombasa and Mogadishu, arose along the East African coast. Islam also flourished in West African commercial centers such as Kano and Timbuktu, where slaves and gold attracted merchants from across Dar al-Islam. Connected to Cairo by southerly trade routes, Timbuktu by the fourteenth century had grown into a city of fifty thousand.[30]

The Persians controlled the even richer trade routes to India and China.[31] In cities such as Isfahan, Tabriz, and Shiraz, burgeoning transcontinental trade, supplemented by local industry, created sprawling bazaars that, along with the mosque, served as the central points of a renewed Iranian urbanism.[32]

By the fourteenth century, both Persian and Islamic cultural influence began to have an impact on nomadic groups such as the Turks and Mongols, whose conquests gave them control over cities in Central Asia and India. These centers had origins that often predated the Islamic conquests, but the new urbane religion sparked brilliant new varieties of city life.

INDIA'S ISLAMIC REBIRTH

India would emerge as a primary case in point. A major center of urban civilization during the Mauryan Empire between the fourth and second centuries B.C.,[33] India would ultimately fall into a decline; with its urban centers largely atrophied, warring, competitive states wreaked havoc on one another, and long-distance trade suffered as a result.[34]

Equally critical, the Hindu-inspired caste system weakened India's urban evolution by stigmatizing trade and depressing curiosity about the outside world. The eleventh-century Arab historian Alberuni observed:

> The Indians believe that there is no country but theirs, no nation like theirs, no king like theirs, no religion like theirs. . . . They are by nature niggardly in communicating what they know, and take the greatest possible care to withhold it from men of another caste from among their own people, still more of course from any foreigner.[35]

The triumphant Muslim sultans, like their Arab predecessors in the Near East and North Africa, quickly reinvigorated India's cities. They professionalized administration, improved roads, constructed inns for travelers, and encouraged trade links with the outside world. This boosted not only bustling trade cities, such as Cambay in Gujerat, but also the emerging administrative center of Delhi, a city conquered at the end of the twelfth century.

When ibn Battuta visited Delhi under the rule of the Muslim Tughluq dynasty, he encountered "a vast and magnificent city . . . the largest city in India, nay the largest of all the cities of Islam in the East." The capital had developed a large marketplace and drew scholars, scientists, artists, and poets from throughout the Islamic world.[36]

Although the vast majority of Indians in the country remained Hindus, Muslims dominated urban centers throughout the subcontinent. Muslim traders, along with some Hindu merchants, managed profitable coastal trade routes between the Persian Gulf and Southeast Asia.[37]

Large portions of India's drugs, spices, luxury goods, and slaves also found their way to the coastal cities of China, where both Muslim merchants and missionaries had established a presence. Yet China was not destined to become part of the Muslim world. Instead, it represented a distinctly different center of urban civilization, one whose magnificence and power rivaled that of Dar al-Islam.

CHAPTER EIGHT

CITIES OF THE MIDDLE KINGDOM

A century before ibn Battuta, a group of Venetian merchants traveled across the vastness of Central Asia to the East. Like their North African counterpart, the Polos found that most cities across these vast tracts followed the faith of Muhammad. It was only in Lop, today located in Xinjiang Uygur Autonomous Region, that Islamic influence began to fade before more distinctly Chinese influence.[1]

Initially, the rise of Islam had represented something of a setback for China's cities. Under the Han dynasty, which flourished at the time of the western Roman Empire, and again under the Tang in the seventh century, Chinese merchants had controlled the lucrative transcontinental trade route all the way to the edges of Afghanistan. Yet when confronted by Muslim forces in 751, the Chinese were decisively beaten.[2]

By the time the Polos arrived in China, the loss of the far periphery was barely remembered, much less mourned. Unlike Islam, which sought to conquer and convert the world, China, noted the historian Bernard Lewis, lacked a powerful missionary zeal. China could slough off defeat in the far periphery, because as the great "Middle Kingdom" it remained largely economically self-sufficient and culturally self-contained.[3]

Chinese influence might, by example or conquest, extend to Korea, Japan, and Southeast Asia, but its culture lacked a transcendental set of values that non-Chinese could adopt. An individual could become a

Muslim; it was not so easy to become truly Chinese, even if one occupied the throne of the Middle Kingdom.

URBAN TRADITION IN AN AGRICULTURAL SOCIETY

In powerful contrast with the city-centered Muslim culture, China's cities arose within the framework of a predominantly agriculturally based civilization. Even as late as the sixteenth century, the Ming emperors continued to perform ritualistic fertility rites in a highly choreographed setting on the palace grounds.[4]

This enduring agrarian reality reflected itself even within the cities. Hangzhou, Guangzhou, Zhangzhou, and Beijing stood as arguably the world's largest and best-planned cities, yet they did not differ so radically from the surrounding, often crowded countryside.[5] China's cities, despite achieving great size, constituted merely a "denser in quality" version of the greater agrarian reality.

China's cities simply did not exercise the influence over the hinterland common in classical Europe or in the Islamic world. Even in the largest cities, most goods were produced primarily for local consumption; most rural needs were fulfilled at the village level. Despite having by far the world's largest population, China was unable to achieve a comparable level of urbanization, as measured by percentage of people living in large cities; China remained less than half as urbanized as Western Europe, the Mediterranean, or, for that matter, Japan from the first millennium until the present day.[6]

"THE ASTRAL CENTER OF THE UNIVERSAL ORDER"

China's most important cities served primarily as administrative centers of the empire. The centers developed during the Zhou period in the first millennium B.C. set the prevailing pattern, with bureaucracy, priestly functions, and the military playing the leading roles. Craft and commercial activities evolved to serve the ruling elites but generally played a secondary role.[7]

Politics, not commerce, propelled the fates of China's cities.[8] The urban fortunes of Chang'an, Loyang, Kaifeng, Nanjing, and Beijing tended to wax and wane based on the locational preferences of dynasties. Issues such as the need for forward defense or access to food supplies largely determined which city or cities would serve as capital.[9]

A shift of capital, and with it the massive weight of the governmental apparatus, was enough by itself to spur a burgeoning marketplace economy. The East Market at Chang'an under the Tang dynasty in the late first millennium A.D. boasted "two hundred streets and alleyways, each surrounded on the four sides with warehouses filled with rare and curious goods from the whole country." As in the Greek agora or Roman Forum, these places became natural settings for their services, including those of printers, entertainers, butchers, and cloth dealers.

City life was highly regulated by imperial bureaucracy. Market times and curfews were announced by the banging of drums.[10] When it came time to lay out a new capital or restore a former one, great priority was placed on following the precepts in the *Zhou Li,* the ancient Chinese protocol governing the way of life, personal conduct, and relationships among things. Each great capital, notes the historian Heng Chye Kiang, was laid out by a formula, surrounded by walls, with strict grid systems, market districts, and an exclusive, virtually self-sufficient district entirely for the emperor, chief ministers, and others connected to the imperial household.[11]

The need to separate the imperial household from the outside world dominated the planning process. The imperial city was cut off from its surroundings by high walls; it did not so much look down upon the surrounding areas, which would be common in Europe or the Near East, as away from them. Military forces, needed to protect the imperial family, often constituted a large proportion of the city's population; one Chinese scholar estimates that as many as one in five residents around the Sung capital of Kaifeng after A.D. 1000 was associated with the armed forces and other parts of the security apparatus.[12]

Some dynasties constructed more than one such capital to administer their domains. The Sui dynasty established three capitals and connected them by roads, canals, and imperial resting pavilions. Sui Wen-ti, who founded the dynasty in A.D. 581, started the Grand Canal to ensure food supplies for the traditional capital of Chang'an, a city that soon grew to rival the size of any contemporary city, including Constantinople.[13]

Beyond the capital cities lay a vast network of smaller centers. In the third century B.C., Shih Huang-ti, the first emperor to unite China, divided the formerly independent Chinese states into provinces, or *zhou*, each with its own administrative center. Below these developed a vast archipelago of smaller administrative districts, or *hsien*. These centers not only secured the empire, but also dispersed food during famine and provided for the sick and aged.[14]

Yet Chinese urbanism centered mostly on its great capitals. These were not merely cities of earthly power under Confucian traditions; they also served as "the astral center of the universal order," the central point of the Middle Kingdom.[15] As centers of veneration, they resembled Islam's holy places, such as Mecca, Medina, and Jerusalem, but with a distinctly different emphasis. The Muslim holy places were sacred but, after the first century of Islamic history, no longer seats of political power. In China, power and divinity shifted in tandem; where the emperor resided, there was the sacred place.

"GREAT CLOUDS IN THE SKY"

By the end of the first millennium A.D. and in the ensuing centuries, there emerged in China another kind of metropolis, one based primarily not on political power, but on mercantile values. The first flowering of commercial cities took place under the Tang dynasty, which ruled China from A.D. 618 to 907. By loosening traditional restrictions on trade, most importantly in land, the Tang helped create a new, potentially powerful class of urban proprietors. The commercial pace hastened under the Sung, who took power in 960 and encouraged the growth of trade.

For the first time, China emerged as a transcontinental trading power. After sweeping Japanese and other pirates from the seas, Chinese merchants established a dominating role over trade routes all the way to India. Chinese navigators were the world's most accomplished, learning the use of the compass, and mapped the seas to as far as the Cape of Good Hope.

By the twelfth century, the Chinese fleet grew to twenty squadrons and over fifty-two thousand men. Chinese economic, cultural, and political influence now spread to a vast expanse of Asia, including Korea, Japan, and much of Southeast Asia.[16] Some of their vessels could carry upwards of five hundred people and store a year's supply of food. Pigs were bred on ships and wine brewed. "The ships that sail the southern seas," wrote the traveler Chou Ch'u-fei, "are like houses. When their sails are spread they are like great clouds in the sky."[17]

The growth of transoceanic business greatly stimulated the development of commercially oriented cosmopolitan cities. A flourishing city by 100 B.C., Guangzhou by the eighth century A.D. had become home to its own powerful Muslim trade community. The Sung established their first customs office there in 971, and for the next century, the port city enjoyed a veritable monopoly of foreign trade. By 1200, Guangzhou's population had grown to more than two hundred thousand, ranking it among the world's four or five largest cities.[18]

Marco Polo marveled at the vast quantity and diversity of the burgeoning urban economy. For every ship that arrived in Alexandria or any Italian port with spices, the Venetian traveler estimated, "a hundred" arrived in Zhangzhou, which had emerged as China's premier port for trading with South Asia. Spices, drugs, gems, and the handiwork of the Near East, India, and Southeast Asia poured from the piers into the warehouses of Chinese cities. These, in turn, exported China's crafts products, technology, and silk.[19]

This represented a potentially auspicious new beginning for Chinese urban history. In the early centuries of the first millennium, rising cities such as Guangzhou, Fuzhou, and Zhangzhou displayed the cosmopolitan mixture then seen in Alexandria, Cairo, Antioch, or Venice. Arab and Jewish traders, living under imperial protection in *fan-fang*, or foreign quarters, were particularly active; a broad diversity of ideas created a fertile artistic, scientific, and creative climate.[20]

These coastal cities attached themselves as well to the strong national internal trade network, most notably in the Sung capital of Kaifeng. The streets beyond the Palace City were "dense as fish scales," lined with bustling shops, drinking houses, and brothels. Significant colonies of Muslims and Jews also settled in the capital. The relaxation of some traditional restrictions of business, such as strict curfews, encouraged the development of a genuine "urban culture," with two- or three-story commercial buildings, lively popular literature, and various kinds of popular entertainment.[21]

The Mongol seizure of China in the early thirteenth century, much lamented by nationalistic Chinese, nevertheless accelerated these trends. With a vast empire in their control, the Mongols extended China's influence across Asia to the edges of Europe. In foreign cities under Mongol control, such as Moscow, Novgorod, and Tabriz, significant Chinese colonies now appeared for the first time.

The Mongols thoroughly terrified their enemies but also spurred trade by providing an unprecedented degree of security over vast expanses of the Asian continent. Under their rule, one Muslim commentator noted, "a man might have journeyed from the land of sunrise to the land of sunset with a golden platter on his head without suffering the least violence from anyone."[22]

The Mongol spirit of religious tolerance also promoted widening commercial and intellectual contacts. Buddhism, Taoism, Christianity, Islam, and other faiths flourished in relative harmony. Mosques, hospitals, and bazaars, administered by Muslim *qadis,* or judges, operated in Guangzhou and Zhangzhou under Islamic commercial and civil law. Many Muslims, and even Europeans like the Polos, rose in the service of the Mongol emperor.[23]

The growth of cross-cultural trade and contacts also accounted for much of the wealth that accumulated in the house of the great Khan. Although far from the coastal trading cities, the great capital and other major interior cities consumed vast quantities of the luxury goods of India, the Near East, and even Africa. "To this city," Marco Polo wrote of Kublai Khan's capital, "everything that is rare and valuable from all parts of the world finds its way."[24]

CHAPTER NINE

OPPORTUNITY LOST

At the time of the Polos and, later, ibn Battuta, it would have been rational to assume that the future of cities and civilization lay in the East. Yet by 1600, the urban dynamism of China and Dar al-Islam—so evident from the docks and warehouses of Zhangzhou to the Qasaba of Cairo—was beginning to dissipate.

THE PROBLEM OF PROSPERITY

Why did the cities of Dar al-Islam and China squander this opportunity? Part of the problem lay in the very prosperity that so impressed European visitors to the East. Viewed from the perspective of a ruler in Beijing, Delhi, Istanbul, or Cairo in the sixteenth century, European cities would have seemed insignificant and backward. Chinese and Muslim technology, drugs, and tools of all kinds were, for the most part, far more sophisticated than those produced in Europe. The agricultural systems of the East, notably those in China, with its highly evolved irrigation and canal systems, also outproduced those in the West.

The leading cities of China and Dar al-Islam appear to have surpassed their European counterparts in both population and architectural magnificence. The Moguls, descendants of the Mongols who seized control of India in 1526, ruled from a capital, Delhi, that an Islamic historian described as "a garden of Eden that is populated." Istanbul, the Islamic city that rested on the remains of vanquished Constantinople, possessed more riches and housed more people than any in Europe.[1]

The magnificence of Eastern capitals further validated long-standing attitudes of superiority. Typical were the attitudes of the Chinese imperial court: The farther one got from the capital city, they believed, one passed from the royal domains to that of princes, then to a "pacification zone," followed by the realm of "half-civilized barbarians," and, finally, the region of "cultureless savagery." Europe, at the far end of the periphery, seemed barely worthy of consideration.[2]

Elite opinion within Dar al-Islam frequently held equally dismissive attitudes toward foreigners, particularly Europeans. A survey of trade, written in Baghdad in the ninth century, mentioned Byzantium, Central Asia, India, and China as having valuable items to offer; the cities of Northern and Western Europe, in contrast, were useful only as sources of selected minerals or slaves. Remarkably, these attitudes did not much change until well into the eighteenth century, when European military and technical superiority was already becoming manifest.[3]

THE LIMITS OF AUTOCRACY

The predominance of autocratic power further slowed the evolution of Asiatic and Islamic cities. Even magnificent cities such as Córdoba in Spain or Chang'an in China all but collapsed when the ruling house was overturned.[4] Autocratic structure also made the Oriental cities particularly vulnerable to what ibn Khaldun described as the natural "life span" of regimes. Most ruling regimes in the Islamic world, he argued, were derived from virile nomadic peoples who had captured cities to plunder their riches. In the first generation, these nomads—early Arabs, Maghrebian tribes, Turks—often exhibited the high energy and imagination necessary for the building of great empires and cities.

The longer they tasted the luxurious life in long-settled places, the Arab scholar observed, the sooner these rulers inevitably lost both their martial spirit and moral resolve. Pampered offspring generations removed from life on horseback, he suggested, could not be expected to retain the virtues of their rougher-hewn ancestors.

When new nomadic invaders arrived on the scene, the results could prove catastrophic for even the most splendid cities. This was the fate of Baghdad in 1258 when Mongol invaders overwhelmed the forces of the enfeebled Abbasid caliphate. They not only executed the last caliph, along with much of his family, but massacred a large part of the populace. Much of the city was left in ruins. Baghdad was never again "the crossroads of the world."[5]

Ibn Khaldun's notions, drawn largely on examples in the Muslim world, could also apply to Chinese dynasties. At their origins, the Sung, Yuan, Ming, and Ch'in each displayed considerable martial virtue and a capacity for effective rule. Yet over time, the regimes became increasingly weak and corrupt. Legions of privileged bureaucrats, aristocrats, and idle soldiers siphoned off the wealth of empire. This inevitably left the dynastic capitals vulnerable to new nomadic invasions.[6]

THE SUPPRESSION OF ENTREPRENEURS

This process of successive enfeeblement is not uniqe to Asian or Islamic societies. Aristocratic classes in Europe also often grew weaker after generations in power. Yet in contrast with the East, Europe's rising urban merchant and artisan classes provided a vital alternative capable of invigorating the urban economy and often forcing changes in regime.

No such surge of middle-class power took place in Japan, Korea, China, India, or Egypt.[7] Everywhere, autocratic regimes undermined the incentive for entrepreneurs through arbitrary taxation, confiscations, and favoritism shown toward court favorites.[8] "Attacks on people's property," ibn Khaldun noted, "remove the incentive to acquire and gain property."[9]

Commercially as well as politically, the capital cities were turning away from the world. Under the influence of neo-Confucianist scholars, China curtailed its bold explorations, to the detriment of its coastal cities.[10] Such decisions ultimately would leave oceanic commerce in the hands of European traders based in cities thousands of miles away.[11]

EUROPE'S REEMERGENCE

These debilitating trends in the East developed just as a new capitalist spirit was rising in European cities, first in Italy and later in Great Britain and the Netherlands.[12] By the late sixteenth century, some of these cities had become as wealthy as those in the East—and the wind was at their backs.

The Chinese, Indian, and Muslim regimes had little knowledge of, or even much interest in, these developments. Wealthy and powerful, secure in their systems, those ruling the great cities of North Africa, the Near East, India, or China did not generally feel threatened when the adventurers from the West appeared in their coastal towns. After all, these were simply traders from a relatively backward part of the world, producing little valued in either the bazaars or the palaces.

Even the Europeans' high-masted, tiny ships seemed unimpressive. Yet soon these little vessels appeared with alarming frequency, becoming progressively faster and capable of ever longer trips. By the end of the seventeenth century, Portuguese, Spanish, and Dutch merchants had gradually seized control of trade with the spice-rich lands of Southeast Asia, capturing as well the lucrative commerce in African slaves, ivory, and gold.

No longer critical as trade entrepôts, cities like Cairo and Istanbul began to weaken commercially.[13] Even coffee, originally an export of the Near East to the West, was being transported to Ottoman bazaars on Dutch ships stocked with beans grown in their Javan colonies.[14]

The Westerners even began to establish a powerful presence in the East. Small commercial settlements on the peripheries of China, India, and Africa evolved slowly into large, commercially vibrant cities. Gradually, the great interior Islamic and Chinese capitals, still magnificent in aspect, began to lose control of even their own domestic trade. Political power and finally cultural influence also would soon slip from their grasp. One era of urban civilization was drawing to a close, and a new one, dominated by Europeans and their descendants, was about to begin.

PART FOUR

WESTERN CITIES REASSERT THEIR PRIMACY

CHAPTER TEN

Europe's Urban Renaissance

In the years following the collapse of the Roman Empire, Europe possessed one powerful cohesive force—the Catholic Church. The Christian clergy, whose presence now sustained Rome in its stunted form, had always been ambivalent at best toward the old classical urban society. Yet in the midst of the collapse of the empire, it was the church that nurtured the first glimmerings of Europe's urban renaissance.

THE SACRED ROOTS OF THE RENAISSANCE

The church contributed in both cultural and political spheres. Christian monks preserved the written languages, the ancient texts, and the traditions of intellectual rigor critical to Europe's urban revival.[1] Equally important, in many of the last surviving towns, diocesan structures served as the basis of urban boundaries and privileges; the bishops, whether in Paris, Rome, or elsewhere in Italy, most often offered the only recognized form of authority.[2]

A full resurgence of urban life required more than ecclesiastical blessings. Cities, as always, needed both a secure periphery and a vital economy. The church lacked the force to fight off invaders, whether Viking, heathen, or Islamic; its own theology was also often diffident, if not outright hostile, toward the commercial values upon which an urban economy depends.

THE RETURN OF THE CITY-STATES

Unable to rely fully on the church, and without strong empires capable of ensuring their security, Europe's beleaguered urban communities were forced to rely on their own resources for survival. With marauding knights and brigands roaming the countryside, the first priority lay in erecting a defensive perimeter. An eighth-century description of Verona, in Italy, tells of a city "protected by thick walls and surrounded by forty-eight gleaming towers." In the years before the introduction of cannons, strong city defenses could resist even the fiercest invaders.

Thus began a new golden age for independent European city-states. Merchants and artisans in places like northern Italy financed their own defensive armed forces.[3] In a world where imperial boundaries were vague and often meaningless, cities constituted the one reliably defined space.[4]

Safe behind their walls, urban merchants and artisans enjoyed an independence unimaginable in the cities of the East. There was no emperor, caliph, or sultan to restrain the private property rights or the guild privileges of the commercial classes.[5] In the West, the autonomous city and nascent capitalism grew together. "The love of gain," writes Henri Pirenne, "was allied, in them, with local patriotism."[6]

Italy emerged as the focal point for the renewal of urbanism. Blessed with an urban infrastructure left over by the Romans, Italy in the early years of the second millennium became *terra di citta,* or "the land of cities."[7]

The First Crusade in 1095 exposed these Italian cities to the model presented by their more advanced counterparts in the Islamic world. Ultimately unable to dominate the Muslims militarily, traders from cities such as Venice, Genoa, and Pisa procured spices, silks, and sophisticated manufactures from their erstwhile enemies.[8] Inland cities like Florence and Padua participated in this commercial expansion not only by manufacturing textiles, but also by financing trade, all this at a time when usury remained largely unacceptable among both Muslims and Christians.[9]

The slow but steady decline of Constantinople opened new opportunities for the Italian city-states. Constantinople would remain Christendom's largest city for centuries, but the old imperial center now lacked the energy to protect its own periphery.[10] By the eleventh and twelfth centuries, the capital city was losing control of the eastern Mediterranean, giving the Italian cities ever greater control of the critical trade routes to the East.

The greatness of these cities did not lie in their girth—even by the fourteenth century, Florence, Venice, Genoa, Milan, or Bologna were home to no more than one hundred thousand souls. Instead, the Renaissance cities' greatest assets lay in their powerful commercial spirit, their willingness to embrace the classical urban tradition, and, decisively, the creativity to improve upon it.

The Italian cities eagerly embraced the long-abandoned classical notions of civic nationalism. They drew on sources such as Marcus Vitruvius Pollio, a Roman architect from the time of Augustus, whose work was rediscovered early in the fifteenth century. Renaissance city builders enthusiastically devoured Pollio's notions of the radial concentric city, with a defined core or forum and residential areas extending outward toward the city walls.[11]

Not content merely to copy old traditions, Renaissance urban visionaries such as Leon Battista Alberti, Antonio Averlino, and Leonardo da Vinci advanced the old Roman art of urban infrastructure, developing new techniques for the construction of defensive fortifications and canals. Filled with pride in their accomplishments, the Italian urban centers—like their classical counterparts—vied with one another in fashioning the most arresting urban landscapes.

VENICE: "JEWEL BOX OF THE WORLD"

In this competition among cities, none exceeded Venice. With its magnificent Grand Canal, Loggia, and Rialto, the city became, as the historian Jacob Burckhardt put it, "the jewel box of the world."[12]

Equally important, Venice also presaged the ultimate shape of the modern city, the greatness of which stems primarily from its economic power. Venice paid for its opulence not through imperial conquest or by its position as a sacred center. Instead, its wealth—like that of Phoenicia—derived almost entirely from its commercial prowess.

The city's origins certainly were plebeian. No dominant religious or imperial figure forged the way to Venice's ascent to greatness. Its own founding myth had little of saints or heroes; the first Venetians were said to be Roman refugees who hid amid the area's marshy islands during a barbarian assault in 421.

From this small band of exiles, the Venetians developed their own urban culture, with each island parish serving as a neighborhood. Their fronts facing the sea, their backs to the mouth of the Po River, the Venetians developed skills as expert fishermen, traders, and seafarers.

Venice's outward thrust initially relied on close ties with Byzantium. Links to the great city gave Venice unique access to the riches of the Levant at a time when most Europeans were largely isolated. Eventually, the Venetians chafed at imperial restrictions on their activities, which were interfering with their profits. Determined to go their own way, they established their own independent republic around 1000.

Essentially an elected oligopoly, the republic was run largely as a business concern, quick to take advantage of trade anywhere profits could be made.[13] The Venetians developed a reputation for being self-serving in both business and politics. They traded with the Muslims when most of Christendom engaged them in bitter armed combat. In 1204, they took full advantage of the seizure of Byzantium by the Crusaders to further consolidate their hold on the eastern Mediterranean.[14] Venetian ships eventually controlled Europe's trade not only with the Arabs, but, frequently through Islamic and Jewish middlemen, also with India, South Asia, and China.

Not content to be merely middlemen or financiers, the Venetians also developed an elaborate production base, further enhancing the city's economy. Long before the notion of specialized "industrial districts" became widespread elsewhere in the West, the Venetians broke up their neighborhoods along distinct functional lines, with specific residential and industrial communities for shipbuilding, munitions, and glassmaking. By the fourteenth century, more than sixteen thousand people worked in these varied industries, making Venice not only the West's trader and banker, but its workshop as well.[15]

By the early sixteenth century, this combination of commerce and industry had transformed Venice into by far the wealthiest city in Europe.[16] More remarkable still was the city's distinctly cosmopolitan character. At a time when most of Europe was darkened by intolerance and violence toward strangers, Venice offered foreigners a "haven of comparative security."[17] Merchants from Germany, Jews and Greek Christians from the

Levant, and other outsiders crowded Venice's streets, bringing goods, ideas, and techniques to the city.[18]

FLORENCE AND THE EMERGENCE OF MODERN URBAN POLITICS

The other Italian cities vied with Venice in the competition for money, talent, and industrial supremacy. Florence challenged Venetian supremacy in everything from banking to the textile trade. The Genoese battled for control of Mediterranean commerce. Smaller cities such as Prato concentrated on dominating specific industrial niches.[19]

The city-states were governed in many ways, more often than not despotically. Rival factions among the guilds, merchants, aristocrats, and clergy vied for control of the cities, often overturning one another with frequency. Yet the break with imperial and ecclesiastical traditions was clear; once again the city remained the supreme value, the basis for all political decisions. Regulations, particularly in reference to commerce, were designed for the economic benefit of the city, or its most powerful citizens, even if they violated traditional concepts of canon law.[20]

In this often contentious setting, urban politics of a distinctly modern type now arose. The Medicis of Florence can be seen as precursors of modern urban political bosses. Their power rested largely on their ability to deliver largesse to their factions and the populace at large. They were acutely opportunistic: The Medicis' primary goal was not the propagation of faith or even the building of a great empire, but achieving for themselves and their city the highest possible level of material wealth.

Throughout northern Italy, urbanites now began to experience a level of affluence that by some modern estimates exceeded that of classical Rome.[21] Niccolò de Rossi, a nobleman studying law in Bologna in the fourteenth century, captured the frankly materialistic spirit of the times:

> Money makes the man,
> Money makes the stupid pass for bright,
> Money buys the treasury of sins,
> Money shows.[22]

IMPERIAL CITIES OVERCOME THE CITY-STATES

Such cynicism revealed what was becoming a critical weakness of the Italian city-states. As they grew more affluent, the Italian cities gradually lost the internal cohesion and intense civic spirit that had undergirded their rise. Having cut themselves off from the ecclesiastical orientation of their medieval past, they also began to lose their classical sense of virtue and moral cohesion. "Blind cupidity," warned Dante early in the fourteenth century, would doom them:

> The new people and sudden gains have begot in
> Thee, Florence, arrogance and excess so that
> Thou weepest for it![23]

By Dante's time, many prominent Florentines, Venetians, and Genoese inherited most of their wealth from previous generations. Seeking higher returns, and contemptuous of work, they spent their fortunes either on their pastoral estates or in ventures outside the city.[24] As capital flowed elsewhere, formerly comfortable artisans descended into a growing propertyless proletariat. The old guild structure buckled further as the remaining industrialists farmed out their work to unorganized peasants in the countryside or to other countries.[25]

These internal problems weakened the city-states just as they faced the revival of new imperial centers that were increasingly stirred by strong nationalistic sentiments. By the 1600s, these cities—London, Lisbon, Madrid, Paris, Vienna—increasingly challenged the supremacy of the city-states. Other, more modest capitals such as Berlin,[26] Copenhagen, and Warsaw also began to achieve significant size.[27]

Like the Sumerian, Phoenician, and Greek city-states before them, Italy's independent municipalities, particularly as they lost their moral cohesion, could not compete alone against urban centers drawing on broader human and material resources. This proved their undoing. For all their artistic and commercial genius, the Italians lacked the collective will that might have allowed them to ward off the new challengers.

Late Renaissance Italy, if united, was home to 13 million people, a population second only to that of France and more than 50 percent greater than Spain's. But Italy's rulers lacked the enlightened self-interest necessary to unite against foreign foes. Instead, as Machiavelli noted in the beginning of the sixteenth century, they "only thought of fleeing instead of defending themselves."[28]

Over time, the city-states also lacked the manpower to protect their trade lifelines, overseas possessions, and ultimately their own independence. As early as the thirteenth century, Venice had to rely largely on Greeks and Catalonians to man their fleets.[29] The plagues that devastated Europe throughout the Renaissance hit the densely packed, trade-dependent Italian cities particularly hard; between the mid-fourteenth and mid-seventeenth centuries, the populations of Milan, Venice, Florence, and Genoa were reduced by roughly half.[30]

These cities recovered less quickly from pestilence than others that could draw on a large agricultural hinterland. Their depleted armies, made up largely of foreign mercenaries, could not match the superior forces of imperial powers such as Spain and France. Slowly, the city-states were swallowed up by these powers. Venice managed to hold on to its independence but was forced to cede parts of its own far-flung archipelago of possessions in the eastern Mediterranean.[31]

THE IBERIAN ASCENDANCY

The position of the city-states was further eroded by dramatic changes in the pattern of world trade. Burning with Christian passion after their successful defeat of the Moors, the newly emergent nations of Portugal and Spain burst forth onto the oceans, starting in the fifteenth century, with an almost messianic frenzy. They opened up new, alluring markets that would eventually undermine the trade routes long dominated by the Italians and their partners.

Tiny Portugal, a backward and impoverished country with barely a million people, delivered the first crushing blow. Portuguese sailors began to reach westward to the Azores by the 1440s and soon were building colonies along the West African coastline. With Vasco da Gama's arrival in Calicut in 1498, the tiny nation opened routes around Africa to Asia that threatened the long-standing Italian monopoly over the lucrative spice trade.

Another critical event took place in 1509, a decade before the conquest of Tenochtitlán, when a small Portuguese fleet defeated a large Muslim armada at Diu, outside Gujerat in India. From then on, the control of world trade, and the future of the cities, fell inexorably out of the control of Arabs, Chinese, and other peoples and into the hands of the Portuguese and Spaniards.[32]

The brutal conquest by Spain and Portugal of the "New World" in the late fifteenth and early sixteenth centuries further undermined Italian commercial preeminence. More and more, the route to riches for ambitious Italians lay in working for the Iberian monarchs. Italians like Christopher Columbus, John Cabot, and Giovanni da Verrazano ranked among the earliest explorers of the vast new domains. The new continents would eventually be named for the explorer Amerigo Vespucci, a onetime agent for the Medici financial interests in Florence.

By the seventeenth century, Lisbon, insignificant just two hundred years earlier, had emerged as a major city, the leading port and administrative center for Portugal's far-flung empire. With a population of more than one hundred thousand, Lisbon now took on airs of a great imperial capital, influencing events on a global scale.[33]

In Spain, newly acquired riches accelerated the growth of the port of Seville as well as the capital cities of Valladolid and, later, Madrid. Conquests within Europe, both in Italy itself and in the Netherlands, added to the wealth of the Spanish court. Private homes and public buildings now reflected their empire's enormous riches. The Escorial monastery complex outside Madrid, started in 1563, was lavishly decorated with the rewards of empire, the rich woods of the Americas, the steel workmanship of Milan, and the tapestries of Flanders.[34]

PARIS: THE ULTIMATE EUROPEAN CAPITAL CITY

The most enduring of these new capital cities evolved not on the peninsula, but in France, the largest, richest, and most coherent continental European empire. Paris's earliest roots lay with the old Roman settlement on an island in the Seine. Largely deserted in the early centuries after Rome, the city survived as an ecclesiastical center. At the close of the tenth century, the Capetian dynasty designated the city as its administrative center.

Capetian kings, benefiting from their rich and growing domain, laid the foundations of a great capital. King Philip Augustus in the twelfth century paved Paris streets for the first time, developed a new central market at Les Halles, and constructed stronger protective walls around the city. Work on Notre Dame Cathedral was begun, although not completed until late in the thirteenth century. By then, the city's population had swelled to roughly 150,000, the largest in Catholic Europe.[35]

Paris lacked the commercial dynamism of its Italian competitors and even of its smaller national rival, Lyon. Its great advantage lay elsewhere, in the expansive power of the monarchy, the flourishing of its university, and its importance as a center of spiritual thought.[36] Like imperial cities in contemporary China, Paris flourished as a city of bureaucrats, priests, students, and scholars; its merchant class grew not as much from exporting goods as by servicing the elites now clustered there.[37]

Long dynastic struggles, followed by bitter religious wars, slowed the city's development until the end of the sixteenth century. Only the conversion in 1594 of the first Bourbon monarch, Henry IV, from Protestantism to the Catholic faith assured both the unity of the kingdom and the city's imperial destiny. *"Paris vaut bien une Messe,"* he is said to have explained: Paris is well worth a Mass.

Henry IV was determined to make Paris a capital worthy of a great empire. He cleaned up the filthy streets, expanded the Louvre, and constructed several public squares along the Italian model. Nobles now flocked to the city. Bureaucracies expanded, and artisans migrated to serve the needs of an expanding population, which doubled over the next century to roughly half a million.[38]

By the 1670s, Paris was bulging past its ancient walls. Although sometimes alarmed by the capital's unruly growth, the rulers sought to embellish its façades. Even as Louis XIV moved his own residence to the suburb of Versailles, his chief minister, Colbert, encircled the city with tree-lined boulevards and began work on the Invalides military hospital, numerous arches of triumph, and the circular Place des Victoires, with a looming statue of Louis covered in twenty-four-karat gold leaf.

Paris aimed now to become the world's great capital city, the new Rome. "Nothing," Colbert suggested, "marks the greatness of princes better than the buildings that compel people to look at them in awe. . . ." Unfortunately, such magnificence also helped to both bankrupt the nation's treasury and impoverish its common people. To prevent starvation and rioting in the capital, grain was requisitioned from the surrounding countryside. Not surprisingly, the rest of the country often regarded Paris as the "bloodsucking Babylon," growing great at their expense.[39]

Yet for all the jealousy and hatred Paris inspired within France, by the seventeenth century, the city had emerged as continental Europe's primary artistic and cultural capital.[40] Throughout the next three centuries, Paris would be considered a paragon of urban centralization and magnificence. Traditions of highly centralized rule—from the monarchy through modern times—have allowed French officials to spend an enormous percentage of the nation's resources on the capital.[41]

Napoleon I, the great architect of modern France, made clear his determination to turn Paris into "something fabulous, colossal and unprecedented." His grandiose plans, however, were sidelined by his defeat in 1815 by the allied powers. The true transformation of the capital instead occurred under his nephew Louis Napoleon. Shortly after taking power in 1851, Louis Napoleon declared Paris "the heart of France. Let us put all our efforts into embellishing this great city."

Under Napoleon's ambitious and often ruthless prefect, Georges-Eugène Haussmann, Paris was organized along broad boulevards brilliantly adorned with magnificent *grands travaux* and well-designed parks. Distinctly French ideas of city building, layout, and architecture would influence city builders from Vienna to Washington, D.C., Buenos Aires, and Hanoi.[42]

CHAPTER ELEVEN

CITIES OF MAMMON

For all the magnificence of Paris, and the other emerging capitals across Europe, the keys to the urban future lay elsewhere. Securing a sacred place and political power remained critical to the growth of cities, but increasingly the best prospects now belonged to those cities whose greatness rested not on God or the power of the state, but on the relentless and successful pursuit of mammon.

EUROPE'S EXPANDING URBAN ORDER

The new routes to Asia and the Americas constituted only part of a vastly expanding field of economic endeavor for cities. New European markets also were opening up in what had been the remotest hinterlands in Roman times. The urban imprint on the continent now expanded for the first time in a millennium. Villages were becoming towns and some towns cities, with their own cathedrals and central markets. Urban centers arose from the upper Rhineland to Riga, Gdańsk, and the steppes of Russia.[1]

For the first time since the classical period, Europe's level of urbanization surpassed that of Asia and the Near East.[2] Between 1500 and 1650, the number of towns of over 10,000 almost doubled to nearly two hundred; the overall percentage of urban dwellers grew from 7.4 to 10 percent. The ranks of new cities over 100,000 also increased dramatically.

Even long-suffering Rome enjoyed an urban renaissance, growing from 17,000 people in the 1370s to roughly 124,000 in 1650.[3]

The key issue now lay in which cities would be best positioned within the growing urban network. Paris and the other sparkling capital cities, although exemplars of advanced urban form and magnificence, remained essentially parasitic, drawing largely on their own hinterlands. History would favor those cities that seized control of the primary avenues to a widening world.

THE FAILURE OF THE IBERIAN EMPIRES

The most likely beneficiaries of the expanding European economy would seem to have been the cities with control over the most extensive overseas empires. But Lisbon, Seville, and, later, Madrid failed to develop the commercial savvy allowing them to reap fully what they had so impetuously sown.[4]

Cultural values stood at the core of this failure. Men like Hernán Cortés, Bernal Díaz's captain and conqueror of Tenochtitlán, were more like medieval knights than builders of cities and economies. Like other *conquistadores,* Cortés strove primarily for glory, God, and precious metals.[5]

A fierce but ultimately debilitating religious intolerance accompanied this swaggering Iberian sensibility. For centuries, Jews and recent converts, known as New Christians, had played pivotal roles in the commercial and professional lives of Europe's burgeoning cities, nowhere more so than in Spain.[6]

Aware of the importance of the Jews to their commerce, some cities, including Seville, Barcelona, and Valencia, protested against the Inquisition. The increasingly absolutist Spanish state, sweeping away the last vestiges of municipal powers, overwhelmed all municipal resistance. Following the expulsion order of 1492, over 180,000 Jews and New Christians left the country. Concerning that fateful year, the historian Barnet Litvinoff observed: "With the voyage of Columbus, Spain gained a continent; with the expulsion of the Jews, they lost a limb."[7]

The remnants of Spain's commercial middle class, operating in a country where the church and aristocrats controlled much of the capital, largely lacked the business skills to take full advantage of the new opportunities before them.[8] Wealth poured into Spain, largely through Seville, only to end up in the hands of Italian middlemen and merchants. Even the exports to Spain's colonies were, for the most part, produced elsewhere. The empire's gold, mortgaged to foreigners to finance incessant wars and purchase luxury goods for the aristocracy, became its curse.[9]

Chronic food shortages, the hemorrhage of young men sent to die in foreign wars, massive public debt, emigration, and, finally, an epidemic at the end of the seventeenth century drastically reduced the size of Spanish cities. Having doubled in the sixteenth century to over nine hundred thousand, the number of people in Spanish cities larger than ten thousand dropped by a third by 1650. By the seventeenth century, Naples, Spain's largest Italian possession and a great port city, easily surpassed any Spanish city in both industry and population.[10]

THE EMERGENCE OF THE NORTH

In contrast, the cities of the north—Antwerp, Amsterdam, and ultimately London—benefited mightily from the rapid expansion of world trade. While the urban centers of Spain and Portugal declined through the seventeenth and eighteenth centuries, those in the Netherlands grew fourfold and in Britain by more than six times.[11]

The decisive weapons for this ascendancy were not those employed by intrepid explorers or warriors; rather, they lay in the more mundane arts of bankers, merchants, and skilled artisans.[12] It was not Spain, with its brave soldiers and intrepid missionaries, that garnered the commercial fruits of empire, but Antwerp and the other commercially oriented cities of the Netherlands.[13]

Had the Hapsburg ruler Charles V accepted the principle of tolerance, Spain, through control of these cities, may still have dominated the rising European urban economy. Instead, the regime's desire to impose Catholicism turned its productive and heavily Protestant northern cities into, as one Spanish general put it, "the graveyard of Europe."

The Great Revolt of 1572, when large portions of the Netherlands rose up against Spain, represented the critical turning point. The Spanish commander, the Duke of Alba, waged a merciless campaign against the Protestants. Although the northern part of the Netherlands resisted successfully, the south remained under Catholic control.

Alba's war had disastrous effects on Spain's commercial prospects. The predominantly Protestant merchant classes now fled those areas under

Spanish control. Antwerp, sacked by Spanish troops in 1576, declined, while much of its talent, money, and business acumen shifted to the newly independent cities of the north.[14]

AMSTERDAM: THE FIRST GREAT MODERN COMMERCIAL CITY

At the end of the war with Spain, Amsterdam emerged the most important of the newly independent Protestant cities. In contrast with most contemporary European cities, Amsterdam was dominated not by aristocrats or priests, but by profit-seeking merchants and tradesmen. The quintessential Dutchman was described by one seventeenth-century British writer as "Nick Frog," the "son of the mud, who worships Mammon."[15]

Amsterdam was barely more than a fishing village in the thirteenth century, until its residents began methodically to expand their trading capabilities by extending their canal system. As the city grew, it slowly strengthened its security perimeter, guarded against fire by mandating brick construction, and took measures to improve sanitation.[16]

Other Dutch commercial centers such as Leiden and Rotterdam also took steps to improve their ability to trade with the world. With their vast fleet of 1,800 seagoing vessels, the entrepreneurs of the great Dutch cities soon seemed to be poking their noses everywhere. In the Mediterranean, Africa, Asia, and the newly discovered Americas, they usually bested their rivals at the critical game of buying low and selling high.

With half its people located in towns and cities by the early seventeenth century, the Netherlands had become the most urbanized society in Europe.[17] Amsterdam, Holland's primary city, was something new and yet remarkably familiar: a dense modern city noteworthy not so much for its heroic statues and great boulevards, churches, or palaces as for its teeming alleys, bustling wharves, and clean and comfortable residences. Having won at great cost their independence, the Amsterdammers did not seek out military adventures to become a new Rome. They simply wanted to carry out their trade with minimum interference.[18]

The Amsterdammers' Calvinist faith also helped bolster a civic culture centered around trade and commerce. Calvinist pastors expunged the old Catholic laws against usury and cast away the age-old prejudices against capitalist enterprise. Indeed, the Hollanders saw their material success as further proof of God's sanction. "Amsterdam," noted a popular seventeenth-century Dutch history, "has risen through the hand of God to the peak of prosperity and greatness."[19]

Like ancient Alexandria, Cairo at its height, and Venice in the fifteenth century, Amsterdam owed much of its commercial success to the presence of a vast diversity of people. The city boasted fully functioning Catholic, Huguenot, Jewish, Lutheran, and Mennonite religious institutions as well as the dominant Dutch Reformed Church; those outside the officially sanctioned religious consensus comprised roughly one in four city residents. "The miracle of toleration was to be found," observed the French historian Fernand Braudel, "wherever the community of trade convened."[20]

The combination of commercial vitality and a diverse population created a climate ideal for bold new innovations in art, technology, and philosophy. In contrast, in Spain, complained Rodrigo Manrique, son of the inquisitor-general, "one cannot possess any culture without being suspected of heresy, error and Judaism."[21] The Dutch cities not only permitted open inquiry and innovation, but nurtured them in their universities, scientific societies, and publishing concerns.

This progressive spirit proved critical to the cities' success. Initially, Dutch trade was heavily dependent on commodities such as wine, timber, sugar, and chemicals. By the seventeenth century, however, the Dutch applied innovative techniques to move more decisively into the "rich trades"—dyes, glazes, ceramics, linen, fine furniture, and tapestries. Dutch entrepreneurs also exported engineering services, industrial expertise, and technology to a vast array of countries throughout Europe and even as far away as Mexico.[22]

Holland's expanding middle class proved critical to its development as a major cultural center. Dutch artists in the sixteenth and seventeenth centuries were frequently the sons of skilled craftspeople—designers of tapestries, fur cutters, goldsmiths, and the like. These artists received support largely from the local merchant and manufacturing elites. Art became a way to achieve not only fame but also money. Rembrandt, as a fashionable portrait painter, made far more than a university professor.[23]

LONDON

The democratization of culture was evident in other European cities. Technological improvements had made books increasingly accessible to the masses; by the 1530s, in France a copy of the New Testament became affordable even to a laborer. Old barriers were breaking down; Jews, such as Spinoza, and women now were able to engage in intellectual and cultural dialogue. The French author Louise Labé exhorted women: "The honor that knowledge will give us will be entirely ours, and it will not be taken from us by the thief's skill . . . or by the passage of time."[24]

Nowhere was this new spirit more evident than in London. During the Elizabethan period in the late sixteenth century, London evolved into a brilliant showcase for everything from drama to intense scientific and theological debate. Long forbidden or frightening, knowledge was now regarded as a supreme value.[25]

Soon London began surpassing Amsterdam in both intellectual achievement and commercial vigor. By the late seventeenth century, the Dutch were clearly losing their once inimitable boldness and tenacity. Dutch capitalists—like those in Venice before them—now often opted to become *rentiers,* investors in land and stock, rather than initiate new ventures.

Interested primarily in short-term financial gain—epitomized by the famous tulip mania of 1636–1637—the Dutch elites lacked the moral resolve to defend some of their key overseas holdings, most portentously their fledgling colony of New Netherland. One early explorer rightly identified the colony's settlement at New Amsterdam as "a great natural pier ready to receive the commerce of the world." Surrounded by rivers and bays that opened to the sea, the tiny colony of barely one thousand souls represented an almost unparalleled opportunity for the expansion of Dutch enterprise.

But faced with the need to ward off intrusions from the surrounding English colonies, Dutch business interests balked at spending the funds needed to defend the tiny colony. What mattered more to them was to keep hold of Suriname, isolated, easy to defend, and also rich in "commodities" like sugar. In 1664, with barely a fight, they surrendered New Netherland to the British, who quickly renamed the capital city New York.[26]

THE WORLD CAPITALIST CAPITAL

Barely a decade after New Amsterdam became New York, London was ready to assume the role as the world capitalist capital.[27] This shift may have proven inevitable in the long run. Like the Italian city-states before them, the Dutch cities were constrained by a lack of resources and people. In contrast, London could draw on Britain's far larger population for settlers, soldiers, and sailors. Britain also possessed critical raw materials such as coal, iron, and tin. Even under the most enlightened administration, these factors likely would have forced the Dutch cities to accept secondary position behind London.[28]

London's emergence rested on its ability to marry the advantages of a great capital city with the commercial abilities of the Dutch trading centers or Italian city-states. From the fourteenth century on, London had attracted an ever greater portion of the country's young and ambitious of all classes. Even as older centers such as Winchester and Lincoln declined, London's population and economy expanded rapidly.

As in the Netherlands, the triumph of Protestantism accelerated London's commercial growth. Henry VIII's sale of church lands, roughly one-sixth of the kingdom, enriched both the state and the property-owning classes, including merchants and artisans. Upstarts rising from middle and working classes—some aspiring to join the aristocracy—constituted an essential component of what the historian F.R.H. Du Boulay would dub "an age of ambition."[29]

Geography had made the British seafaring people. Now the irrepressible desire to "better" their station propelled individual Britons toward long-distance trade.[30] Britain's successful imperial thrust ultimately gave it control of possessions from the coast of China to the wilds of North America. Arguably the most critical was the gradual takeover of India and its vast trade. In 1601, Britain's revenues were less than a tenth of Mogul India's; within two hundred years, the relationship was totally reversed in England's favor.[31]

This venturesome spirit reflected a great surge in national ambition and purpose. "Unbounded Thames," Alexander Pope predicted in 1712, "shall flow for all mankind."[32] In the sixteenth century, London itself grew from 60,000 to nearly 225,000 souls. Rebuilt on a grand scale after the great fire of 1666, it would soon grow into Europe's largest city.[33] By

1790, London's population had swelled to almost 900,000 people, more than four times that of Amsterdam.[34]

Seeing a vast new realm of opportunities, Italian, Dutch, and German merchants and bankers increasingly gravitated to the British capital.[35] Of the seventeen leading London-based merchant banks to survive into the twentieth century, fifteen could trace their origins to various immigrants, many to this early period. The city also benefited from the migration of entrepreneurs and skilled laborers seeking religious freedom from such places as Flanders, Germany, and France.[36]

London's rise was not only greater in degree, but also markedly different in character from that of imperial rivals such as Paris, Madrid, Vienna, or St. Petersburg. Like London, these great capitals boasted grand cathedrals, palaces, and parks, expressions of their national greatness. But only London created the vital economic institutions essential to the control and administration of an ever expanding world economy. It also acquired that critical sense of moral purpose underpinning great cities since the earliest times. Like imperial Rome at its height, London prepared to both lead the world and improve it.[37]

PART FIVE

THE
INDUSTRIAL
CITY

CHAPTER TWELVE

THE ANGLO-AMERICAN
URBAN REVOLUTION

London's commercial and imperial ascendancy laid the foundation for the next critical shift in the evolution of cities, one driven by a revolution in manufacturing technology. Although industry had been an important component in urban life from Mesopotamian times, in the late eighteenth century Britain would pioneer the creation of a new kind of city, one tied primarily to the mass production of goods.

Many natural factors favored Britain's early industrial emergence, such as closeness to the Atlantic, the convenient rivers for power and transport, and later on ample coal resources. More important still, Britain enjoyed a social and political climate ideal for the growth of manufacturing endeavors. Unified for much of its history, it suffered neither the pervasive fragmentation of power that bedeviled Italy nor France's tumultuous upheavals. Britain's shift to a new economic paradigm also benefited from the elimination of both the Catholic hierarchy and its vast estates, which broke the "stratified Christian co-operative" of the Middle Ages.[1]

This created an ideal climate for early innovators rising up from the old artisan class, men such as Richard Arkwright, who developed the "spinning jenny" in 1768. Aristocracy remained powerful in Britain, but men of property, no matter what their ancestry, enjoyed a wider latitude to build enterprises than in most other European countries, much less than in the more constricted East.

Finally, Britain's advent as the world's dominant empire unlocked both vast sources of raw materials and new markets outside Europe. "The dawn of the era of capitalist production," in Karl Marx's phrase, coincided with the consolidation of empire. Capital from imperial ventures— cotton, tobacco, slaves—provided much of the financing needed for the island's headlong leap forward into the industrial frontier.[2]

LANCASHIRE: ORIGINATOR OF THE REVOLUTION

With its specialized institutions employing tens of thousands of clerks, administering the world's trade in equities as well as commodities such as coal and wool, London clearly occupied the commanding heights of the British economy.[3] But the most radical transformation—and the greatest source of Britain's wealth—took place in cities far from the great metropolis.

The epicenter for this new urban revolution lay in Lancashire. Long among Britain's poorest regions,[4] in the early nineteenth century Lancashire emerged as the world's most dynamic economic area. The population of its principal city, Manchester, soared from 94,000 to more than 270,000 during the first thirty years of the century and would more than double again by its end.

Some smaller cities experienced even more rapid growth. In 1810, the worsted manufacturing center of Bradford was an obscure small town with 16,000 people. As the capacity of the city's factories rose by more than 600 percent in the first half of the nineteenth century, the population exploded to more than 103,000, the fastest growth experienced by any city in contemporary Europe.[5]

Unlike London, which remained both a traditional commercial center and an imperial capital, these cities represented something entirely new: urban centers whose prominence rested primarily on the mass production of manufactured goods. This evolution would mark the beginning of an urban revolution that would transform cities all around the world.

The rapid growth of these industrial cities greatly accelerated Britain's unprecedented rate of urbanization. Between 1750 and 1800, England, although it accounted for barely 8 percent of Europe's population, was responsible for roughly 70 percent of all urban growth. By the mid-nineteenth century, Britain became the first country with a majority of its people living in large cities; by 1881, urbanites accounted for two-thirds of its population.[6]

"WITH COGS TYRANNIC"

The Industrial Revolution profoundly transformed the urban environment in often hideous ways. Visitors remarked about the persistent smell of the tanneries, breweries, dyeworks, and gasworks. Living conditions, particularly for the poor, were often abominable.[7] Friedrich Engels wrote this account of a working-class ward in Manchester:

> Everywhere one sees heaps of refuse, garbage and filth.... One walks along a very rough path on the river bank, in between clothes-posts and washing lines to reach a chaotic group of little, one storied, one room cabins. Most of them have earth floors and working, living and sleeping all take place in one room.[8]

This squalor created lethal health problems. Death rates in early-nineteenth-century Manchester were one in twenty-five, almost three times that of surrounding rural hamlets. Death from disease, malnutrition, and overwork became so pervasive that factories could be kept running only by tapping a continuous supply of workers from the distant countryside and from impoverished Ireland.[9] Extreme poverty in what was now easily the world's greatest economic power, noted Alexis de Tocqueville, appeared more pervasive than in such backwaters as Spain or Portugal.[10]

The treatment of young children was particularly shocking. Traditionally, children had labored alongside their parents at home, in a small workshop, or in the fields; now they often worked by themselves, servicing machines in vast impersonal industrial plants. One West Indian slaveholder, on a visit to Bradford, thought it impossible for "any human being to be so cruel as to require a child of nine to work twelve and a half hours a day."

In part, this "cruel" treatment may have resulted from lack of intimate contact between owners and workers. The capitalist controlling a small factory might have had some casual familiarity with his workers and their children. The great capitalists owning the largest factories, in contrast, often lived far away, in London or at their country estates.[11]

In contrast to the creators of the classical or Renaissance cities, such beneficiaries of the new order initially scorned the cities of their creation. These were places to make money, not to spend one's leisure time. "There are no pleasant rides, no pleasant walks," a socially prominent Bradford doctor complained, "all being bustle, hurry and confusion."[12]

This new industrial society may have been creating unprecedented wealth, but at the cost of every basic human value. There seemed little ' place for either compassion or God in the factory; the industrial city seemed largely devoid of sacred space or any compelling social morality other than what Marx called "the cash nexus." By the 1850s, religious attendance, once almost universal, had dropped to less than 50 percent and to less than a third in such cities as Manchester.[13] William Blake expressed his alarm at the impact of this mechanistic age:

> Washed by the Water wheels of Newton, black the cloth
> In heavy wreathes folds over every Nation; cruel Works
> Of many Wheels I view, Wheel without wheel, with cogs tyrannic
> Moving by compulsion each other: not as those in Eden.[14]

"HERO OF THE AGE"

By the 1850s, signs of the new order were evident everywhere in British cities: looming railway bridges, vast tunnel systems, sprawling factories. Gradually, some began to sense something monumental was afoot. There was in Britain, noted the usually even-tempered Tocqueville, at "every step . . . something to make the tourist's heart leap."[15]

Where Blake saw only the soulless "cogs tyrannic," some now envisioned the factory as the harbinger of a glorious and prosperous future. Sir George Head, traveling in Leeds in 1835, described a mechanized cloth factory as "a temple dedicated by man, grateful for the stupendous power that moved within, to Him who built the universe." The "hero of the age," he noted, was not the knight or aristocrat, but the "hardworking mechanic, blackened by smoke, yet radiant in the light of intelligence."[16]

By midcentury, this sense of optimism had spread as even ordinary Britons now began to enjoy the benefits of mechanization. Wages, spurred by the growth of trade unions, now rose. Working-class consumers, who before could hardly have hoped to afford them, could now purchase such items as stockings or dining utensils. Some, particularly in the skilled trades, ascended into the middle class; children from the industrialist class now entered the elite universities. Having become great lords without proper titles, some now, by marriage or through influence, acquired noble status.[17]

Social reform movements—led usually by the clergy and a rising professional class—now organized to address the most obvious defects of the industrial system. Reform legislation, such as the Municipal Corporations Act in 1835 and the first Public Health Act by Parliament in 1848, brought more efficient administration to the sprawling, chaotic cities. Reformers established parks, baths, and washhouses for the poor. New sanitary measures and improvements in medicine lowered urban rates of mortality significantly. Crime, once rampant, dropped dramatically.[18]

By the turn of the century, wrote Liverpool's Thomas Baines, cities like Manchester, Liverpool, Leeds, and Bradford—for all their undoubted ugliness, polluted skies, and terrible slums—could not be dismissed merely as crude places spewing out goods. They now constituted, like Tyre or Florence in the past, "nurseries of intelligence" whose inventions were improving the lot of mankind.[19] Wealth allowed these once dreary cities to erect magnificent new public buildings—town halls, libraries, and hospitals—that in the words of one Bradford writer rivaled "the far famed palaces of Venice...."[20]

URBANIZING THE "GARDEN OF THE WORLD"

In the first half of the nineteenth century, no European country came close to matching Britain's industrial might. Paris, the largest city on the continent, remained mainly a city of small enterprises. After 1850, the conscious policy of Napoleon III and Baron Georges-Eugène Haussmann, fearful of proletarian unrest, actually discouraged large-scale industrial growth in the capital.[21]

The new focus of industrial growth lay instead in the still largely underdeveloped expanses of North America—a place some Europeans romanticized as the "garden of the world." Here the factory town not only took root, but did so on a scale exceeding that of Britain itself.[22]

Industrialism would bring many changes to the United States, ultimately transforming a primarily rural landscape into one of large cities. As late as 1850, the United States had only six "large" cities with a population of over one hundred thousand, constituting barely 5 percent of the population. This reality would change dramatically in the next fifty years. By 1900, there were thirty-eight such cities, and they now housed roughly one in every five Americans.[23]

The spectacular growth of American cities was driven by several factors—immigration, investment from Europe, the overall growth of the North American consumer base, and most of all, the rapid development of manufacturing industries, particularly in mass production. The country had proved uniquely suited to the rapid evolution of capitalist enterprise. Adam Smith's "voice had been ringing in the world's ears for sixty years," wrote one observer in 1838, "but it is only in the United States that he is listened to, reverenced, and followed."[24]

NEW YORK'S NINETEENTH-CENTURY INDUSTRIAL AGE EMERGENCE

Large numbers of British and other European immigrants sought new lives in this booming capitalist economy, especially in the great port city of New York.[25] By 1860, Gotham's population had topped 1 million, 42 percent foreign born.[26]

Some of these immigrants lived in squalid conditions comparable to those found in Britain. Disease was rampant throughout the crowded working-class sections of Manhattan: Between 1810 and 1870, the rate of infant mortality in New York *doubled*.[27] Class distinctions, defined more by wealth than pedigree, persisted as well in the new land. "A few moments from salons superbly furnished in the style of Louis XIV," noted the writer Lydia Child, lay the abodes of "dreary desolate apartments" inhabited by "shivering urchins."[28]

Yet what most impressed many observers about New York was its extraordinary social mobility. A manual worker in an American factory still enjoyed a far better chance, and his offspring an even better one, of rising into the middle or even upper class than his European counterpart.[29] Lowly artisans and mechanics, many of them immigrants, were prominent among the owners of the more than four thousand manufacturing establishments on Manhattan island, which at the time may well have been the most rapidly industrializing place in the world.[30]

CITIES OF THE HEARTLAND

Equally dramatic changes took place out on the western frontier, where Americans were moving to in massive numbers. New cities appeared seemingly overnight on places hitherto only lightly settled by native peoples. Among the first was Cincinnati, located on a bend in the Ohio River, which grew from a tiny frontier settlement of barely 750 residents in 1800 to a booming city of more than 100,000 forty years later.

Cincinnati and other midwestern cities proved ideally suited for manufacturing growth. The region's huge agriculture surplus created an opportunity for mass production of animal products on a hitherto unimagined scale. Soon dubbed "Porkopolis," Cincinnati boasted vast slaughterhouses that dropped "rivers of blood" into Deer Creek and from there into the Ohio.

Other cities enjoyed similarly rapid growth.[31] St. Louis, home to a few hundred hardy souls at the opening of the nineteenth century, was by century's end a mature metropolis of half a million. Detroit, a rugged outpost of barely 20,000 in 1850, shot up to more than 200,000 fifty years later. Chicago's explosive growth outpaced them all. A settlement of barely 350 in 1835, it expanded to 100,000 at the time of Abraham Lincoln's election in 1860 and housed over 1 million forty years later.

These midwestern cities differed in many ways from the older coastal hubs. Unlike New York or Boston, with their thousands of small industrial shops and thriving mercantile districts, the heartland metropolis was more often dominated by giant factories, sometimes with thousands of workers, producing such hard goods as steel, agricultural implements, and cars.[32] The United States was becoming the world's leader in heavy manufacturing—and its beating heart lay in the cities of the Midwest.[33]

These cities competed ferociously, and often recklessly, with one another for preeminence. Chicago, following the panic of 1837, one speculator wrote, "resounded with the groans of ruined men and the sobs of defrauded women who entrusted all to greedy speculators." Undaunted, the city's elites proved relentless in their ambition, lobbying Washington and Wall Street for dominant position in the burgeoning east-west trade. St. Louis businesspeople, noted the *Chicago Tribune* in 1868, "wore their pantaloons out sitting and waiting for trade to come to them," while Chicago's "wore their shoes out running after it."[34]

THE CHALLENGE OF "PROGRESS"

As in Britain, America's early period of rapid industrialization left in its wake a pitifully barren urban landscape. After two years in Cincinnati, the British writer Frances Trollope wrote, "every bee in the hive is actively employed in the search for honey . . . neither art, science, learning, nor pleasure can seduce them from their pursuit." Chicago, a Swedish visitor commented in 1850, was "one of the most miserable and ugly cities" of America.[35]

The existence of grinding poverty was even more disturbing than the degraded environment. Two journalists writing in the late 1870s, in language reminiscent of Engels's picture of Manchester a generation earlier, described one St. Louis slum:

> Some of the largest and worst tenement buildings . . . are built on back lots, and instead of fronting on the street, they look out upon dirty alleys that always emit a foetid odor. They are dilapidated, grimy and foul beyond our powers of description.[36]

Such gross inequality, particularly in an avowedly egalitarian country, sparked intense class conflict. In the 1870s, St. Louis workers marched down the streets singing "La Marseillaise" and speaking of revolution. The city, the British consul warned, was "practically in the hands of the mob." Chicago, Detroit, Cleveland, and other, smaller midwestern cities experienced similar, often violent distrubances.[37]

As in Britain, some prominent citizens questioned the fundamentally utilitarian values associated with the industrial age. Some, like Josiah Strong, a Protestant minister from Ohio, even challenged the American faith in "progress." Rather than embrace economic change, Strong abjured it, believing that the industrial expansion was pushing the nation toward the "final doom of materialism."

Others, such as Chicago's Jane Addams, believed only massive intervention could address the rampant crime, deepening class conflict, and growing evidence of deviancy, from alcoholism to prostitution, common among the working poor. A host of American cities soon followed her example of providing recreation and educational opportunities in slum areas.

Reformist urges also spilled into the political world, transforming often corrupt governments in cities such as Milwaukee, Cleveland, Toledo, and Detroit.[38] Cities everywhere in America began modernizing their administrations. In 1853, for example, New York, following London's lead from a generation earlier, introduced uniformed policemen. In many cities, services such as fire protection and transportation were organized systematically for the first time.[39]

Attention now also turned to improving the urban environment, nowhere more so than in the Midwest's great metropolis of Chicago. Rebuilding after the devastating fire of 1871, the city embarked on an ambitious program of civic improvement, constructing over the next three decades a major library system, a new home for the Arts Institute, the Field Columbian Museum, and a large expansion of the University of Chicago.[40]

Reformers also began to make concerted efforts to save some of the natural environment for their increasingly harried, city-bound citizens. In the 1870s, St. Louis acquired what would later become Tower Grove and Forest Park. Similarly ambitious efforts were made in Chicago, Philadelphia, Boston, and New York.[41] "One great purpose" of New York's Central Park, noted Frederick Law Olmsted, a leader in this movement, was "to supply to the hundreds of thousands of tired workers . . . a specimen of God's handiwork."[42]

NEW YORK: THE ULTIMATE VERTICAL CITY

Owing to their nation's awesome industrial power, America's cities now stood out as the cutting edge of the world's urban civilization. Nowhere was this more evident than in New York, which by 1900 enjoyed an economic and cultural preeminence unprecedented in American history. Twice as populous as second-place rival Chicago, Gotham controlled well over 60 percent of all the bank clearings in the entire nation. Its port accounted for upwards of 40 percent of all the trade into and out of the United States.[43]

Located on a granite island in the midst of a great natural harbor, Manhattan was peculiarly suited for the construction of "a vertical city." The tight boundaries of the island had placed a premium on the use of space.[44] Rising demands for space by the diverse sectors of the city's economy—light manufacturing, trade, finance, and other services—fostered irrepressible pressure for concentration.

Manufacturing still employed many New Yorkers, but the most dramatic increases in the workforce now took place among white-collar employees as well as a swelling army of "pink collar" female clericals. The opening in 1904 of the subway system allowed increasingly large numbers to be shuttled between residential neighborhoods elsewhere on the island and the downtown and midtown office districts.

New York's annexation of Brooklyn and other adjacent areas in 1898 provided Manhattan with a sprawling hinterland from which to draw even more workers to its congested streets. Burrowing under the East River, New York's subways carried ever more commuters, inciting more office construction. New York, the writer O. Henry famously remarked, would be "a great place if they ever finished it."[45]

The burgeoning demand required structures accommodating hundreds and even thousands of office workers. The first skyscraper went up in 1895 and was quickly followed by others.[46] The key breakthrough came with the erecting in 1902 of the Flatiron Building, widely known as "Burnham's Folly," after its designer, the Chicago architect Daniel H. Burnham, because some thought it would fall of its own weight. Within a decade, an even larger building, the sixty-story Woolworth Building, rose in lower Manhattan.[47]

"LIKE A WITCH AT THE GATE OF THE COUNTRY"

As with past mercantile cities such as Athens, Alexandria, Cairo, and London, New York's commercial growth also engendered an efflorescence of cultural life.[48] More and more the global center of marketing, advertising, and mass entertainment, New York sent around the world melodies, images, and ideas for every level of cultural taste. One turn-of-the-century British writer complained that "our jokes are being machine made in the offices of New York publishers, even as [British] babies are fed on American food and their dead buried in American coffins."[49]

New York's culture also transcended European norms. Reflecting an increasingly polyglot society, Gotham served as the nursery for a wide diversity of ethnic humor, jazz, and all forms of modern art. "New York," noted James Weldon Johnson, the Harlem Renaissance poet, "is the most fatally fascinating thing in America. She sits like a witch at the gate of the country."[50]

New Yorkers themselves often saw their town as the progenitor of a new kind of city.[51] The city's glass towers and darkened streetscapes seemed to reflect a new, bold expression of the modern metropolis. The novelist John Dos Passos drew the setting in the mid-1920s:

> Glowworm trains shuttle in the gloaming through the foggy looms of spider-web bridges, elevators soar and drop in their shafts, harbor lights wink.[52]

AMERICA GOES HIGH-RISE

In much of the world as well, these images became synonymous with urbanity itself. George M. Cohan may have remarked that "after you leave New York, every town is Bridgeport," but other American cities—not only Chicago—sought to imitate Gotham's urban landscape.[53] Within a year of the completion of the Woolworth Building, Seattle had constructed the forty-two-story Smith Tower, bringing architectural giantism to the Pacific. Chicago, Detroit, Cleveland, and St. Louis all rushed to erect new monuments to their commercial vitality.[54]

Even lesser cities raced to make their statement. At a time when neither London, the world's largest city, Berlin, nor Paris boasted a single high-rise, steel-framed towers were rising in such obscure places as Bangor, Maine; Tulsa, Oklahoma; and Galveston, Texas. More tradition-bound Philadelphia, Boston, and Washington, D.C., imposed height limits, but in most places the only restraint was the exuberance of the local downtown real estate market. A "real metropolis," *The Denver Post* argued, needed such structures to assert its status.[55]

Still, the center of the new urban world lay in New York. Its growing dominance of international trade, finance, and media had made it the unsurpassed business capital of America and increasingly the world. The journalist A. H. Raskin remarked that "in a single afternoon in a single Manhattan skyscraper," decisions would be made that would determine what movies would be played in South Africa, whether or not children in a New Mexican mining town would have a school, or how much Brazilian coffee growers would receive for their crop.[56]

The soaring high-rises of America's great cities lifted the steel-and-concrete façade of the factory town to the sky. In physical terms, and as inspirers of awe, they represented the commercial city's answer to the great spired cathedrals of Europe, the elegant mosques of the Islamic world, and the imperial complexes of East Asia.[57]

Still, these towers of concrete and steel could not provide the sense of sacred place that had so shaped the urban past. Essentially structures for business, they presumed to say little about an enduring moral order or social justice. Constructed largely for profit by private interests, they could not shield the city from attack by those who now sought to impose other, radically divergent visions of the urban future.

CHAPTER THIRTEEN

INDUSTRIALISM AND ITS DISCONTENTS

After disembarking from his ship at Kobe in the fall of 1922, G. C. Allen boarded a train bound for the Japanese city of Nagoya. For the first few hours, the twenty-two-year-old British scholar traveled through an exotic and thoroughly alien landscape of terraced rice fields, tea plantations, and misty, forested hillsides.

Gradually, as the train chugged toward its destination, the scenery turned increasingly familiar. Suddenly, Allen saw a city "submerged by a swelling wave of factories, tall blocks of offices, concrete elevated roads and new tracks and bridges for high speed trains." It was almost as if he had transported back home to the great industrial metropolis of Birmingham.[1]

In Nagoya, as in Britain, the industrialization of the urban landscape had transformed the city that had existed before. "Beauty and squalor rubbed shoulders," Allen noted, often on the same block. Hidden amid the factories and creaking trolley cars could be found the running of a tiny stream or a well-kept garden tucked amid the "dull and featureless streets."[2]

THE GLOBAL IMPLICATIONS OF INDUSTRIALISM

As industrial growth spread across the world, it ushered in a new era of rapid urbanization on an unprecedented scale. By the late nineteenth century, large urban centers were appearing on every continent, in South America, Africa, Australia, and, most portentously, Asia. More than 5 percent of the world's population now lived in cities of more than one hundred thousand, nearly three times the percentage of a century earlier.[3]

In much of the world, this growth was driven by that of administrative services, trade, and export of raw materials. Industrial expansion remained limited by the mercantile policies of colonial powers and the underdevelopment of transportation systems and other modern infrastructure. In much of continental Asia and Africa, the exceedingly low cost of labor and lack of a large consumer base also discouraged the local use of machinery in favor of more dispersed, primitive rural industry.[4]

Far more dramatic progress took place in other regions. By the early part of the twentieth century, three critical countries—Japan, Germany, and Russia—boasted large and expanding industrial cities. Tokyo, Osaka, Berlin, and St. Petersburg now competed directly with New York, Manchester, and London, not only locally but often on a global scale.

As Allen noted on his way to Nagoya, these cities shared the outward appearance—the crisscrossing train tracks, the smoky factories, the office buildings—of the Anglo-American manufacturing centers. Yet they would respond to industrialism in ways strikingly different from those of Britain or America, seeking to forge alternative paths to the making of modern cities.

This search for another approach grew from the fact that all three of these countries industrialized without the democratic traditions that had helped America or Britain adjust to the shock of the new urban condition. These societies—making a rapid shift to the industrial city under essentially medieval political systems—lacked the legal structures and social attitudes to cope with what Sigmund Freud, in his landmark *Civilization and Its Discontents*, described as the "cultural frustration" with life in the large, often impersonal world of the modern metropolis.[5]

JAPAN'S SUDDEN INDUSTRIALIZATION

Freud wrote these words in Vienna just four years before that city fell to National Socialism. He would have recognized as well in Japan the familiar symptoms of a "cultural frustration." Japan's transformation to the industrial age was made all the more difficult by both its suddenness and its enormous rapidity. After the overthrow of the Tokugawas in 1868, Japan embarked full-bore on modernization. The architects of the Meiji Restoration worked busily to catch up with the dominant industrial powers, giving priority to both infrastructure investment and importation of Western technology.

Prior to Meiji, Japan's urban development had been slowed by the decision of the Tokugawa *bakufu* to ban most contact with foreigners.[6] Yet when Commodore William Perry's gunships in Tokyo Bay broke this isolation in 1853, Japan's cities—blessed with a highly literate population, a developed national market, talented artisans, and a strong entrepreneurial tradition—were better positioned than any outside Europe to meet the challenges of the industrial age.[7]

As in Britain and America, the rise of the manufacturing economy brought with it a rapid surge in the urban population. Doubling in the first half century after the Meiji revolution, city dwellers already accounted for nearly one in four Japanese by the 1920s. Osaka, with a vast assortment of smaller factories, was now dubbed the "Manchester of the East"; its population more than quintupled between 1875 and the 1920s. Nagoya, too, was transformed from an old castle town to a major industrial center, including the base for what was to become one of the world's most dominant industrial corporations, Toyota Motors. Provincial factory towns like Kawasaki, Fukuoka, and Sapporo grew even faster.[8]

Tokyo emerged as the first among all Japanese cities. Replacing Kyoto as home to the emperor, the city gained "instant legitimacy" as the spiritual as well as temporal capital of the nation.[9] Many leading business institutions now found it advantageous to locate their main offices there in preference to traditional commercial centers such as Osaka or one of the many rising industrial towns.[10]

Even after its devastation in the Kanto earthquake of 1923, which killed one hundred thousand and left millions homeless, Tokyo continued to consolidate its dominant position. By the 1930s, Tokyo boasted an imposing downtown hub, complete with tall buildings, department stores, and sophisticated mass transit.[11] For the first time since industrialization, Asia possessed a city that could compare itself with New York or London. And, for a time, it could even dream of surpassing them.

"THE IRON MONSTER"

Amid these signs of progress, industrialism also wreaked widespread social, moral, and environmental havoc. Even in the late nineteenth century, a writer noted, "red crested cranes could still be seen soaring through the skies" above Tokyo. Foxes and badgers proliferated, and the waters of the Sumida River could still be used for brewing tea.[12] Yet by the 1920s, Japanese city dwellers endured widespread pollution, numbing ugliness, and the devastation of a splendid natural environment fundamental to their traditional religious beliefs and ancient culture. Canal-laced Osaka, once known as "the city of water," had become a "city of smoke," its canals now fetid and filled with noxious chemicals.[13]

The new technologies assuredly also brought many wonders. Former peasants rode trains and streetcars to factories operated by electrical power. Lowborn artisans or impoverished samurai transcended ancient class barriers to become the new leaders of Japan's rising industrial economy. Information once limited to scholars and government officials now became widely available through universal education, mass-market books, newspapers, and eventually radio.

Yet there remained a pervasive sense that traditional ideas and nobler ways of life were now under assault by impersonal and dangerous foreign forces. Maps issued in the 1860s still referred to the mythological and historical interest of places; the railway maps of the new era eschewed poetics, concentrating instead on precise measurements.

The author Natsume Soseki, writing in 1916, protested against the "violent way" that "the iron monster" tore through the countryside and threatened one's sense of individuality.[14] The "iron monster" seemed to be devouring the brightly colored ancient central symbols of traditional Japanese urban life—walls, temples, great central markets—and replacing them with belching factories and dull gray concrete office buildings.[15]

RECONSTRUCTING JAPANESE CITIES

The severe economic downturn of the late 1920s and early 1930s led many Japanese to question the validity of Western models. More and more, Japanese leaders now thought about reconciling the demands of their ever more urban industrial society with a deeply traditionalist, often aggressively xenophobic sensibility. Rather than accept the conflict and anomie associated with industrial cities in America and Europe, some Japanese sought ways to build urban society around the more familiar and less contentious notion of extended family networks—what the sociologist Setsuko Hani calls "the idea or consciousness of the house."[16]

Asserting the hierarchy of the "house" had the effect of reinforcing the authority of parents, firm owners, military and political leaders, and, ultimately, the emperor. Many government and intellectual leaders now deemed Western notions about coping with dissent and gradual democratic change inappropriate for Japan. Instead, they sought ways to, in the words of the Ministry of Education's Spiritual Culture Institute, "perfect and unify the nation with one mind."[17]

To impose such moral unanimity on an increasingly sophisticated, urbanized society required high degrees of regimentation and repression. Working-class organizations were either co-opted or suppressed.[18] Authorities also initiated a cultural crusade against Western influences— attacking everything from Western fashions and jazz to Hollywood movies and women's emancipation. Tokyo, Osaka, and other great Japanese cities, where Western influences were most pervasive, now would be purged of cultural norms emanating from New York, Los Angeles, and London.[19]

In addition to these moral reforms, Japanese urban planners dreamed of ways to refashion urban life that would be more congruent with traditional lifestyles. With the riches of a growing empire to draw on, some devoted themselves to developing ideal new urban centers in Manchuria, Korea, and other parts of the emerging Japanese "co-prosperity sphere."

Closer to home, they worked on plans, particularly around Tokyo and Nagoya, to replace sprawling apartment blocs with greenbelts and neat, satellite communities. Uzo Nishiyama, one of the most influential planners, based his urban vision on the traditional neighborhood structure, the *machi*. Work and housing would be integrated as much as possible, promoting a way of life closer to that of the traditional village. Nishiyama's traditionalist sensibility also led him to oppose the high-rise construction increasingly emblematic of American cities, favoring instead the development of what he called "life spheres," decentralized, self-governing neighborhoods.

THE NAZI EXPERIMENT

Nishiyama and other Japanese planners drew some of their inspiration from neotraditionalist ideas developed by the National Socialist theorist Gottfried Feder. In his book *Die nue Stadt*, Feder forcefully advocated the creation of decentralized urban zones surrounded by agricultural areas.[20] Feder also shared the unease of Nishiyama, and other Japanese, about the negative impact of cosmopolitan, Anglo-American society on what he considered traditional values.[21]

As in Japan, the Industrial Revolution arrived late in Germany, but also with sudden and unsettling consequences. Nowhere was this more evident than in Berlin, the capital of the newly united German state. After centuries as a stodgy and rather unimpressive Prussian "barracks town," Berlin at the end of the nineteenth century suddenly had developed into a vast metropolis of over 1.5 million. The city was ringed with vast industrial plants where, as one observer noted, "every chimney [was] spewing out great showers of sparks and thick billows of smoke, as if it was the fire city of Vulcan."

Widely acknowledged as the most modern city in Europe, the capital of the newly united Germany was also known as "America in miniature" or "Chicago on the Spree."[22] This rapid evolution brought with it the familiar problems of industrial cities—slum housing, crime, and a startling rise of illegitimacy. By 1900, Berlin was both the most crowded city in Europe and a prime center for radical Socialist agitation.[23]

Berlin's thriving industry attracted Germans from the rural provinces as well as immigrants from the impoverished Polish hinterlands. Many of these newcomers felt alternately inspired and appalled by a city where "the money economy" overwhelmed traditional values. A native Berliner, the sociologist George Simmel, observed:

With each crossing of the street, with the tempo and multiplicity of economic, occupational and social life, the city sets up a deep contrast with small town and rural life with reference to the sensory foundations of psychic life.[24]

As in Japan, this assault on Germans' "psychic life" engendered a sharp rise in xenophobia. The Jews, long objects of European hatred, fear, and resentment, bore the brunt of this growing antiforeign model.[25] In 1895, voters in Vienna, the sophisticated cultural capital of the German-speaking world, elected an avowed anti-Semite, Karl Lueger, as their mayor.

The mayor's successful exploitation of anti-Semitism impressed one young provincial, Adolf Hitler, then a struggling artist in the Austrian capital. Decades later, the National Socialist führer would call Lueger "the mightiest Mayor of all times."[26] Like Lueger, Hitler and the National Socialists, including his adviser Gottfried Feder, identified the Jews—both for their capitalist savvy and their prominence among the leading Socialist agitators—as the primary economic and moral threat to the German urban middle class.[27]

Like the Japanese, the Nazis waged a broader cultural war against what they saw as foreign art, music, and culture. They campaigned against Anglo-American styles of dress, "degenerate" jazz, and literature, then widely popular in German cities. Such decadence was identified most particularly with Berlin—a place the local party boss Joseph Goebbels derided as "that sink of iniquity."[28]

Once in power, Hitler jettisoned much of Feder's program for deconcentration of urban areas and sent his old mentor off to a respectable semiretirement. Rather than return to the village past, the Nazis now sought to mold their cities into their own "alternative form of modernity."[29] Hitler now insisted Berlin be "raised to a high level of culture that it may compete with all the capital cities of the world."

Following the brilliantly staged 1936 Olympics, Hitler's chief architect, Albert Speer, developed elaborate plans to transform Berlin into Germania, a massive metropolis that would serve as a modern-day equivalent of ancient Rome or Babylon. The city would be graced with massive boulevards and ceremonial centers, including a domed meeting hall capable of holding 125,000 people and an Adolf Hitler Square, which could accommodate a throng of 1 million.

Still, not all of Feder's ideas were discarded. In their plans for their new occupied eastern territories, the Nazis envisioned an archipelago of compact German-dominated industrial centers, surrounded by agricultural settlements and traditionalist villages.[30] These grandiose plans, like those of the Japanese imperialists, ended with the devastating loss of World War II. Utterly ruined, Japanese and German cities, at least in the West, would rise again, but only under American tutelage.

RUSSIA: THE THIRD ALTERNATIVE

Russia's urbanization lagged behind that of other countries, including both Japan and Germany. Czar Peter, who assumed the crown in 1689, had traveled extensively in Europe, visiting great cities like London and Amsterdam. He wanted his empire's capital to be both modern and outward looking. Only when Russia had caught up with its European rivals, he believed, could they "show their ass" to the West.[31]

Peter's new capital of St. Petersburg, founded in 1703, was envisioned to combine the commercial energy of the Dutch capital with the glorious architecture of Italy and Versailles. It was to be everything Moscow—"Asiatic, anti-western, heavy-handed, vulgar, oppressive and provincial"—was not.[32]

As the new locus of political power, St. Petersburg expanded rapidly, attaining a population of two hundred thousand by Czarina Catherine's death in 1796 and half a million by the mid-nineteenth century.[33] Its development as a manufacturing center, however, was slow. Russia, like North America, was naturally well positioned for industrial growth, with both enormous resources and a vast inland network of rivers. These physical advantages were largely offset by an exceedingly regressive social order; as late as 1861, much of the population, including many residing temporarily in the capital, consisted of serfs legally bound to their agricultural villages.[34]

Even after emancipation, Russian cities suffered from the absence of the large independent property-owning class so critical to urban growth in Britain or America. Most economic resources remained in the hands of the state, the aristocracy, and, increasingly, foreign investors. The middle ranks consisted largely of petty traders and officials, academics, and other professionals serving the regime.[35]

This highly inflexible class structure, and an authoritarian political system, served to widen the gap between the urban population and the ruling elite. With little hope for gradual reform, or a stake in their nation's progress, the middle and working classes became increasingly radicalized.[36]

THE ROAD TO REVOLUTION

The Russian workers and middle class had ample reason for their rage. As Russia began to industrialize, its municipal institutions and basic physical infrastructure lingered in the feudal past. The ancient capital of Moscow remained a haphazard collection of one-story wooden buildings, often wretchedly constructed and without basic sanitation. The city also lacked a professional police force and adequate medical care.

The chasm between these realities and the luxurious life of the ruling classes was most evident in St. Petersburg, where, as the playwright Nikolay Vasilyevich Gogol noted, "everything's an illusion, everything's a dream, everything's not what it seems." A stone's throw from the Italianate elegance of the Winter Palace, workers lived in poorly ventilated, fetid slums in what was contemporary Europe's most disease-ridden city.

St. Petersburg's industrial structure was dominated by large manufacturing facilities, which inadvertently facilitated the mass organization of workers. After failing in their demands for more food and better working conditions, these workers organized into "soviets," or self-governing committees, and turned on the regime itself.[37] In October 1917, St. Petersburg's factory laborers, a tiny urban minority in a largely agricultural country, helped put into power a new regime that would create the third, and most long-lasting, alternative to the Anglo-American industrial city.

THE SOVIET SYSTEM

The triumphant Bolshevik regime turned out to be, if anything, more autocratic than that of the czar. Their rejection of Western materialism was even more far-reaching than that of the Japanese or the Nazis. "Everything was cancelled," recalled the novelist Aleksey Tolstoi. "Ranks, honors, pensions, officer's epaulettes, the thirteenth letter of the alphabet, God, private property, and even the right to live as one wished."[38]

The Communists embraced Czar Peter's dream of creating a highly urbanized Russia. Even in 1917, observed one historian, Russian cities were little more than "islands in an ocean of peasants"; only 15 percent of the population lived in urban centers. With their consolidation of power, the Communists determined to reverse history, making these "islands" ever larger and more powerful.[39]

As the chosen capital of the Soviet revolution, Moscow regained its favored position. Keeping Moscow's population contented now constituted a key political concern of the Bolshevik leaders. "The salvation of the Moscow workers from starvation," Lenin noted, "is the salvation of the revolution." Food was taken, often by force, from the farmers to feed what was deemed the new ruling class, the urban proletariat.[40]

Moscow's population fell drastically during the civil war that raged between 1917 and 1921 but began expanding rapidly again in the mid-1920s, reaching over 2 million people by the late 1920s. With the reimposition of order, death rates dropped and birthrates soared. Seeking work in the new center of power, tens of thousands of ambitious, often hungry people migrated every year into the city.[41]

More cosmopolitan St. Petersburg, renamed Leningrad after the Soviet founder's death in 1924, fared worse. Well in advance of their counterparts in Japan or Germany, the Communists launched a sweeping assault against Western urban culture. Anyone even receiving letters from abroad, a group most concentrated in the old capital, could be hauled off to the ever expanding gulag. The great purges of the 1930s stripped away much of the city's intellectual and artistic elite, including some fifty curators at the Hermitage.[42]

"SHARPENING OUR AXES"

The Soviets had equally little reverence for the role of sacred place or the past in the evolution of cities. In short order, Nizhniy Novgorod became Gorky; Tsaritsyn was renamed Stalingrad; Yekaterinburg, where Czar Nicholas II and his family were liquidated, became Sverdlovsk, after another Soviet leader. In elegant, newly renamed Leningrad, the urban landscape became dominated by massive new housing blocs, office buildings, and commercial spaces designed in what one writer called "a ponderously neoclassical" style.[43]

Moscow underwent an even more dramatic transition. Joseph Stalin, a provincial from distant Georgia, displayed even less appreciation for urban values than Hitler, who had spent his formative years in Vienna and Munich, or the Japanese nationalists, who still revered aspects of that country's urban past. To the horror of much of the architectural community, the Soviet dictator ordered the construction of a new Palace of Soviets—a monument to what Stalin called "the idea of the creativity of the multi-million Soviet democracy"—on the site of the city's magnificent Cathedral of the Savior, a structure built with the pennies of Russia's faithful.

Nikita Khrushchev, who eventually would follow Stalin as leader of the "Soviet democracy," shared these less than delicate sensibilities. "In reconstructing Moscow," he said in 1937, "we should not be afraid to remove a tree, a little church or some cathedral or other."[44] Khrushchev proceeded to destroy much of the old city, including its Triumphal Arch, its old towers, and its walls. When his own architects pleaded with him to spare historic monuments, he replied that his construction crews would continue "sharpening our axes."[45]

The Communist drive to expand manufacturing capacity—by the 1930s, the Soviets had surpassed czarist industry by a wide margin—engendered an ambitious surge in town building. Magnitogorsk, rising adjacent to a giant iron and steel factory on the steppe, typified the new Soviet city: no mosques, churches, or free markets, a population of forced laborers driven by legions of zealous Young Communists. Like the victims of Britain's early capitalist industrialization, the forced workers of the Socialist state endured wretched conditions, subject to epidemics of typhus, typhoid, and other infectious diseases.[46]

In one respect, Soviet urban policies did succeed: They utterly transformed a predominantly rural country into a largely urban one. By the 1930s, cities such as Moscow and Leningrad ranked among the largest in Europe; other smaller cities, particularly factory towns like Sverdlovsk, Gorky, Stalingrad, and Chelyabinsk, expanded even more rapidly. Between 1939 and 1959, the urban population of the Soviet Union grew by 30 million people, while the rural component dropped by 20 million. By 1960, 50 percent of Soviet citizens were city dwellers.[47] There were also some notable accomplishments, such as the Moscow subway and major new electrification systems.

COMMUNISM'S URBAN LEGACY

After World War II, urban conditions in the Soviet Union gradually improved. Food became more plentiful and the long acute housing shortage less acute. Nevertheless, as places to live, Communist cities remained gray and cheerless; spontaneous commercial activity was restricted to the occasional farmer's market or the hidden machinations of a growing underground economy. Social life centered less in the streets or public spaces than among friends crowded into small but often cheerily maintained apartments.

Most telling—particularly given the system's "materialist" value system—the Soviets failed to create an urban standard of living even remotely comparable to those in the the West. Khrushchev's boasts as late as 1970 that the USSR would "outstrip" the United States in quality of life must have seemed incongruous, if not painfully comic, to city dwellers whose level of amenities lagged well behind those of not only the West, but also some rising Asian countries.[48]

As the Communist regime slouched toward its inglorious dénouement in the late 1980s, conditions worsened. The vast complex of high-rise apartments around Moscow and other major cities became increasingly dilapidated. Two-thirds of heavily urbanized European Russia's water supply no longer met minimal standards; air pollution levels in most large Soviet cities were many times worse than those in any city in the West.[49]

Born to remedy the failures of the industrial city, Communist urbanism failed in virtually every respect to meet its promise, and nowhere more than in the moral sphere. Communism, Nicolas Berdyaev once noted, sought to develop a "new man" of higher aspirations, but its materialist philosophy ultimately transformed its subject into a "flat two dimensional being." Robbing cities and individuals of their sacred character and often their history, the Soviet experiment left behind a somber and destitute urban legacy.[50]

PART SIX

THE MODERN METROPOLIS

CHAPTER FOURTEEN

THE SEARCH FOR A "BETTER CITY"

Like so many who came to Los Angeles in the waning days of the nineteenth century, Dana Bartlett could sense the emergence of "a great city . . . forming by the sunset sea."[1] Los Angeles, then a settlement of fewer than one hundred thousand souls, was abuzz with new construction as developers struggled to keep pace with newcomers streaming in from the East.

The business leaders in the once sleepy Mexican pueblo envisioned a metropolis, in the words of the railroad magnate Henry Huntington, "destined to become the most important city in this country, if not the world."[2] Bartlett, a Protestant minister, heartily shared the booster faith but also yearned for something more—the promise of a healthful and beautiful urban form.

THE PROMISE OF LOS ANGELES

Before arriving in Los Angeles, Bartlett had ministered in St. Louis, where crowded slums and belching factories seemed to scar both souls and the landscape. With its mild climate and spectacular scenery, its clear vistas, ample land, and lightly industrialized economy, Los Angeles, Bartlett hoped, could become "a place of inspiration for nobler living."[3]

In his book *The Better City*, written in 1907, Bartlett laid out a vision for a planned "City Beautiful" that would offer its residents easy access to beaches, meadows, and mountains. Taking advantage of the wide-open landscape, manufacturing plants would be "transferred" to the periphery, and housing for the working class would be spread out to avoid over-crowding. Rather than confined to stifling tenements, workers would live in neat, single-family homes.[4]

Many in Los Angeles's political and economic elites embraced this more sprawling notion of urbanism. The city's form did not develop by happenstance; it was designed to be an intentional paradise. In 1908, for example, Los Angeles created the first comprehensive urban zoning ordi-nance in the nation, one that encouraged the development of subcenters, single-family homes, and dispersed industrial development.[5]

Huntington's sprawling Pacific Electric Railway had set the pattern for the city's expansive geography. Later, the growing use of the automobile further accelerated Los Angeles's dispersion. As early as the 1920s, Ange-lenos were four times as likely to own a car as the average American and ten times as likely as a Chicago resident. At the same time, in contrast with most contemporary American cities, Los Angeles's historic down-town was already becoming less important as the region's economic and social center.[6]

The usual motivations—the quest for greed and power—motivated these developments. But many among the region's bureaucrats and devel-opers also believed they were creating a superior, more healthful urban environment. In 1923, the director of city planning proudly proclaimed that Los Angeles had avoided "the mistakes which have happened in the growth of metropolitan areas of the east." This brash new metropolis of the West, he claimed, would show "how it should be done."[7]

The local press, eager for new residents and readers, promoted such notions. The city had laid out its tracts and transit lines, boasted the edi-tor of the *Los Angeles Express,* "in advance of the demands." The prevalence of single-family residences, with their backyards, would transform the city into "the world's symbol of all that was beautiful and healthful and inspiring." Los Angeles, he continued, "will retain the flowers and or-chards and lawns, the invigorating free air from the ocean, the bright sunshine and the elbow room."[8]

By the 1930s, large elements of this vision had been realized. Single-family residences accounted for 93 percent of the city's residential build-ings, almost twice the rate in Chicago. These houses spread over an area that made Los Angeles the world's largest city in terms of square miles.[9]

The city proved markedly less successful in achieving the ideals espoused by Bartlett and his contemporaries. Turning aside a 1930 detailed open-space plan known as the Olmsted-Bartholomew Plan, Los Angeles for all its vastness sadly included only a small amount of park space. Increasingly, the city not only lacked the great public areas of earlier cities, but was also rapidly losing the small-town atmosphere advertised so heavily by the city's promoters.[10]

Los Angeles, however, could not be dismissed as a failure. Sprawling from the ocean to the deserts and down the coast to the edge of San Diego, it had provided for its many millions a "better city," experienced not in great public spaces, but in individual neighborhoods, private homes, and backyards. In the late twentieth century, the ranks of Angelenos swelled with a large number of immigrants, largely from Latin America and Asia. Like earlier generations, they began buying homes, starting businesses, and building new lives in the region.[11]

Most important, Los Angeles demonstrated to the world a new model of urban growth—dispersed, multicentered, and largely suburbanized. For modern cities, whether elsewhere in America, in old Europe, or emerging in Asia, Los Angeles now represented the prevailing form of urbanity, the original, as one observer put it, in the Xerox machine.

A SHORT HISTORY OF SUBURBIA

The rise of the suburban model in Los Angeles suggested a radical break with the evolution of cities. Throughout history, cities have gloried in their towering landscapes and the liveliness of their public spaces. The most sacred and awesome public structures inevitably rose in or around the core. The most dynamic ancient cities—Tyre, Carthage, and Rome—responded to a burgeoning population by building upward and cramming ever more residents into the central space.

The onset of the Industrial Revolution greatly accelerated the rate of urban growth, placing unprecedented pressure on the geography of cities. By 1800, European cities had become at least twice as dense as their medieval antecedents; some American cities, notably New York, were even more crowded.[12] Once refuges of security, the inner city had also become increasingly crime-ridden.[13]

Even so, early in the industrial era, it was not at all clear that the future lay in the periphery. Initially, it was the poor who led the move to the urban periphery, in effect exchanging longer commutes for lower rents. "Even the word suburb," noted the historian Kenneth Jackson, "suggested inferior manners, narrowness of view, and physical squalor."[14] Suburbs often remained the abode of all manner of undesirables, the rejects of the city.[15]

"ONIONS FIFTY TO A ROPE"

One solution to managing the growth of cities would be to reorganize and revitalize the core urban space, as occurred in the mid-nineteenth century in Paris under the leadership of Napoleon III and his prefect, Baron Haussmann. Britain, the world's most urbanized country, chose a dramatically different direction, one that would ultimately find its most complete expression in distant Los Angeles.

To start with, London's problems were of a different order from those of Paris; by 1910, it was the world's largest city, with three times the population of the French capital.[16] Even to affluent Londoners in the nineteenth century, the city appeared to be choking of its own growth. Pleasant neighborhoods like Bloomsbury, Belgravia, and Regent's Park increasingly seemed like isolated islands of graceful urbanization amid a sea of gray, dense, and staggeringly unattractive industrial slums.[17]

In their search for a "better city," London authorities could not command massive resources, like Paris, to redevelop the core of its capital. Instead, the British simply allowed what had been occurring naturally, a gradual, inexorable expansion of the urban space.[18] It started initially with the most affluent residents, but as the nineteenth century evolved, the increasingly prosperous middle and working classes joined the exodus to the countryside. If a nice apartment in the middle of the city was the dream of the upwardly mobile Parisian, the Londoner's aspiration fixed upon a cottage, detached or semidetached, somewhere out on the periphery of the city. London, one observer noted in 1843, "surrounds itself, suburb clinging to suburb, like onions fifty to a rope."[19]

Other major British cities evolved in a similar manner. In the great industrial centers of Lancashire and the Midlands, everyone from great industrialists to clerks sought to move away from the belching factories and congested commercial districts. "The townsman," noted one observer of

Manchester and Liverpool in the 1860s, "does everything in his power to cease being a townsman, and tries to fit a country house and a bit of country into a corner of the town."[20]

A NEW URBAN VISION

Many Britons saw this pattern of dispersion as the logical solution to Britain's long-standing urban ills. H. G. Wells predicted that improvements in communication and transportation technology, most especially commuter rail lines, would eliminate the need to concentrate people and industry in the central core. Instead of "massing" people in town centers, Wells foresaw the "centrifugal possibilities" of a dispersing population. He predicted that eventually all of southern England would become the domain of London, while the vast landscape between Albany and Washington, D.C., would provide the geographic base for New York and Philadelphia.[21]

This vision was widely embraced by those who, like Dana Bartlett, were horrified by the ill effects of industrial urbanism. With the overthrow of capitalism, Friedrich Engels predicted the end of the large megacity and dispersal of the industrial proletariat into the countryside. The dispersing city dwellers would "deliver the rural population from isolation and stupor" while finally solving the working class's persistent housing crisis.[22]

Suburbanization also appealed to more conservative thinkers. Setting the stage for later reformers, Thomas Carlyle believed the growth of the industrial city had undermined the traditional ties between workers and their families, communities, and churches. Moving the working and middle classes to "villages" in the outlying regions of major cities could "turn back the clock" to the more wholesome and intimate environment. In the small town or village, he hoped, women and children could be protected from the injurious influences of the city, with its bawdy houses, taverns, and pleasure gardens.[23]

The British planner Ebenezer Howard emerged as perhaps the most influential advocate for dispersing the urban masses. Horrified by the disorder, disease, and crime of the contemporary industrial metropolis, he advocated the creation of "garden cities" on the suburban periphery. These self-contained towns, with a population of roughly thirty thousand, would have their own employment base and neighborhoods of pleasant cottages and would be surrounded by rural areas. "Town and country *must be married*," Howard preached, "and out of this joyous union will spring a new hope, a new life, a new civilization."

Determined to turn his theories into reality, Howard was the driving force behind two of England's first planned towns, Letchworth in 1903 and Welwyn in 1920. His "garden city" model of development soon influenced planners around the world, in America, Germany, Australia, Japan, and elsewhere.[24]

"A SIX ROOM HOUSE WITH A BIG YARD"

Even before the first "garden cities" were being developed in Britain, America also embraced the notion of urban deconcentration. By the 1870s, prominent Philadelphia families already were escaping the crowded streets of William Penn's old city for the leafier west side and toward Germantown to the north. The ensuing development of suburban railroads carried much of the city's business and professional establishment away from the central Rittenhouse Square area to residences in Chestnut Hill and other Main Line communities.[25]

The shift to the suburbs was particularly robust in the far West and across the industrial Midwest. Land was generally less expensive and urban culture far less developed. The reasons for moving to the periphery seemed self-evident to working-class people, like one Chicago meatcutter who in the 1920s exchanged "a four bedroom house on the second floor of an apartment house" for "a six room house with a big yard" in Meadowdale in the far western suburbs.[26]

As automobile registrations soared in the 1920s, suburbanization across the rest of the country also picked up speed, with suburbs growing at twice the rate of cities. Cities, noted *National Geographic* in 1923, were "spreading out."[27] The Great Depression temporarily slowed the outward migration, but not the yearning among Americans.[28] At the nadir of national fortune in 1931, President Herbert Hoover noted:

> To possess one's home is the hope and ambition of almost every individual in this country, whether he lives in a hotel, apartment or tenement. . . . The immortal ballads, *Home Sweet Home, My Old Kentucky Home,* and the *Little Gray Home in the West,* were not written about tenements or apartments. . . .[29]

CHAPTER FIFTEEN

SUBURBIA TRIUMPHANT

Following World War II, the pace of suburbanization in America again accelerated, accounting for a remarkable 84 percent of the nation's population increase during the 1950s. Thanks in large part to the passage of legislation aiding veterans, home ownership became an integral aspect of middle- and even working-class life. By the mid-1980s, America enjoyed a rate of home ownership, roughly two-thirds of all families, double that of such prosperous countries as Germany, Switzerland, France, Great Britain, and Norway. Nearly three-quarters of AFL-CIO members and the vast majority of intact families owned their own homes.[1]

Once a nation of farms and cities, America was being transformed into a primarily suburban country. No longer confined to old towns or "streetcar suburbs" near the urban core, suburbanites increasingly lived in ever more spread-out new developments such as Levittown, which arose out on the Long Island flatlands in the late 1940s and early 1950s.[2] New York planning czar Robert Moses, who helped devise the road system that made developments like Levittown viable, understood the enormous appeal of these new communities:

> The little identical suburban boxes of average people, which differ only in color and planting, represent a measure of success unheard of by hundreds of millions on other continents. Small plots reflect not merely the rapacity of de-

velopers but the caution of owners who do not want too much grass to cut and snow to shovel—details too intimate for historians.[3]

The suburbs, noted the historian Jon C. Teaford, provided an endless procession of lawns and carports, but also "a mixture of escapism and reality."[4] They offered a welcome respite from both crowded urban neighborhoods and old ethnic ties. There one could make new friendships and associations without worrying about old social conventions. And with their ample yards, new schools, and parks, noted the novelist Ralph G. Martin, the suburbs seemed to offer "a paradise for children."[5]

THE "SLEEP OF DEATH"

Clearly the preference of millions, the suburbs won few admirers among the sophisticated social critics and urban scholars of the time. The new peripheral communities were decried for everything from scarring the landscape to being cultural wastelands. Over the last half of the twentieth century, suburbs were held responsible for turning America into "a placeless collection of subdivisions," for "splintering" the nation's identity, and even for helping to expand the nation's waistlines.[6] As the poet Richard Wilbur wrote in the mid-twentieth century:

> In the summer sunk and stupefied
> The suburbs deepen in their sleep of death.[7]

As subdivisions ran into old, established communities, particularly in the Northeast and Midwest, they often undermined long-standing economies and ways of life. One observer wrote about an old Connecticut mill that, once the center of the local economy, had been shut down and now sat mute, "intimidated by the headlights of commuters as they race up and down the valley, weary from the city and hungry for home."[8]

The harshest critics tended to be dedicated urbanists and impassioned city dwellers. Lewis Mumford identified the suburbs as "the anti-city," sucking the essence out of the old urban areas. As more residents and businesses headed for the periphery, he argued, the suburbs were turning cities from creative centers into discarded parcels of "a disordered and disintegrating urban mass."

Perhaps the most telling criticism of suburban migration focused on an expanding racial divide between the heavily white suburbs and the increasingly black inner cities. Clearly, some new suburbanites, and the developers catering to them, shared a deep-seated racism: In 1970, nearly 95 percent of suburbanites were white. "In some suburbs," complained the author William H. Whyte, "[you] may hardly see a Negro, a poor person, or, for that matter, anyone over fifty."[9]

Long concentrated in the rural South, African Americans now dominated the populations of many large cities, particularly in the North and Midwest. By the 1960s, more than 51 percent of African Americans lived in the inner cities, compared with only 30 percent of whites.[10] This pattern was most notable in industrial cities such as Detroit, Newark, St. Louis, Cleveland, and Oakland, California.[11]

The ensuing social crisis caused by the growing gap between the city and the suburbs threatened to tear the nation apart—and devastate the urban cores. In 1968, Lewis Mumford could write convincingly about the "progressive dissolution" of American cities.[12] At the time, many cities seemed consumed with social pathologies, from illegitimacy to crime and drug addiction.[13] "Social disorder," *The New York Times* complained in 1968, "is rampant in New York."[14] In contrast, the suburbs appeared to many whites as a welcome refuge from high crime rates in the inner city.

SKYSCRAPERS AFLAME

Faced with both a rising suburban tide and increasing rancor among their largely impoverished residents, the central cities worked with increasing desperation to secure their historic primacy. New technology, some suggested, now made possible not only sprawl, but an unprecedented degree of urban concentration. The old city centers could be saved, they insisted, if only the encumbrances of the past were swept away and replaced with something more thoroughly modern.

In the Swiss-born architect Charles-Édouard Jeanneret, known more widely as Le Corbusier, this viewpoint found its most articulate advocate. Le Corbusier looked with disdain on the contemporary city's hodgepodge of cottages, small apartments, and tenements. In its stead, he envisioned vistas of sixteen-story apartment blocs, amid massive towers set aside for commerce. His ideal—published in his *La Ville radieuse*—separated the functions of housing, commerce, recreation, and transport and provided ample green space for the enjoyment of city residents.

Le Corbusier detested the ornamentation of previous cities as wasteful and antimodern. To secure the future, he urged cities to demolish their past. He even supported the efforts of planners in the Soviet Union—whose postwar construction of superblocs reflected his ideas—to demolish much of historic Moscow.

New York's old brownstones, downtown narrow streets, and eclectic mix of architectural styles possessed no more appeal to him than the onion spires of the Kremlin. He was appalled by the squalor of the city's vast tenement complexes, the disorder of the teeming crowds jostling in the subways. What excited him were the possibilities suggested by the yawning bridges and high-rise towers of Manhattan, where, he wrote, "as twilight falls the glass skyscrapers seem to flame."

In his vision, New York reached even farther into the sky. Le Corbusier saw a city where "glass skyscrapers would rise like crystals, clean and transparent in the midst of the foliage of trees." Le Corbusier's idealized New York would be a "fantastic, almost mystic city . . . a vertical city, under the sign of new times."

Although he desired Europe to reassert itself as the leader in urban design and build on a "magnificent ripening" of its civilization,[15] Le Corbusier's notions did not appeal much to Europeans, who were largely satisfied with the continent's nineteenth-century legacy. Yet aspects of his thinking over time would find adherents elsewhere, not only in the United States, but in the burgeoning cities of the developing world—in Brazil, South Korea, Japan, China, Malaysia, and Singapore.

"GRAND ACHIEVEMENTS" AND THEIR LIMITATIONS

The soaring modernist vision espoused by Le Corbusier also left a powerful imprint on America's cities. Between 1960 and 1972, office space in central Chicago expanded by 50 percent, while New York's soared an astonishing 74 percent, creating skylines that the British author Emrys Jones described as "always dramatic and sometimes awe-inspiring." Huge towers also arose in cities such as Boston, San Francisco, Houston, and even Los Angeles.[16]

Such massive buildings, suggested Minoru Yamasaki, one of the world's premier modern architects, reflected "a society such as ours, which is one of large-scale and grand achievements."[17] Yet these "grand achievements" of concrete-and-glass structures also exacted a terrible price in already existing urban neighborhoods. Yamasaki's ill-fated World Trade Center, constructed between 1966 and 1977, not only displaced thousands of small businesses centered around the old electrical district, but essentially cut off whole sections of New York's West Side from one another.[18]

Clearly, such massive redevelopment failed to halt the migration of people and businesses to the periphery. Indeed, as the noted urbanist Jane Jacobs suggested, they may instead have accelerated dispersion. As the nation's population rose by over 60 million in the last decades of the century, that of the central cities stagnated and in some cases continued to drop. By 1990, even New Yorkers seemed to have lost their faith in the cult of urban grandiosity; roughly six in ten told surveyors that they would live somewhere else if they could.[19]

THE FINAL AGONIES OF THE INDUSTRIAL CITY

By millennium's end, for every two of the world's major cities that were adding population, as many as three were losing people. The greatest declines took place in the old industrial cities—St. Louis, Manchester, Leipzig—that a century earlier had stood at the cutting edge of urban development. In some cases, not only did the inner core hollow out and the surrounding neighborhoods decline, but the city's very sense of identity eroded beyond recognition.[20] Writing of his hometown, the novelist Jonathan Franzen asked:

> What becomes of a city no living person can remember of an age whose passing no one survives to regret? Only St. Louis knew.[21]

The identities of America's other world-powerful manufacturing centers—Newark, Cleveland, St. Louis, and Detroit—were now overrun by images and ideas from New York and, if not from there, sprawling upstarts like Los Angeles or Silicon Valley. Although their suburbs often remained relatively healthy, these no longer constituted major urban centers. Midwestern cities, noted the historian Jon Teaford, had been transformed into a "cultural colony . . . down at the heel dowdy matrons, sporting last year's cultural fashions." Once proud and independent urban beacons, they had evolved into "vast conurbations defying definition."[22]

This drift toward oblivion reflected a worldwide phenomenon. In Japan, Osaka, Nagoya, and other manufacturing-oriented cities lost their most talented citizens and much of their distinctiveness to Tokyo. Similarly, once world-leading industrial powerhouses such as Manchester fell to relative insignificance against London, with its world-class cultural institutions, global connectivity, and concentration of advertising agencies. Other old European industrial centers such as Turin and Düsseldorf also stagnated and declined.[23]

THE "UNIVERSAL ASPIRATION"

Suburbia, triumphant in the world's leading economy, also swept successfully through virtually every part of the advanced industrial world. Compared with the option of living closely packed in apartment complexes, most human beings seemed to define their personal "better city" as a little more space and privacy, and perhaps even a spot of lawn. Noted Edgardo Contini, the prominent Los Angeles urbanist and an Italian immigrant:

> The suburban house is the idealization of every immigrant's dream—the vassal's dream of his own castle. Europeans who come here are delighted by our suburbs. Not to live in an apartment! It is a universal aspiration to own your own home.[24]

ARGENTINA AND AUSTRALIA

This "universal aspiration" emerged early in former colonial cities in Argentina and Australia. Urbanites in these land-rich countries were quick to take advantage of peripheral locations. By 1904 Buenos Aires had spread out so far that, as one Spanish observer commented, it "was not a city, but a combination of adjoining cities." This trend would continue throughout the rest of the century.[25]

Much the same occurred in Australia. As the rural population dropped precipitously after 1930, the suburbs around the great Australian cities, notably Melbourne and Sydney, grew as rapidly as in the United States. Like their American counterparts, Australian intellectuals generally despised the suburbanizing trend, but the population still gravitated to these less than culturally effervescent places, which, as one writer charitably observed, appealed to "the Australian's concentration on his home and family."[26]

BRITAIN AND THE MODERN "GARDEN CITY"

Following the devastation of World War II, British planners consciously sought to move both industry and population out of the crowded core of London to the periphery. The Abercrombie Plan, first unveiled in 1943, placed great emphasis on the development of "new towns," surrounded by green space, that would expand the capital's periphery.[27]

The plan was only partially implemented, but in ensuing decades the increased use of automobiles, as elsewhere, accelerated the shift to the suburbs. Between 1980 and 2000, the built-up area of Britain more than doubled, even though the rate of population growth was slight.[28] Perhaps more revealing, some 70 percent of those still dwelling in the urban centers in 2000 told surveyors they'd prefer living somewhere else.[29]

Nowhere was this trend more marked than in London, the first great global city and still a major financial capital. In the postwar era, the city's outer rings offered many middle- and even working-class residents what was impossible to achieve in the core—the opportunity to own a house. Over 60 percent of outer London residents were property owners, more than twice the percentage for those living closer to the city.[30]

This search to fulfill "the universal aspiration" altered the basic geography of the region. After 1960, central London began to lose population while the overall region, particularly the outer fringes, experienced considerable growth.[31] As H. G. Wells had predicted a century earlier, much of southern and even central England was rapidly becoming a vast, dispersed suburb of London. Even once distant rural areas such as Kent and Cornwall felt the vagaries of London's housing market. Not all heading to the country were daily commuters; some headed in two to three times a week while working at home or in a satellite office.[32]

SUBURBANIZATION IN WESTERN EUROPE

Similar patterns could be seen in Western Europe's other cities, despite powerful regulatory biases against suburban growth and low rates of population growth.[33] In the 1980s, populations in such cities as Madrid and Düsseldorf fell even as the outer ring expanded dramatically.[34] Germany, which had the largest economy in Europe, displayed this trend in convincing fashion. This occurred despite German planners' general inclination toward neighborhood-centric "urbanity."[35]

Between 1970 and 1997, Frankfurt, the nation's financial center, saw its core population drop while the less densely populated suburban periphery, now extending as much as thirty to fifty miles away, surged dramatically. Employment followed, dropping in the city while growing in surrounding areas. Hamburg experienced a similar pattern.[36]

As in Britain or America, this outward movement reflected the "universal aspiration" for home ownership, which increasingly could be achieved only in new housing developments on the periphery. The home in suburbia was not so much a rejection of the metropolis, noted one German scholar, as a step "forward to a happy life."[37]

THE GHETTOIZATION OF EUROPEAN CITIES

Negative factors, notably fear of crime, also began to accelerate in the dispersion from Europe's major cities.[38] In some cities, this growing sense of insecurity stemmed in large part from an influx of immigrants, mainly from Africa and the Middle East. These newcomers had been recruited to Europe during labor shortages in the 1950s and 1960s, but many remained, increasingly underemployed or out of work, as the continent's economy stagnated.[39]

In several places, such as Rotterdam and Amsterdam, where immigrants accounted for as much as 30 and 40 percent of the population, they represented an increasingly angry and sometimes violent element in what long had been remarkably peaceful urban areas.[40] As the immigrants increasingly dominated large parts of the inner city, many native-born Netherlanders began moving out to prosperous suburban developments in the periphery.[41] A similar pattern of suburban migration and increasingly immigrant-dominated inner cities also evolved in nearby Brussels.[42]

EVEN IN PARIS

Even Paris, long the bastion of urban centralization, began to experience an outward movement. Despite the assumption that Parisians are "addicted" to dense living, many now seemed as anxious as Americans for a suburban lifestyle. Throughout the last decades of the twentieth century, middle-class families, as well as employment, headed out of the core city for the *grande couronne* far outside the capital, skipping over the poorer, heavily immigrant suburbs closer to the center.[43]

JAPANESE "GARDEN CITIES"

Before World War II, Japanese planners had been attracted to the British ideal of the "garden city," although the effort dissipated amid the demands of the wartime economy. Once the economy recovered from the war, there ensued a marked shift of residents, and some business, to the periphery, where land prices were lower and space for new development available. By the mid-1970s, Osaka, the nation's second largest city, was already beginning to lose population, while peripheral communities grew rapidly. More heavily industrialized smaller cities suffered far more rapid loss, paralleling the experience of their European and North American counterparts.[44]

Tokyo, by the 1970s the advanced world's largest metropolis, also expanded outward in dramatic fashion. The first step was to relieve pressure on the historic core by constructing new subcenters such as Shinjuku, Shibuya, and Ikebukuro. These megadevelopments initially followed the basic precepts of Ishikawa Hideaki, whose decentralist ideas also included the creation of a greenbelt around the capital.

Over time, these and other subcenters would evolve into vibrant parts of the metropolis, housing many of Japan's tallest buildings, including the Sunshine Tower and the Tokyo Metropolitan Government Building.[45] Plans to develop more green space farther outside the core city did not fare nearly as well. Like the Olmsted plans for Los Angeles, Hideaki's "garden city" aspirations fell victim to economic expediency and the political power of landowners.[46]

This vast outward movement occurred largely because of escalating land costs in the Tokyo core area. By the 1970s, the dream for middle-class Tokyo residents of owning a home, even the smallest one-bedroom apartment, escalated out of reach. Forced to the periphery for affordable homes, almost 10 million settled in the suburban regions around the main cities of the Kanto plain between 1970 and 1995.[47]

CHAPTER SIXTEEN

The Postcolonial Dilemma

Gladys García, a character in Carlos Fuentes's ironically titled first novel, *Where the Air Is Clear,* lives amid the sprawling concrete of "the great flat-snouted suffocating city, the city forever spreading like a creeping blot." A cocktail waitress, she inhales not the fragrances of the flowers that bloomed once everywhere in Mexico City, but the old garbage, cigarette smoke, and rotting animals of the backstreets.

Extending beyond limits imagined by either Aztec founders or Spanish conquerors, Mexico City has spread out over 620 square miles. In the world's second most populous city, people are swallowed in chaotic traffic, choked by smog, overcome by stenches, threatened by crime.[1]

García has little notion of the spectacular nature that rings the ancient city. "She knew neither the sea nor the mountains, mustard bloom, the meeting of sun and horizon, ripeness of medlar trees, nor any simple loveliness."[2]

THE COLONIAL LEGACY

Contemporary Mexico, like many cities in the developing world, struggles with both headlong growth and the consequences of a colonial past. At the time of the Spanish conquest in the early sixteenth century, the city known as Tenochtitlán, with between eighty thousand and three hundred thousand people, surpassed any city in Spain[3] and almost any in

Europe.[4] The capital of the Aztecs also exceeded these ill-planned, often pestilential European cities in cleanliness, public hygiene, and general orderliness.[5] According to soldiers who traveled with Cortés, the market-place at Tlatelolco, Tenochtitlán's sister city, excelled in both size and variety over those of Constantinople, Rome, or any city in Spain.[6]

The conquest of Mexico, like those of cities in other parts of the developing world, demolished this old urban culture, its religion, and its political and economic way of life. As an Aztec poet was to write a few years after the conquest:

> Broken spears lie in the roads . . .
>
> The houses are roofless;
> The walls are red with blood.
> Our city, our inheritance
> Is lost and dead;
> The shields of our warriors
> Could not save it.[7]

However brutal the eradication of the old cultures, most European invaders did not eradicate the places of conquest, but recast them in their own image. The great conquistador Cortés understood the political significance of the city he destroyed. He invited the former residents of the city to return and purposely located his main administrative buildings on the site of the central palace, what is now known as the Zocolo.[8] In the same way, the church erected its great cathedral on the site that had been Tenochtitlán's center of religious worship—much as it earlier had built cathedrals on the sites of mosques constructed by the hated Moors.[9]

Replacing ancient sources of sacred power proved far easier than reviving a great metropolis. Cortés had pledged to his emperor, Charles I, that he would create there a great city, but Mexico's resurgence proved slow in coming. More than two centuries after the conquest, the Spanish city of Mexico remained essentially an economic backwater, housing less than half the population of the former Tenochtitlán.[10]

Mexico finally surpassed its preconquest population at the turn of the twentieth century. As it began to connect with the broader world economy, through trains, over roads, and finally by air, the city reached 1 million residents in 1930. Massive new waterworks such as the Lerma aqueduct, completed in 1951, allowed the city, which had exhausted its surrounding lakes, to begin its evolution into one of the globe's largest urban centers.[11]

Yet if the modern city had achieved great size, it often did so in a disorderly and troubling manner. As millions poured in from tiny *ejidos* and small towns, the center of the city became more crowded and less elegant. By the 1920s, the affluent had already begun to flee to the periphery, following the highly mobile, car-oriented lifestyle associated with North American cities.

Many of the poor and working class crowded into illegal settlements. One, Ciudad Nezahualcoyotl, sprouted on a former lake bed so saline that even the hardiest shrubs and trees had trouble growing. This desolate expanse was home to sixty-five thousand people in 1960 and ten times that number a decade later. By 2000, some 2 million people eked out their lives in Nezahualcoyotl; many millions more inhabited other such areas.

Residents of these areas were not too dissimilar, noted one sociologist, from "primitive hunters and gatherers of preagriculture societies," ever on the lookout for odd jobs and whatever else was "left over" from the more affluent members of society.[12] By 2000, the capital suffered a crime rate 2.5 times higher than Mexico's second city, Guadalajara, and 8 times that of Monterrey, the capital of the rapidly growing north.[13] The newcomers, Carlos Fuentes observed, often had to let go of "their migrant nostalgia" and traditional moral restraints. "Sharpen your knives," he warned, "deny everything, feeling no pity, without parleying, without even looking."[14]

"THE URBANIZATION OF THE COUNTRYSIDE"

Such places now define urban reality in much of the world. Between 1960 and 2000, the urban share of population in developing countries doubled from 20 to 40 percent. With the slowing of population growth in European and American cities, the clear majority of the world's urbanites— and over 90 percent of all new city dwellers—resided in the cities of Latin America, Asia, and Africa.[15] By 2007, their growth will establish urban dwellers, for the first time, as an absolute majority of the global population.

These developments were evident in the changing roster of the world's largest megacities. In 1950, only two cities, London and New

York, possessed populations greater than 10 million; half a century later, there were nineteen, all but three in the developing world. In 2015, according to the United Nations, there will be twenty-three such urban behemoths, nineteen of them located in developing countries. By that same date, there will be three urbanites in developing nations to every advanced-country city dweller.[16]

This process reflects a broader, longer-term historical trend that Karl Marx referred to as "the urbanization of the countryside." In his day, Marx noted, the movement of European capitalism had created a "social revolution" undermining the older, largely village-based societies in Asia, South America, and Africa. The current megacities of the developing world represent the ultimate consequence of that revolution.[17]

With the arrival of the Europeans, the urban order in the East, long on a par with or more evolved than that of the West, was transformed and subordinated to a second-class status. The fates of cities in Asia, Latin America, and Africa were determined no longer by emperors, sultans, or local potentates, but by European bankers and government officials. Many of the older capitals that remained, such as Beijing, Istanbul, and Delhi, surrendered much of their historic influence.[18]

"EUROPEAN MICROCOSMS"

A host of relatively new cities serving as "European microcosms" now arose throughout Asia and Africa—Jakarta, Singapore, Bombay, Calcutta, Shanghai, Hong Kong, Cape Town, Johannesburg, and Lagos. Much as Trier, Antioch, Alexandria, and Marseilles had played subordinate roles in Rome's far-flung urban network a millennium and a half earlier, these colonial centers drew their sustenance and direction from European capitals. Local trade diasporas, whether Arab, Lebanese, Chinese, or Indian, shared in the growth of these cities, but not to the extent enjoyed by those most closely aligned with the metropolitan cores.[19]

The evolution of some of these cities was often remarkably rapid. Calcutta, founded in 1690 by Job Charnock, an agent for the British East India Company, arose from a small village to become the largest city on the subcontinent and for 140 years the capital of British India. Along with Bombay, which passed into British hands in 1665, and Madras, the leading port in the south,[20] the city dominated the economy of the subcontinent.

Calcutta served as the ultimate colonial metropolis, taking in the manufacturers of Britain and sending back silk, jute, cotton, rice, sugar, and scores of other products. Alongside the local merchant class, a small European elite presided confidently over the vast city. The splendid Esplanade, where the fashionable took their weekend drives, and magnificent new buildings—the High Court, the Standard Chartered Bank, the Great Eastern Hotel—spoke of a permanent sense of domination.[21]

Similarly favored cities, such as Shanghai, Hong Kong, and Lagos, also rose rapidly to dominate regional economies. Administered by a British elite and populated largely by indigenous peoples or migrants from other possessions, these cities grew swiftly while more traditional centers—Kano and Timbuktu in Africa, Beijing, and Delhi—suffered relative declines in importance and economic power.

European influence could also be felt in cities that, at least nominally, remained outside direct colonial control. In Egypt, French and British influence encouraged the growth of both European populations and ethnic minorities from throughout the region. By the 1930s, a full quarter of Alexandria's residents came from groups outside the mainstream Muslim Arab population. Cairo, too, was changed. By the 1930s, more than 16 percent of Cairo's population were foreigners and minorities, compared with barely 10 percent in 1800.

On the surface, cities such as Cairo appeared increasingly modern and European. Wide avenues and broad streets able to accommodate motorcars were cut through the often labyrinthine streets. New concepts of urban design, emphasizing such European ideas as the development of suburban "garden cities" and broad shopping streets, impinged ever more on the traditional Islamic pattern.[22]

Yet in the end, there remained two Cairos. One, under substantial European influence, grew into a modern, commercial, and heavily secularized metropolis. The other remained largely unchanged, bound tightly by old Islamic social and religious traditions. "Cairo," commented one late-nineteenth-century observer, "is like a cracked vase whose two parts can never be put together."[23]

Many cities in developing countries suffered a similar bifurcation between a Westernized modern metropolis and a poorer, more traditional one. Often unspeakable poverty, filth, and disease existed side by side with great wealth and privilege. In addition, many restraints imposed by Islamic and other traditional moral systems no longer applied. Even arch-colonialists were frequently appalled by the social and physical reality they had created. The eighteenth-century imperialist Robert Clive, for example, described Calcutta—with its slums, criminality, semislavery, and pervasive corruption—as "the most wicked place in the universe."[24]

Perhaps no city suffered more in reputation than Shanghai, the emerging Chinese industrial capital. In 1900, the city's population was a mere thirty-seven thousand compared with the more than 1 million residents of Beijing. By 1937, Shanghai was home to over 3.5 million, better than twice the population of the old imperial capital.[25] Besides serving as a bustling European business center, Shanghai stood out as a hotbed of gangsterism, drug running, and prostitution. "If God lets Shanghai endure," suggested one missionary, "he owes an apology to Sodom and Gomorrah."[26]

"THE HALCYON DAYS"

The end of colonial domination in the 1950s and 1960s created a dilemma for the newly empowered rulers of colonial cities. They had inherited "microcosms" of European influence, with both some modern infrastructure and enormous entrenched inequality. A small, European-educated elite coexisted with a large population that continued to adhere to traditional values and ways of life.

Initially, it was widely hoped that these cities would emerge as vital centers of modernization while serving as proud symbols of political, economic, and cultural renaissance. The 1960s, in the words of Janet Abu-Lugoud, were "the halcyon days" for cities in the Arab and Muslim worlds.[27] Much the same could be said for the rulers of cities in other developing countries.

In many cases, the local European-trained elites moved into the elegant quarters once occupied by Europeans. Hoping to make their cities competitive with those in Europe and North America, they often seized control of major enterprises and simultaneously expanded their own government bureaucracies.

The prospect of great new possibilities made these cities irresistible, not only to the entrepreneurial and professional elites, but also to a swelling migrant population made up of dispossessed farmers and small-town artisans. Cities such as Bombay, Calcutta, Delhi, Lahore, Lagos, Cairo, and Manila swelled to many times their size under colonial rule.

Bombay's population, for example, increased from less than 1.5 million in 1941 to more than 15 million by century's end.[28]

A FATEFUL BREAK IN URBAN HISTORY

In many cases, this huge expansion of cities occurred without a corresponding increase in either wealth or power. Such a development represents a tragic and fateful break in urban history. Whether in the Greco-Roman world, the Chinese or Islamic empires, the Italian cities of the Renaissance, or Northern Europe in the industrial age, large cities usually have developed as a consequence of accelerating economic and political fortunes.

As people migrated to the expanding cities, they either found work in expanding industries or tapped the largesse drawn from imperial conquests. In contrast, many of the largest cities in the contemporary world have grown ever more enormous amid persistent economic stagnation as well as social and political dysfunction. In most cases, these urban areas have failed, as one analyst noted, to perform "their assumed function as the generators of modernization and development."

Superficially, many of these cities retained a Western face, often a legacy from colonial times. There are impressive offices of the global companies, first-class hotels, and elegant residential districts. But in reality, most of these cities have remained mired in underdevelopment, their fates largely subordinate to decisions made by corporations in the United States, Europe, or increasingly East Asia.[29]

Without reliable economic engines to power their growth, such urban regions often lack the wherewithal to maintain, much less expand, their most basic infrastructure. Throughout the developing world, as much as 30 to 50 percent of their garbage goes uncollected, and clean water is often in short supply. Air pollution has become more lethal than in the most congested cities of Europe or North America.

THE RISE OF SQUATTER CITIES

In the early twenty-first century, at least 600 million urbanites in developing countries survive in squatter settlements—called variously *barriadas, bidonvilles, katchi adabis, favelas,* and shantytowns. These settlements, according to one United Nations study, account for the bulk of all new growth in the developing world. Spending upwards of three-fourths of their meager incomes on food, many of these slum dwellers subsist on the fringes of the formal economy.[30]

Despite such miserable conditions, migrants continue to pour into these cities, in large part because prospects in their native rural communities have grown far worse.[31] In many countries, drought and deforestation along with declining commodity prices have left little choice between migration and starvation. "In Sertão," suggests a local saying from that drought-plagued district of Brazil, "one stays and dies or leaves and suffers."[32]

For these rural people, the urban centers, particularly politically influential capital cities, at least offer some basic public services, access to international food aid, and the prospect of informal employment.[33] As in Mexico City, these rural refugees account for a large proportion of both newcomers and residents of informal slum communities.

The industrial city of São Paulo, which by 2000 was ranked the third or fourth largest metropolis in the world, has seen some of the fastest growth experienced by such neighborhoods.[34] Although the city boasts a considerable middle class, São Paulo has evolved into a highly bifurcated city, what the Brazilian sociologist Teresa Caldeira labels "a city of walls."

AFRICA'S URBAN TRAGEDY

Similar or even worse conditions persist elsewhere in cities throughout the developing world. In Africa, long one of the least urbanized regions of the world, the percentage of natives living in cities more than doubled to some 40 percent between 1960 and 1980. Declining agricultural exports, lack of large-scale industry, the ravages of epidemic disease, and persistent political instability have left African cities among the most ill prepared to accommodate massive demographic growth.[35]

These pathologies evolved on a grand scale in Lagos, whose population expanded almost ninefold in the forty years following the departure of the British in 1960. A small minority live in well-appointed neighborhoods, but most residents eke out their existence in crowded quarters, averaging 3.5 people per room, often on the outskirts of the city. Nearly 1 in 5 residents squat in illegal settlements.[36]

In many African cities, the affluent escape the congestion by heading for more comfortable homes on the periphery. Large-scale Western-style suburbs, attracting both whites and upwardly mobile blacks, have evolved in the countryside outside Cape Town, Durban, and Johannesburg in South Africa. As occurred earlier in North America, businesses often have followed this outward migration.[37]

"SOCIAL TIME BOMBS"

Long a center of urban civilization, since the 1950s the Middle East has experienced some of the most explosive urban growth in the world, and little of it has been successful. Cairo, the largest city in the region, has expanded its land area to fifteen times its 1900 levels, while its population has grown to over 10 million. Baghdad, a city of five hundred thousand in the 1940s, after tripling in size by the 1960s, swelled to well over 2 million by the end of the millennium. Once obscure cities—such as Amman, Kuwait City, and Riyadh—enjoyed even more rapid rates of growth.[38]

Owing to the region's prodigious energy resources, the Middle Eastern cities might have been expected to possess the wherewithal to deal with their rising populations. Islam's early success as a city-based religion could have provided some glue for constructing a workable urban moral order.[39] Tragically, even at the height of the oil boom of the 1970s and 1980s, few of these cities created either large-scale manufacturing or world-class service industries capable of employing the growing ranks of city dwellers. And to date, Islam has not been notably any more successful than other belief systems in coping with the ill effects of mass urbanization.

The economic prospects of Middle Eastern megacities, like those in much of the developing world, have been further eroded by the rise of what the historian Manuel Castells labels "informationalism." The increased importance of technology, and the evolution of global economic networks, hurt cities whose populations were largely unable or unwilling to participate successfully in the evolving international economy.[40]

With the notable exceptions of secular-oriented Turkey and pariah Israel, few Near Eastern cities possessed high levels of computer and technical literacy. Barely 1 percent of the population in other Near Eastern countries, for example, used the Internet in 2000. The Middle East, noted the Syrian academic Sami Khiyami, now stood in danger of being "left behind again" in the information age, just as had occurred in the industrial era.[41]

Equally critical, these cities have lost large numbers of entrepreneurial and educated people, who now seek out opportunities in North America and Europe. This exodus has been particularly noticeable among highly urbanized ethnic and religious minorities.[42] Since the 1960s, many groups, such as Arab Christians and Jews, have departed cities like Cairo, Baghdad, and Tehran even after having been resident there for centuries.[43]

These migrations have left behind a population that is generally too poor and unskilled to lay the basis for the kind of modern economy capable of financing an urban infrastructure. As urban populations passed over 50 percent in most Arab countries, sewer and water systems failed to keep pace. Housing also remained in short supply. In Cairo, Casablanca, and Alexandria, as many as three or four people crowd one room. Illegal settlements surround most of the major cities, constituting more than half of all new housing in urban parts of Egypt. A United Nations study estimated that by the 1990s, 84 percent of Cairenes could be characterized as slum dwellers.[44]

The Iranian capital of Tehran stands as another tragic failure. A relatively young city—becoming the country's capital only in 1788—Tehran, as home to the ruling shahs, had enjoyed spectacular growth throughout the twentieth century. The country's oil wealth, expanding middle class, and educated population all pointed to the potential for the building of a great modern city.

Unfortunately, the frequently corrupt and authoritarian regime had failed to distribute the benefits of the nation's prosperity to its growing urban population. As the economy grew, rates of poverty in Tehran more than doubled between the 1940s and the 1970s.[45] Social problems, including crime and prostitution, festered as newcomers crowded once tightly knit neighborhoods, turning Tehran, in the words of one Iranian planner, into "a city of strangers."

Such alienated, impoverished urbanites, like the European working class of the nineteenth century, increasingly embraced radical ideologies, including Islamic fundamentalism. In 1979, these "marginalized Tehranis" and hard-pressed *bazaris* poured into the streets to overturn the shah's rule and bring to power a fundamentalist government.

Cities in other countries not yet under Islamist control have suffered similar economic and social problems. From North Africa to Pakistan, these agglomerations incubated often violent movements with strongly antimodernist tendencies. Urban areas in the region, noted one top UN official, now represent "nothing less than social time bombs" that threaten to undermine the entire global order.[46]

CHAPTER SEVENTEEN

"QUEENS OF THE FURTHER EAST"

Asia experienced the world's largest urban migration—in terms of absolute numbers—during the second half of the twentieth century.[1] In contrast with the growth of the Middle East, much of Latin America, and Africa, Asia's metropolitan development generally occurred more along classic historical lines. Cities not only burgeoned in numbers, but also experienced considerable economic expansion, as well as often greater degrees of both political and social order.

Rather than suffer from the dilemma of postcolonial rule, many of Asia's cities have lived up to the promise of what one nineteenth-century colonialist called "queens of the further east."[2] This optimistic picture was not universal, of course. At the dawn of the new millennium, nearly 40 percent of Karachi's 10 million people lived in squatter settlements. Political instability, particularly the growth of anti-Western and anti-modernist Islamic movements, has since slowed the successful integration of Pakistani cities into the global economy.[3]

Other major cities in Asia—Jakarta, Bangkok, and Manila—have also suffered from political upheavals. Most experienced economic growth, but often barely enough to offset their own demographic expansion. The majority of residents remained very poor, although generally not in the proportions found in the cities of Africa and the Near East.

INDIA'S URBAN REVOLUTION

In the last decades of the twentieth century, India reemerged as a major center of global urban life. In contradiction to Mahatma Gandhi's ideal vision of a village-centered nation, the nation's economy shifted from a predominantly rural and agricultural system to one that was increasingly industrialized (even postindustrial) and urban. Spurred by state-led investment in manufacturing and modern infrastructure, cities in India more than doubled their share of the national gross domestic product between 1950 and 1995.[4] The reform of India's once quasi-Socialist system, which had long suppressed entrepreneurial ventures, further accelerated urban growth.

Much of the new urban growth was concentrated less in the old colonial hub, Calcutta, than in the capital city of New Delhi and the other great outpost of imperialism, Bombay. In contrast with those of cities in much of the developing world, the prospects for Bombay, whose name was changed to Mumbai in 1995, are not entirely bleak. Projected to be the world's second largest city, after Tokyo, by 2015, Mumbai already assumed a commanding position in a whole series of industries from financial services to manufacturing and entertainment. In the late 1990s, steps toward constructing new poles of development such as the "new city" of Navi Mumbai helped create new environments attractive to the city's growing middle class.[5]

More than anything, the presence of a large group of educated, technically proficient workers—by 2000, India accounted for roughly 30 percent of the world's software engineers—constituted the critical advantage for the nation's metropolitan areas. This proved particularly true for several smaller Indian cities such as Bangalore.[6]

By the 1980s, Bangalore had emerged as India's fastest-growing city, its population soaring from barely 1 million in 1960 to over 4.5 million by century's end. With over nine hundred software firms, the city had become widely regarded as India's "Silicon Valley," and its development largely followed that of the original American version—sprawling, car oriented, and full of largely self-contained, research-oriented industrial parks.[7]

Following Bangalore's lead, other Indian cities, such as Hyderabad, developed new office parks, academic institutions, highways, and airports conducive to the growth of advanced industries. In the late 1990s, Andhra

Pradesh State, which includes Hyderabad, housed more than fifteen thousand software workers and saw its software exports increase twenty-six-fold.

As global demand for talent expanded, the technology and service industries began to spread even to lagging megacities such as Calcutta.[8] None of this brought an end to poverty in Calcutta, renamed Kolkata, or other Indian cities. In even the most economically dynamic centers, large pockets of unemployment and impoverished laborers, including millions of children working for pitifully low wages, struggled alongside an expanding middle class.[9]

EAST ASIA BREAKS THE MOLD

Without question, the most spectacular urban evolution in Asia took place farther east, among cities influenced directly or indirectly by the rich urban culture of China. Long before India's urban economy began to show signs of maturation, these Asian cities followed the path trod earlier by Osaka and Tokyo, financing their urban expansion from the fruits of rapid economic growth.

In the 1960s, most cities in Asia had been considered parts of the largely undifferentiated, impoverished "developing world," alongside the likes of Cairo, Lagos, or Calcutta. By the end of the millennium, urban areas such as Seoul, Taipei, Singapore, and Hong Kong had evolved into something much more. Like modern Asiatic versions of the vigorous trading city-states of Phoenicia, classical Greece, or Renaissance Italy, they now strode the world stage, looking for new industries and markets to conquer.[10]

SEOUL'S EMERGENCE

Until 1876, Seoul served as capital of the Korean "hermit kingdom," cut off almost entirely from the rest of the world economy. Only under intense prodding from commercial interests from Japan did it slowly open itself to outside influence. Early in the twentieth century, the Japanese occupied the country outright. During Japan's often brutal reign, Seoul subordinated itself to Osaka or Tokyo, much as Bombay and Calcutta serviced the needs of London, Birmingham, and Liverpool. Like European colonialists in India and elsewhere, the Japanese also helped to transform Seoul, turning an old imperial capital into a modern city with manufacturing industries, streetcars, and a growing professional class.

Seoul regained its independence after the defeat of Japan in 1945, serving as the capital and principal city of the new Republic of Korea. Five years later, a surprise attack from the Communist-controlled north devastated the city. Over the ensuing three-year-long conflict, the city and its environs served as a critical battleground between Allied and Communist forces.

The South Korean capital emerged from the Korean War both battle-scarred—47 percent of its standing buildings were destroyed—and desperately poor. Like many cities in the developing countries, it swelled with rural migrants; in the 1960s and 1970s, over three hundred thousand people migrated annually to the still largely devastated capital city.

As migrants poured in from the countryside, Seoul's population increase paralleled that of Cairo, São Paulo, Mumbai, and a host of other cities in the developing world. In 1960, the city was home to 3 million people; by 2000, it had grown to more than 11 million, with a surrounding metropolitan area accounting for an additional 9 million.[11]

Initially, Seoul also displayed the familiar ill effects of this growth—ramshackle squatter settlements, perpetually overburdened transport, substandard sanitary and health facilities.[12] What proved the critical difference was an economy that expanded faster than almost any in the world.

Seoul's growing wealth provided the wherewithal to meet many challenges posed by its rapid demographic expansion. New roads, housing, office buildings, and research parks arose throughout the region. To make way for the development of the central parts of the city, sprawling squatter settlements were demolished throughout the 1960s and again in the 1980s, in part to prepare for the 1988 Olympic Games. Although many people were displaced, poverty was effectively reduced.[13] By 1988, only 14 percent of Seoul's population, according to one UN study, lived in slums, roughly one-sixth the level of Cairo's.[14]

By that time, the Korean capital had more in common with crowded, congested, and expensive Tokyo, or modern Western cities, than with the impoverished urban centers of Africa or the Middle East. Seoul dominated the Korean economy even more than the Japanese capital; it was home to forty-eight of the country's fifty largest companies, the main government agencies, and most foreign corporate headquarters.[15] The city also served as home to as many of these megacorporations as such older commercial centers as Frankfurt or Osaka.[16] Seoul's dominance was so overwhelming that by the early twenty-first century, some advocated moving the capital to rural areas to the south.[17]

BRITAIN'S SUCCESSFUL OFFSPRING

Seoul's emergence represented part of a remarkable, wider-ranging late-twentieth-century pattern among East Asian cities. The progenitors of this event in modern urban history lay in the evolution of two commercial cities, Singapore and Hong Kong, spawned under the authority and economic power of the British Empire.

Hong Kong, granted outright to Britain in 1841, had emerged as a European microcosm, which helped it supplant Canton (Guangzhou) as the primary trading port in southern China. Increasingly, it also nurtured a formidable Chinese economic culture that would soon spread throughout East Asia. A new kind of urban society, a blending of Chinese and European influences, now evolved rapidly, as the population soared from a few thousand at the onset of the twentieth century to more than a million in 1937.

A decade later, the Communist revolution in China devastated that country's commercial centers. Hong Kong now established itself, after Tokyo, as Asia's second business capital. Crammed with refugees from the Maoist regime, it more than tripled in population by the 1980s. The city's ascendancy rode on more than swelling numbers; it benefited from the presence of entrepreneurs and professionals from across China, most notably the former financial and industrial elites of Shanghai.[18]

SINGAPORE: ASIA'S MODEL CITY

Founded in 1819 by Sir Stamford Raffles as an imperial trading post, Singapore became a full-fledged British colony in 1867. Located far to the south of the Chinese mainland, the city attracted masses of migrants from that country. Sizable populations of Indians, Malays, Arabs, and Jews, as well as colonial representatives, transformed Singapore into a dynamic cosmopolitan society, connected not only to London, but to

Baghdad, Jakarta, Canton, and Shanghai. Described by Joseph Conrad as "riotous with life," the city teemed with merchants, sailors, and a primarily Chinese working class.[19]

The Japanese occupation during World War II severely disrupted this colonial society. Humiliated by an Asian power, Britain lost its claim to unchallenged supremacy. Pressure for independence grew, and in 1965, the British finally left the old colonial city.

Initially, the prospects for the tiny, 225-square-mile republic appeared dubious at best. The city suffered all the usual problems associated with developing countries—large, crowded slums, criminal gangs, and a relatively unskilled population. The country also faced hostility from neighboring, far more populous, and predominantly Muslim Malaysia from which it had broken away.

Singapore's great achievement—so rare in the postcolonial world—was using its new sovereign power not to promote a small, and corrupt, elite, but to construct one of the stunning urban success stories of the late twentieth century. Under the authoritarian leadership of Cambridge-educated Lee Kuan Yew, Singapore broke dramatically with much of its colonial past and forged a new model for Asian urbanism. Tenements and low-slung shops were replaced by planned apartment complexes; congested streets were supplanted by a modern road system under which ran an advanced subway system; and crime, once rampant, was nearly eliminated.

As in Seoul and Hong Kong, the key lay in large-scale economic growth. Lee and his government worked assiduously to exploit Singapore's natural advantage as a harbor and transit center for trans-Asian trade. Moving rapidly from low-wage industries like textiles to high-technology and service industries, Singapore by the end of the twentieth century boasted among the world's best-educated and economically productive populations. Class divisions remained, but most now achieved a standard of living and wealth unimaginable for the masses in other cities of the postcolonial world. Income levels, barely $800 per person in 1964, had risen to over $23,000 in 1999.[20]

Singapore's literate, English-speaking middle class, lack of corruption, and modern infrastructure also attracted a great deal of investment by global multinationals. Lee was not only interested in improving the short-run economic prospects for his tiny city-state; he wanted to develop a new Asian urban culture capable of competing globally well into the twenty-first century. "Having given them a clean city, modern amenities and a strong economy," one of his ministers declared, "we are now thinking of what culture we should give them."[21]

THE REVITALIZATION OF
CONFUCIAN DISCOURSE

By the mid-1980s, Lee had decided upon what "kind of culture" he wanted for his people—one built on the bedrock of the city's Asian, and particularly Chinese, value system. The self-described Anglophile, who once suggested he was no more Chinese than President Kennedy was Irish, now promoted an essential Confucianist ethos, based on respect for the authority of a wise and powerful mandarin elite. Without this culture, he suggested, Singapore would soon degenerate into what he scathingly described as "another Third World society."[22]

This revitalization of the Confucian discourse increasingly shaped perceptions not only in Singapore, but also in the Chinese-dominated economies of Taiwan, under nationalist direction, and in Hong Kong.[23] Confucian attitudes of "collective egocentrism," combining Western and traditional notions of personal and familial improvement, provided a sense of moral order and collective will not apparent in many other parts of the developing world.

By the 1980s, even China's Communist leaders, long contemptuous of their capitalistic-minded overseas brethren, began to shift their attitudes toward this perspective. In 1992, China's paramount leader, Deng Xiaoping, openly expressed particular admiration for Singapore's "social order," embracing the city-state's authoritarian approach to capitalism as the best blueprint for the rapid development of China's own cities.[24]

CHINESE CITIES UNDER MAOISM

Such attitudes would have been unthinkable in the early years after the Communist revolution. The Communists had risen to power largely through their support of peasants and rural villagers. Their vanquished rivals, the Kuomintang, drew their strongest backing in the coastal cities and their cosmopolitan elites.[25]

Once in control in 1949, Communist leader Mao Zedong sought to steer his country's development away from the "corrupt" coastal commercial centers and toward countryside and interior towns. He consciously curbed big-city growth by restricting rural migration. Periodically, as during the Cultural Revolution in the late 1960s, the Communists also "sent down" large numbers of young urbanites to the countryside to learn from the peasantry and provide manpower for massive development schemes.

As a result, China urbanized at a slower pace than elsewhere in East Asia and the rest of the developing world. At a time when cities such as Hong Kong, Bombay, and Mexico were enjoying rapid population growth, many of the country's established commercial centers—Guangzhou (Canton), Tainjin, and Shanghai—expanded only modestly. In contrast, Beijing, center of the all-powerful Communist bureaucracy, continued to grow, adding twice as many people as Shanghai between 1953 and 1970.

In all cities under the Maoist regime, many traditional aspects of Chinese urban life were suppressed. Old shrines were either abandoned or destroyed. Public markets, a critical component of Chinese cities for millennia, were discouraged. Once "riotous with life," China's commercial cities became largely drab places, albeit with drastically less crime, prostitution, and open corruption.[26]

THE FOUR MODERNIZATIONS AND THE REVIVAL OF CHINESE CITIES

China's urban evolution shifted dramatically following Mao's death in 1976. Under Deng Xiaoping's "Four Modernizations," Beijing gradually loosened its strict control over municipalities. Local officials now encouraged private initiative and outside investment. The creation of special economic zones, such as that in Shenzen between Hong Kong and Canton, attracted the largest amounts of foreign capital, much of it from Hong Kong, Taipei, and Singapore. Within fifteen years, the area around the Pearl River Delta had become much like the British Midlands in the mid-nineteenth century, not only the "country's workshop," but rapidly the workshop of the world.[27]

Arguably more so than at any time in Chinese history, the country's cities now assumed primacy as central places in the national life. Freed from strict controls on their movements and seeking new opportunities, rural migrants streamed toward the cities by the tens of millions.

In less than a generation, street-level life in China changed dramatically. Streets previously filled with bicycles were now choked with automobile traffic. New modern office buildings, hotels, and high-rise apartments dwarfed the old Stalinist-style state buildings along the major boulevards. Public markets reappeared, offering an ever wider variety of meats, vegetables, and fruits to an increasingly affluent public.

SHANGHAI'S RESURGENCE

The cosmopolitan culture Maoism had sought to stamp out once again returned, particularly in the coastal cities.[28] This was especially true in the old colonial bastion of Shanghai, which progressively challenged both Hong Kong and Tokyo for the role as Asia's premier business center and location for foreign investment.

Shanghai also embarked on some of the world's most ambitious infrastructure projects, including a new subway system and airport improvements. The largest development, the massive Pudong New Area, across the Huangpu River from Shanghai, started construction in 1990; within a decade, a whole new city had arisen, complete with a greenbelt area, luxury hotels, 140 high-rise office buildings, sleek roadways, a modern ferry terminal, subways, and an underground pedestrian tunnel.[29]

China's rapid urban resurgence brought with it many of the challenges associated with rapid development. Millions of migrant workers—the "floating population"—have followed the path trod earlier by impoverished Lancashire farmers, Irish peasants, and European immigrants in Chicago or New York. They crowded into small apartments at often exorbitant prices. Millions of Chinese urbanites worked at jobs that were dirty, dangerous, and often insecure. Prostitution, bald-faced corruption, petty crime, and other "vices" associated with the old China now returned, sometimes with a surprising vengeance.[30]

SUBURBIA COMES TO EAST ASIA

For all these similarities with the old industrial cities, the rising urban centers of Asia are products of a primarily decentralized age. Unlike the highly centralized urban centers of Europe or North America, these regions are developing in an era where the automobile, telecommunications, and industrial technology shape the contours of urban geography.

As great towers rose over Shanghai, Hong Kong, and Seoul, the pressures for outward development accelerated. Some among East Asia's expanding urban middle class increasingly coveted the fast-paced urban lifestyles of New York or Tokyo, but much of the new housing, factories, and shopping malls headed out to the periphery. This phenomenon could also be seen in such other Asian cities as Jakarta, Kuala Lumpur, Bangkok, and Manila, all of which developed elaborate suburban areas that attracted both affluent residents and industry.[31]

Some of those working in the new office parks, factories, and research facilities sought to move into comfortable and rapidly expanding auto-dependent suburban developments that sometimes looked suspiciously like somewhat denser versions of the outskirts of Los Angeles or San Jose.[32] Like their counterparts in the established Western cities, these Asian urbanites were finding their "better city" in an expanding archipelago of suburbs.[33]

THE URBAN FUTURE

The process of ascent and decline of cities is both rooted in history and changed by it. Successful urban areas today must still resonate with the ancient fundamentals—places sacred, safe, and busy. This was true five thousand years ago, when cities represented a tiny portion of humanity, and in this century, the first in which the majority live in cities.[1]

The world's urban population, only 750 million in 1960, grew to 3 billion by 2002 and is expected to surpass 5 billion in 2030. These swelling ranks of city dwellers face a vastly changed environment in which even the most powerful urban area must compete not only with other large places, but with an ever wider array of smaller cities, suburbs, and towns.[2]

THE CRISIS OF THE MEGACITY

These shifts will be felt most acutely among the sprawling megacities of the developing world. In the past, size allowed cities to dominate the economies of their hinterlands. Today, the very girth of the most populous megacities—Mexico City, Cairo, Lagos, Mumbai, Kolkata, São Paulo, Jakarta, Manila—is often more a burden than an advantage.[3]

In some places, these urban giants have been losing out to smaller, better-managed, and less socially beleaguered settlements. In East Asia, the critical nursery of twenty-first-century urbanism, Singapore and, to a lesser extent, Kuala Lumpur have integrated themselves into the global economy more successfully than the far more populous Bangkok, Jakarta, and Manila.[4]

Similarly, bloated size has, as one observer noted, "robbed Mexico City of its economic logic."[5] Burdened by crime, congestion, and pollution, *La Capital* is often bypassed by entrepreneurs and ambitious workers for faster-growing, better-run cities such as Chilango, Guadalajara, and Monterrey, or across the border to urban areas of *el norte* itself.[6]

In the Near East, megacities like Cairo and Tehran have suffered to keep pace with their exploding populations, while smaller, more compact centers such as Dubai and Abu Dhabi have flourished. Dubai, a dusty settlement of twenty-five thousand in 1948, saw its population approach 1 million fifty years later, while avoiding the economic stagnation that has haunted most of the Arab world.[7]

As in Dubai, cosmopolitan attitudes and the accumulation of unique skills continue to have a major impact in determining successful cities. Openness to varied cultures and the clever employment of talent helped relatively small cities such as Tyre, Florence, and Amsterdam play outsize roles in their times. Similarly, in the twenty-first century, a small cosmopolitan city such as a Luxembourg, Singapore, or Tel Aviv often wields more economic influence than a sprawling megagiant of 10 or even 15 million.[8]

THE LIMITS OF THE CONTEMPORARY URBAN RENAISSANCE

As the twentieth century drew to a close, megacities in the advanced countries seemed to be enjoying brighter economic prospects. There was a statistically small but notable increase in residential development even in some long-abandoned downtowns. Many people now predicted that the most cosmopolitan "world cities"—London, New York, Chicago, Tokyo, and San Francisco—had indeed irrevocably "turned the corner."[9] "Neither Western civilization nor Western cities," suggested one keen observer, the historian Peter Hall, "show any sign of decay."[10]

This new optimism rested largely on the impact of global integration and the worldwide shift from a manufacturing to an information-based economy. Cities like New York, London, and Tokyo, argued the theorist

Saskia Sassen, occupy "new geographies of centrality" that provide "the strategic sites for management of the global economy."[11] Behind these giants, she identified a secondary list of global centers, including variously Los Angeles, Chicago, Frankfurt, Toronto, Sydney, Paris, Miami, and Hong Kong.

These cities clearly enjoyed far better prospects than the rapidly shrinking great industrial cities such as Manchester, Liverpool, Leipzig, Osaka, Turin, and Detroit, which increasingly suffered from technological obsolescence and competition from developing countries. "The 'things' a global city makes," Sassen suggested, "are services and financial goods." These products, it was widely assumed, needed the unique skills and capabilities that existed only within the "global city."[12]

THE "DESTRUCTION OF DISTANCE"

Such an assessment may be replacing the excessive pessimism of the 1960s with a magnified sense of optimism. Even the most evolved "global cities" now find the advantages of scale diminished by the rise of new technologies that, in the words of the anthropologist Robert McC. Adams, have accomplished "an awesome technological destruction of distance."[13]

The ability to process and transmit information globally, and across great expanses, undermines many traditional advantages enjoyed by established urban centers. Throughout the last third of the twentieth century, secular trends, particularly in the United States, pointed to a continued shift even of corporate headquarters to the suburbs and smaller cities.[14] In 1969, only 11 percent of America's largest companies were headquartered in the suburbs; a quarter century later, roughly half had migrated to the periphery.[15]

These developments contradict the notion that a handful of megacities exercised the ultimate "command and control" centers of the global economy. Many elite service and financial firms remained in the established centers, such as Boston, New York, or San Francisco, but the clients "calling the plays" were just as likely to be operating in distant suburbs of Seattle, Houston, and Atlanta, or from abroad.[16]

Even high-end services, the supposed linchpin of "global city" economies, have continued to disperse toward the periphery or smaller cities. This was even more marked among firms in the largest generator of new growth, the entrepreneurial sector.[17] Improvements in telecommunications promise to further flatten economic space in the future, with choice jobs able to shift to exurbs and even small cities such as Fargo, Des Moines, and Sioux Falls.[18] One result has been the shift in the very landscape of growth, with suburban office parks widely favored over gleaming high-rise towers.[19]

The global securities industry, for example, once overwhelmingly concentrated in the financial districts of London and New York, has gradually shifted an ever larger share of their operations to their respective suburban rings, other smaller cities, and overseas. The headquarters might remain in a midtown high-rise, but more and more the jobs are located elsewhere.[20]

One particularly striking case comes from the retail industry. For much of the twentieth century, New York dominated a great deal of the retailing world; by 2000, not one of the sector's twenty largest firms was located there. New York–based fashion designers, advertising executives, trade show organizers, and investment bankers continued to play an important supporting role. The most critical power-shaping global retail lay elsewhere, in firms such as Wal-Mart, which operated effectively from Bentonville, Arkansas.[21]

These decentralizing trends have taken an unmistakable toll on the overall economic relevance of New York, still the most important of the advanced world's megacities. In the last three decades of the twentieth century—a period of explosive job growth across the United States—the city's private sector created virtually no new net employment. A powerful service economy still remained, but as the historian Fred Siegel suggested, the long-term trends showed the city slipping further behind the nation "with each new turn of the cycle."[22]

Even in highly centralized Japan, software and other technology-centered activities have begun to move away from the great centers of Osaka and Tokyo and outward to outlying prefectures. In the same way, Hong Kong has hemorrhaged both high-tech manufacturing and engineering positions to surrounding parts of mainland China. The rise of "telecities" around the world suggests the emergence of new high-end industrial pockets, including in the less urbanized sections of France, Belgium, and Korea.

The increased application of home commuting threatens to reduce even further the roles once played exclusively by urban regions. The evolution of a home-centered economy, in its infancy today, promises elite knowledge workers an unprecedented latitude in choosing where they live and work.[23]

THE RISE OF THE EPHEMERAL CITY

Under these circumstances, even the best-positioned urban areas face severe demographic and economic challenges. Many of the young people lured to these cities in their twenties often depart when they start families and businesses. Increasingly, upwardly mobile immigrants, critical contributors to the urban resurgence, join the exodus. European, Japanese, and other East Asian urban centers face an even more extreme demographic crisis. Low birthrates are reducing the ranks of young people, the group most attracted to large cities, while choking off the traditional pool of immigrants from the countryside.[24]

With economic growth, even in high-end services, shifting elsewhere, many leading cities in the advanced world increasingly rest their future prospects on their role as cultural and entertainment centers. These cities may now be morphing, as H. G. Wells predicted a century earlier, from commanding centers of economic life toward a more ephemeral role as a "bazaar, a great gallery of shops and places of concourse and rendezvous."[25]

Cities have played this staging role since their origins. Central squares, the areas around temples, cathedrals, and mosques, long provided ideal places for merchants to sell their wares. Natural theaters, cities provided the overwhelmingly rural populations around them with a host of novel experiences unavailable in the hinterland. Rome, the first megacity, developed these functions to an unprecedented level. It boasted both the first giant shopping mall, the multistory *Mercatus Traini,* and the Colosseum, a place where urban entertainment grew monstrous in its size and nature.

In the industrial era, noted the French philosopher Jacques Ellul, "the techniques of amusement" became "more indispensable to make urban suffering bearable." By the twentieth century, industrialized mass entertainment—publishing, motion pictures, radio, and television—occupied an ever larger hold on the life of urban dwellers. These media-related businesses also accounted for a growing part of the economy in such key image-producing cities as Los Angeles, New York, Paris, London, Hong Kong, Tokyo, and Bombay.[26]

By the early twenty-first century, this focus on the cultural industries began to inform economic policies in many urban areas. Instead of working to retain middle-class families and factory jobs or engage in economic competition with the periphery, urban regions placed increased focus on such ephemeral concepts as fashionability, "hipness," trend, and style as the keys to their survival.

In Rome, Paris, San Francisco, Miami, Montreal, and New York, tourism now stands as one of the largest and most promising industries. The economies of some of the fastest-growing centers, such as Las Vegas or Orlando, rely largely on the staging of "experiences," complete with uniquely eye-catching architecture and round-the-clock live entertainment.[27]

Even in such unlikely places as Manchester, Montreal, and Detroit, political and business leaders hoped that by creating "cool cities," they might lure gays, bohemians, and young "creatives" to their towns.[28] In some places, the accoutrements of this kind of growth—loft developments, good restaurants, clubs, museums, and a sizable, visible gay and single population—succeeded in reviving once desolate town centers, but hardly with anything remotely reminiscent of their past economic dynamism.[29]

Cities in continental Europe—notably Paris, Vienna, and post–cold war Berlin—particularly embraced this reliance on a culturally based economy. Having largely failed to regain its status as a world business center, Berlin now celebrated its bohemian community as its primary economic asset. The city's relevance was increasingly defined not by the export of goods or services, but by its edgy galleries, unique shops, lively street life, and growing tourist trade.[30]

THE FUTURE, AND LIMITS, OF GENTRIFICATION

In the twenty-first century, some cities or parts of cities may survive, and even thrive, on such an ephemeral basis and, with the support of their still dominant media industries, market that notion to the wider world. The brief but widely acclaimed rise of urban technology districts—such as New York's "Silicon Alley" or San Francisco's "Multimedia Gulch" during the dot-com boom of the late 1990s—even briefly led some to identify hipness and urban edginess as the primary catalyst for information-age growth.[31]

Both of these districts ultimately shriveled as the Internet industry contracted and then matured, yet the market for new housing continued to grow. This demand came partly from younger professionals, but also from a growing population of older affluents, including those hoping to experience "a more pluralistic way of life." These modern-day nomads often reside part-time in cities, either to participate in its cultural life or to transact critical business. In some cities—Paris, for one—these occasional urban nomads constitute, by one estimate, one in ten residents.[32]

The rush in many "global cities" to convert old warehouses, factories, and even office buildings into elegant residences suggests the gradual transformation of former urban economic centers into residential resorts. The declining old financial center of lower Manhattan seemed likely to revive not as a technology hub, noted the architectural historian Robert Bruegmann, but as a full- or part-time home for "wealthy cosmopolites wishing to enjoy urban amenities in the elegantly recycled shell of a former business center."[33]

Over time, however, this form of culturally based growth may not be self-sustaining. In the past, achievement in the arts grew in the wake of economic or political dynamism. Athens first emerged as a bustling great mercantile center and military power before it astounded the world in other fields. The extraordinary cultural production of other great cities, from Alexandria and Kaifeng to Venice, Amsterdam, London, and, in the twentieth century, New York, rested upon a similar nexus between the aesthetic and the mundane.[34]

Broader demographic trends also pose severe long-term questions for these cities. The decline in the urban middle-class family—a pattern seen in both the late Roman Empire and eighteenth-century Venice—deprives urban areas of a critical source for economic and social vitality. These problems will be particularly marked in Japan and Europe, where the numbers of young workers are already dropping. Superannuated Japanese cities face increasing difficulties competing with their Chinese counterparts, enriched by the migration of ambitious young families from their vast agricultural hinterlands.[35]

Under these circumstances, it is difficult to imagine the continued dominance of the Italian fashion industry or Japan's preeminence in Asian popular culture as their populations of young people continue to decline.[36] Over time, the economically ascendant cities around the world—Houston, Dallas, Phoenix, Shanghai, Beijing, Mumbai, or Bangalore—seem certain to generate their own aesthetically based industries.[37]

Finally, the ephemeral city seems likely to face often profound social conflicts. An economy oriented to entertainment, tourism, and "creative" functions is ill suited to provide upward mobility for more than a small slice of its population. Focused largely on boosting culture and constructing spectacular buildings, urban governments may tend to neglect more mundane industries, basic education, or infrastructure. Following such a course, they are likely to evolve ever more into "dual cities," made up of a cosmopolitan elite and a large class of those, usually at low wages, who service their needs.[38]

To avoid the pitfalls of an ephemeral future, cities must emphasize those basic elements long critical to the making of vital commercial places. A busy city must be more than a construct of diversions for essentially nomadic populations; it requires an engaged and committed citizenry with a long-term financial and familial stake in the metropolis. A successful city must be home not only to edgy clubs, museums, and restaurants, but also to specialized industries, small businesses, schools, and neighborhoods capable of regenerating themselves for the next generation.

SECURITY AND THE URBAN FUTURE

Over time, no urban system can survive persistent chaos. Successful cities flourish under a strong regime of both law and order. Citizens must feel at least somewhat secure in their persons. They also need to depend on a responsible authority capable of administering contracts and enforcing basic codes of commercial behavior.

Maintaining a strong security regime can do much to revive an urban area. One critical element in the late-twentieth-century revival in some American cities, most notably in New York, can be traced to a significant drop in crime. This was accomplished by the adoption of new policing methods and a widespread determination to make public safety the number one priority of government. Indeed, the 1990s represented arguably the greatest epoch of crime reduction in American history, providing a critical precondition for both the growth of tourism and even a modest demographic rebound in some major cities.[39] Even Los Angeles, following the devastating riots of 1992, managed to curtail crime and then stage a significant economic and demographic recovery.[40]

Yet even as security concerns in American cities improved, new threats to the urban future surfaced in the developing world.[41] By the end of the twentieth century, crime in megacities such as Rio de Janeiro and São Paulo had devolved into what one law enforcement official called "urban guerrilla war." Drug trafficking, gangs, and general lawlessness also infest many parts of Mexico City, Tijuana, San Salvador, and other cities.

Inevitably, such an erosion in basic security undermines city life. Fear of both crime and capricious authority usually also slows the movement of foreign capital, sometimes in favor of safer locations in the suburban periphery. Even in relatively peaceful countries, "kleptocratic" bureaucracies deflect business investment to safer and less congenitally larcenous locales.[42]

Perhaps even more insidious are the effects of the polluted environment and growing health-related problems in many cities of the developing world. At least 600 million city residents worldwide lack access to even basic sanitation and medical care; these populations naturally become breeding grounds for deadly infectious diseases, against which neither foreign nationality nor affluence can always immunize.[43] Such threats also drive both indigenous professionals and foreign investors to seek more healthful environments abroad or in secured suburbs.[44]

THE TERRORIST THREAT

The Islamic Middle East poses the most immediate lethal threat to the security of cities globally. Here the familiar woes of developing countries have been exacerbated by enormous social and political dislocations. In trying to adopt Western models of city building during the twentieth century, many Islamic cities weakened traditional bonds of community and neighborhood without replacing them with anything both modern and socially sustainable.

This transformation, suggests the historian Stefano Bianca, "sapped the shaping forces of cultural identity," leaving behind a population alienated from its increasingly Westernized environment.[45] This alienation has been further deepened by political conflicts, most importantly the struggle with an economically and militarily advanced Israel. The aspirations of Islamic, and particularly Arab, cities were perpetually thwarted not only by economic, social, and environmental failures, but also by repeated humiliations on the battlefield.

To a large extent, Islamic societies have also failed to adjust to the cosmopolitan standards necessary to compete in the global economy. Beirut, the Arab city best positioned for cosmopolitan success, foundered because of incessant civil strife and only in the late 1990s began to make any serious efforts to rebuild itself. Other potentially successful Islamic cities such as Tehran and Cairo still lack the social stability or transparent legal system critical for overseas investors. Even the best-run of these countries, such as the United Arab Emirates, still suffer from political and legal systems far more arbitrary than those in the West or in such Asian cities as Singapore, Taipei, Seoul, or Tokyo.[46]

From this difficult milieu has emerged perhaps the most dangerous threat to the future of modern cities—Islamic terrorism. This phenomenon differed from the radical nationalism associated with writers such as Frantz Fanon. A black psychiatrist from Martinique deeply affected by his experiences during the Algerian war for independence, Fanon saw the struggle of the developing world as "starting a new history of man" that still embraced the urban culture of the West.[47] In contrast, the Islamic terrorists regarded the West, and particularly its great cities, as intrinsically evil, exploitative, and un-Islamic.

One Arab scholar has labeled the leaders of the Islamic movement as "angry sons of a failed generation"—the ones who saw the secularist dream of Arab unity dissolve into corruption, poverty, and social chaos. For the most part, their anger has been incubated not in the deserts or small villages, but in such major Islamic cities as Cairo, Jiddah, Karachi, or Kuwait. Some have been longtime residents in such Western urban centers as New York, London, or Hamburg.[48]

This experience abroad seemed only to deepen their anger against Western cities. As early as 1990, one terrorist, an Egyptian resident in New York, already spoke of "destroying the pillars such as their touristic infrastructure which they are proud of and their high world buildings that they are proud of."[49] Eleven years later, that anger shook the urban world to its foundation.

In the years following the 2001 attack on New York, both individuals and businesses began rethinking the advisability of locating close to prime potential terrorist targets in high-profile, central locations. To the already difficult challenges posed by changing economic and social trends, cities around the world now have to contend with the constant threat of physical obliteration.[50]

THE SACRED PLACE

Throughout history, cities have faced many challenges to their prosperity and survival. Even the nature of the most immediate current threat— loosely affiliated marauders rather than states—is not unique. Some of the greatest damage done to cities in history has been inflicted not by organized states, but by nomadic peoples or even small bands of brigands.

Despite such threats, the urban ideal has demonstrated a remarkable resilience. Fear rarely is enough to stop the determined builders of cities. For all the cities that have been ruined permanently by war, pestilence, or natural disaster, many others—including Rome, London, and Tokyo— have been rebuilt, often more than once. Indeed, even amid mounting terrorist threats, city officials and developers in New York, London, Tokyo, Shanghai, and other major cities continue to plan new office towers and other superlative edifices.[51]

Far more important to the future of cities than constructing new buildings will be the value people place on the urban experience. Great structures or basic physical attributes—location along rivers, oceans, trade routes, attractive green space, or even freeway interchanges—can help start a great city, or aid in its growth, but cannot sustain its long-term success.

In the end, a great city relies on those things that engender for its citizens a peculiar and strong attachment, sentiments that separate one specific place from others.[52] Urban areas, in the end, must be held together by a consciousness that unites their people in a shared identity. "The city is a state of mind," the great sociologist Robert Ezra Park observed, "a body of customs, and of unorganized attitudes and sentiments."[53]

Whether in the traditional urban core or in the new pattern of development in the expanding periphery, such issues of identity and community still largely determine which places ultimately succeed. In this, city dwellers today struggle with many of the same issues faced by the originators of urbanity anywhere in the world.

Progenitors of a new kind of humanity, these earliest city dwellers found themselves confronting vastly different problems from those faced in prehistoric nomadic communities and agricultural villages. Urbanites had to learn how to coexist and interact with strangers from outside their clan or tribe. This required them to develop new ways to codify behavior, to determine what was commonly acceptable in family life, commerce, and social discourse.

In earliest times, the priesthood usually instructed on these matters. Deriving their authority from divinity, they were able to set the rules for the varied residents of a specific urban center. Rulers also gained stature by claiming their cities to be the special residences of the gods themselves; the sanctity of the city was tied to its role as the center for worship.

The great classical city almost everywhere was both suffused with religion and instructed by it. "Cities did not ask if the institutions which they adopted were useful," noted the classical historian Fustel de Coulanges. "These institutions were adopted because religion had wished it thus."[54]

This sacred role has been too often ignored in contemporary discussions of the urban condition. It barely appears in many contemporary books about cities or in public discussions about their plight. This would have seemed odd not only to residents of the ancient, classical, or medieval cities, but also to many reformers in the late Victorian age.

"New urbanist" architects, planners, and developers, for example, often speak convincingly about the need for city green space, historical preservation, and environmental stewardship. Yet unlike the Victorian-era progressives, who shared similar concerns, they rarely refer to the need for a powerful moral vision to hold cities together.[55]

Such shortcomings naturally reflect today's contemporary urban environment, with its emphasis on faddishness, stylistic issues, and the celebration of the individual over the family or stable community. The contemporary postmodernist perspective on cities, dominant in much of the academic literature, even more adamantly dismisses shared moral values as little more than the illusory aspects of what one German professor labeled "the Christian-bourgeois microcosmos."[56]

Such nihilistic attitudes, if widely adopted, could prove as dangerous to the future of cities as the most hideous terroristic threats. Without a widely shared belief system, it would be exceedingly difficult to envision a viable urban future. Even in a postindustrial era, suggested Daniel Bell, the fate of cities still revolves around "a conception of public virtue" and the "classical questions of the polis."

Cities in the modern West, Bell understood, have depended on a broad adherence to classical and Enlightenment ideals—due process, freedom of belief, the basic rights of property—to incorporate diverse cultures and meet new economic challenges.[57] Shattering these essential principles, whether in the name of the marketplace, multicultural separatism, or religious dogma, would render the contemporary city in the West helpless to meet the enormous challenges before it.[58]

This is not to suggest that the West represents the only reasonable way to achieve an urban order. History abounds with models developed under explicit pagan, Muslim, Confucian, Buddhist, and Hindu auspices. The cosmopolitan city well predates the Enlightenment: It may have surfaced first in pagan Greek Alexandria, but it also flourished later in coastal China and India as well as throughout much of Dar al-Islam.

In our time, perhaps the most notable success in city building has occurred under neo-Confucianist belief systems, mixed with scientific rationalism imported from the West. This convergence, an amalgam of modernity and tradition, eventually overcame Maoism, which was intent on destroying all vestiges of China's cultural past. Today, it struggles both with the ill effects of unrestrained market capitalism and, particularly in China itself, with the self-interested corruption of a ruling authoritarian elite.[59]

It is to be hoped that the Islamic world, having found Western values wanting, may find in its own glorious past—replete with cosmopolitan values and a belief in scientific progress—the means to salvage its troubled urban civilization. The ancient metropolis of Istanbul, with more than 9 million residents, has demonstrated at least the possibility of reconciling a fundamentally Muslim society with what one Turkish planner called "a culturally globalized face." The future success of such a cosmopolitan model, amid the assault from intolerant brands of Islam, could do much to preserve urban progress around the world in the new century.[60]

Indeed, in an age of intense globalization, cities must manage to meld their moral orders with an ability to accommodate differing populations.

In a successful city, even those who embrace other faiths, like *dhimmis* during the Islamic golden ages, must expect basic justice from authorities. Without such prospects, commerce inevitably declines, the pace of cultural and technological development slows, and cities devolve from dynamic places of human interaction into static, and ultimately doomed, congregations of future ruins.

Cities can thrive only by occupying a sacred place that both orders and inspires the complex natures of gathered masses of people. For five thousand years or more, the human attachment to cities has served as the primary forum for political and material progress. It is in the city, this ancient confluence of the sacred, safe, and busy, where humanity's future will be shaped for centuries to come.

NOTES

PREFACE

1. Jacques Ellul, *The Meaning of the City,* trans. Dennis Pardee (Grand Rapids, Mich.: William B. Eerdmans, 1970), 5.
2. Witold Rybczynski, *City Life: Urban Expectations in the New World* (New York: Scribner's, 1995), 49.

INTRODUCTION: PLACES SACRED, SAFE, AND BUSY

1. Bernal Díaz del Castillo, *The Discovery and Conquest of Mexico,* 1517–1521 trans. A. P. Maudslay (New York: Farrar, Straus, and Cudahy, 1956), xii. In the American introduction, Irving Leonard fixes Bernal Díaz's "approximate" birth date as 1492, the same year Columbus sailed to the Americas.
2. Ibid., 119.
3. Ibid., 190–92.
4. Tertius Chandler and Gerald Fox, *Three Thousand Years of Urban Growth* (New York: Academic Press, 1974), 365.
5. Herodotus, *The Histories,* trans. Aubrey de Sélincourt (London: Penguin, 1954), 5.
6. Kevin Lynch, *The Image of the City* (Cambridge, Mass.: Technology Press, 1960), 4.
7. Henri Pirenne, *Medieval Cities: Their Origins and the Revival of Trade* (Princeton, N.J.: Princeton University Press, 1925), 55–57.

CHAPTER ONE: SACRED ORIGINS

1. A.E.J. Morris, *History of Urban Form: Before the Industrial Revolution* (London: Longman, 1994), 1.

2. Ibid., 2–5; William H. McNeill, *Plagues and Peoples* (Garden City, N.Y.: Anchor Press, 1974), 27.

3. Werner Keller, *The Bible as History* (New York: William Morrow, 1981), 3.

4. Gordon Childe, *What Happened in History* (London: Penguin, 1957), 89.

5. Hans J. Nissen, *The Early History of the Ancient Near East, 9000–2000 B.C.* (Chicago: University of Chicago Press, 1988), 56.

6. Grahame Clark, *World Prehistory: An Outline* (Cambridge, Eng.: Cambridge University Press, 1961), 85–90.

7. Childe, *op. cit.,* 92–96.

8. For example, in Sir Peter Hall's magisterial and comprehensive work, *Cities in Civilization* (New York: Pantheon Books, 1998), there is virtually no sustained mention of religion in general, Islam, Christianity, or cathedrals in the making of urban history. Similarly, in Tony Hiss's well-written *The Experience of Place* (New York: Knopf, 1990), there is loving treatment of parks, apartment houses, office buildings, and train stations, but little of places of worship.

9. Childe, *op. cit.,* 137.

10. Mason Hammond, *The City in the Ancient World* (Cambridge, Mass.: Harvard University Press, 1972), 35; Keller, *op. cit.,* 8.

11. Mircea Eliade, *The Myth of the Eternal Return,* trans. Willard R. Trask (Princeton, N.J.: Princeton University Press, 1971), 13.

12. Hammond, *op. cit.,* 37–38.

13. Ibid., 28.

14. *The Epic of Gilgamesh,* trans. Andrew George (London: Penguin, 1999), 1; Keller, *op. cit.,* 17.

15. Childe, *op. cit.,* 102; Hammond, *op. cit.,* 44.

16. Eliade, *op. cit.,* 14.

17. Clark, *op. cit.,* 107–9.

18. Robert W. July, *A History of the African People* (New York: Scribner's, 1970), 14.

19. Childe, *op. cit.,* 114–18.

20. A. Bernard Knapp, *The History and Culture of Ancient Western Asia and Egypt* (Belmont, Calif.: Wadworth Press, 1990), 109–10.

21. Clark, *op. cit.,* 109–11; Morris, *op. cit.,* 11–14.

22. Hammond, *op. cit.,* 73.

23. Chandler and Fox, *op. cit.,* 300–301.

24. Lewis Mumford, *The City in History: Its Origins, Its Transformations, and Its Prospects* (New York: Harcourt Brace, 1961), 80.

25. Childe, *op. cit.,* 129.

26. Clark, *op. cit.,* 182–85.

27. Joseph Levenson and Franz Schurmann, *China: An Interpretive History, from the Beginnings to the Fall of Han* (Berkeley: University of California Press, 1969), 19–22.

28. Morris, *op. cit.,* 2.

29. Paul Wheatley, *The Pivot of the Four Quarters: A Preliminary Enquiry into the Origins and Character of the Ancient Chinese City* (Chicago: Aldine Publishing Company, 1971), 71.

30. Ibid., 175, 179.

31. G. C. Valliant, *Aztecs of Mexico* (Garden City, N.Y.: Doubleday, 1944), 35, 44–45; Jeremy A. Sabloff, *The Cities of Ancient Mexico: Reconstructing a Lost World* (London: Thames and Hudson, 1989), 28, 41; Jorge E. Hardoy, "Two Thousand Years of Latin American Civilization," in *Urbanization in Latin America: Approaches and Issues,* ed. Jorge E. Hardoy (Garden City, N.Y.: Anchor Books, 1975), 4; Rene Million, "The Last Years of Teotihuacán Dominance," in *The Collapse of Ancient States and Civilizations,* ed. Norman Yoffee and George L. Cowgill (Tucson: University of Arizona Press, 1991), 108–12; Clark, *op. cit.,* 225–30; Garcilasco de la Vega, *The Incas,* trans. Maria Jolas (New York: Orion Press, 1961), 57, 119.

32. J. Alden Mason, *The Ancient Civilizations of Peru* (London: Penguin Books, 1957), 40–48.

33. Sabloff, *op. cit.,* 28; Million, *op. cit.,* 108–12; Clark, *op. cit.,* 225–30; de la Vega, *op. cit.,* 57, 119.

34. Sabloff, *op. cit.,* 134–35, 144–45.

CHAPTER TWO: PROJECTIONS OF POWER—
THE RISE OF THE IMPERIAL CITY

1. Hammond, *op. cit.,* 56–57; Knapp, *op. cit.,* 156.

2. Knapp, *op. cit.,* 85–92; H.W.F. Saggs, *The Greatness That Was Babylon: A Sketch of the Ancient Civilization of the Tigris-Euphrates Valley* (New York: Hawthorn Publishers, 1962), 61.

3. Saggs, *op. cit.,* 50–53.

4. Knapp, *op. cit.,* 97–100.

5. Chandler and Fox, *op. cit.,* 300–301.

6. Hammond, *op. cit.,* 52.

7. Saggs, *op. cit.,* 72; Knapp, *op. cit.,* 151.

8. Herodotus, *op. cit.,* 70–71; Chandler and Fox, *op. cit.,* 301.

9. Chandler and Fox, *op. cit.,* 300.

10. Hammond, *op. cit.,* 51–55; Knapp, *op. cit.,* 224–25; Mumford, *op. cit.,* 111.

11. Romila Thapar, *A History of India,* vol. 1 (New York: Penguin, 1990), 55–61; Clark, *op. cit.,* 190–91.

12. Clark, *op. cit.,* 226–28.

13. Hardoy, *op. cit.*, 6–10; Clark, *op. cit.*, 224.

14. Wheatley, *op. cit.*, 7, 182.

15. Sen-Dou Chang, "Historical Trends of Chinese Urbanization," *Annals of the Association of American Geographers* 53, no. 2 (June 1963): 109–17; Morris, *op. cit.*, 2.

16. Laurence J. C. Ma, *Commercial Development and Urban Change in Sung China*, Michigan Geographical Society, 1971.

17. Alfred Schinz, *Cities in China* (Berlin: Gebruder Borntraeger, 1989), 10–15; Chandler and Fox, *op. cit.*, 302.

18. Paul Wheatley and Thomas See, *From Court to Capital: A Tentative Interpretation of the Origins of the Japanese Urban Tradition* (Chicago: University of Chicago Press, 1978), 70–75, 110–15.

19. Ibid., 131–33; Nicolas Fieve and Paul Waley, "Kyoto and Edo-Tokyo: Urban Histories in Parallels and Tangents," in *Japanese Capitals in Historical Perspective: Place, Power and Memory in Kyoto, Edo and Tokyo*, ed. Nicolas Fieve and Paul Waley (London: Routledge Curzun, 2002), 6–7.

CHAPTER THREE: THE FIRST COMMERCIAL CAPITALS

1. T. R. Fehrenbach, *Fire and Blood: A History of Mexico* (New York: Macmillan, 1979), 42; Sabloff, *op. cit.*, 41; Elman R. Service, *Origins of the State and Civilization: The Process of Cultural Evolution* (New York: W. W. Norton, 1975), 221–31; Wheatley, *op. cit.*, 371; July, *op. cit.*, 28–29.

2. Victor F. S. Sit, *Beijing: The Nature and Planning of a Chinese Capital City* (New York: John Wiley, 1995), 6–28; Wheatley, *op. cit.*, 126–27, 133, 176, 188–89; Levenson and Schurmann, *op. cit.*, 99–100.

3. Michael Grant, *The Ancient Mediterranean* (New York: Scribner's, 1969), 62–63.

4. Ibid., 74–76.

5. Sabatino Moscati, *The World of the Phoenicians*, trans. Alastair Hamilton (New York: Praeger, 1968), 99, 101.

6. Chandler and Fox, *op. cit.*, 300.

7. Childe, *op. cit.*, 140.

8. Isaiah 23:8; Hammond, *op. cit.*, 89–91.

9. Herodotus, *op. cit.*, 126.

10. Gerhard Herm, *The Phoenicians: The Purple Empire of the Ancient World* (New York: William Morrow, 1975), 79–81, 88–89.

11. Hammond, *op. cit.*, 75–86.

12. Knapp, *op. cit.*, 190–91; Grant, *op. cit.*, 77–78; Clark, *op. cit.*, 161; Herodotus, *op. cit.*, 299.

13. Moscati, *op. cit.*, 10.

14. Ibid., 123–26.

15. Ibid., 116–21; Herm, *op. cit.,* 129.

16. Herm, *op. cit.,* 144–60.

17. Ibid., 214; Chandler and Fox, *op. cit.,* 302.

18. Moscati, *op. cit.,* 131–35; Grant, *op. cit.,* 125, 129–30.

19. Moscati, *op. cit.,* 135.

CHAPTER FOUR: THE GREEK ACHIEVEMENT

1. Knapp, *op. cit.,* 198; Gordon Childe, *The Dawn of European Civilization* (New York: Knopf, 1925), 24–28; Grant, *op. cit.,* 63, 88.

2. Knapp, *op. cit.,* 202–4.

3. Childe, *The Dawn of European Civilization,* 42–43.

4. Mumford, *op. cit.,* 120–23.

5. Grant, *op. cit.,* 108–10; Clark, *op. cit.,* 150–51.

6. Grant, *op. cit.,* 136–37.

7. Ibid., 192.

8. G.E.R. Lloyd, "Theories of Progress and Evolution," in *Civilization of the Ancient Mediterranean,* ed. Michael Grant and Rachel Kitzinger (New York: Scribner's, 1988), 27.

9. Aristotle, *The Politics,* trans. Carnes Lord (Chicago: University of Chicago Press, 1984), 90.

10. Oswyn Murray, "Greek Forms of Government," in *Civilization of the Ancient Mediterranean,* 439–53.

11. Ibid., 439.

12. Hall, *op. cit.,* 35; Chandler and Fox, *op. cit.,* 300–301.

13. Philip D. Curtin, *Cross-Cultural Trade in World History* (Cambridge, Eng.: Cambridge University Press, 1984), 75–78; Alison Burford, "Crafts and Craftsmen," in *Civilization of the Ancient Mediterranean,* 367.

14. Peter Walcott, "Images of the Individual," 1284–87, and Stanley M. Burstein, "Greek Class Structures and Relations," 529–31, in *Civilization of the Ancient Mediterranean;* Hall, *op. cit.,* 61; Aubrey de Sélincourt, *The World of Herodotus* (Boston: Little, Brown, 1963), 193–97.

15. Hall, *op. cit.,* 41; Mumford, *op. cit.,* 163; McNeill, *op. cit.,* 105.

16. Clark, *op. cit.,* 162.

17. Thomas D. Boyd, "Urban Planning," in *Civilization of the Ancient Mediterranean,* 1693–94; Mumford, *op. cit.,* 149–51.

18. M. M. Austin, "Greek Trade, Industry, and Labor," in *Civilization of the Ancient Mediterranean,* 727.

19. Ibid., 725–34.

20. Edith Hamilton, *The Greek Way* (New York: W. W. Norton, 1930), 137.

21. Grant, *op. cit.,* 168–80, 208–10; J. B. Ward-Perkins, *Cities of Ancient Greece and Italy: Planning in Classical Antiquity* (New York: George Braziller, 1974), 16.

22. R. Ghirshman, *Iran* (New York: Penguin, 1954), 86, 130–33, 203–5; Knapp, *op. cit.*, 256–59.
23. Hall, *op. cit.*, 66–67; Hamilton, *op. cit.*, 142–46; Ghirshman, *op. cit.*, 196–99; Austin, *op. cit.*, 747.
24. Ghirshman, *op. cit.*, 208–9.
25. Hall, *op. cit.*, 38.
26. Curtin, *op. cit.*, 80.
27. Michael Grant, *From Alexander to Cleopatra: The Hellenistic World* (New York: Scribner's, 1982), 107–10; Ghirshman, *op. cit.*, 211.
28. Boyd, *op. cit.*, 1696.
29. Mumford, *op. cit.*, 190–97.
30. Grant, *From Alexander to Cleopatra*, 40–44.
31. Ibid., 37–40, 194–96, 198–203.
32. Burstein, *op. cit.*, 545–46.
33. Samuel Sandmel, *Judaism and Christian Beginnings* (New York: Oxford University Press, 1978), 30–31.
34. Grant, *From Alexander to Cleopatra*, 80–88; Piggot, *op.cit.*, 4, 22.

CHAPTER FIVE: ROME—THE FIRST MEGACITY

1. Petronius, *The Satyricon*, trans. J. P. Sullivan (New York: Penguin, 1986), 11–13.
2. Morris, *op. cit.*, 37–38; Jérôme Carcopino, *Daily Life in Ancient Rome*, trans. E. O. Lorimer (New Haven: Yale University Press, 1940), 16–20; Hall, *op. cit.*, 621; Chandler and Fox, *op. cit.*, 302–3.
3. Mumford, *op. cit.*, 237.
4. McNeill, *op. cit.*, 104.
5. Carcopino, *op. cit.*, 174.
6. John E. Stambaugh, *The Ancient Roman City* (Baltimore: Johns Hopkins University Press, 1988), 7–8.
7. Ibid., 11–12.
8. Massimo Pallottino, *The Etruscans*, trans. J. Cremona (Bloomington: Indiana University Press, 1975), 95–97.
9. F. E. Adcock, *Roman Political Ideas and Practice* (Ann Arbor: University of Michigan Press, 1964), 16.
10. Numa Denis Fustel de Coulanges, *The Ancient City: A Study on the Religion, Laws, and Institutions of Greece and Rome* (Baltimore: Johns Hopkins University Press, 1980), 17–52.
11. Ibid., 132–34.
12. Ibid., 182.
13. Ibid., 91.
14. Stambaugh, *op. cit.*, 12, 18–19; Clark, *op. cit.*, 164–66.

15. Stambaugh, *op. cit.,* 33–35.
16. Keith Hopkins, "Roman Trade, Industry and Labor," in *Civilization of the Ancient Mediterranean,* 774; Stambaugh, *op. cit.,* 36–37; Morris, *op. cit.,* 44.
17. Morris, *op. cit.,* 45; Stambaugh, *op. cit.,* 44–45.
18. Stambaugh, *op. cit.,* 51.
19. E. J. Owens, *The City in the Greek and Roman World* (London: Routledge, 1991), 121–40, 150–52, 159.
20. Herbert Muller, *The Uses of the Past: Profiles of Former Societies* (London: Oxford University Press, 1952), 219–20.
21. Carcopino, *op. cit.,* 20–27, 65.
22. Ibid., 45–51.
23. Petronius, *op. cit.,* 129.
24. Morris, *op. cit.,* 46–47; Stambaugh, *op. cit.,* 150–53.
25. Stambaugh, *op. cit.,* 144–45.
26. Morris, *op. cit.,* 39–44.
27. Edward Gibbon, *The Decline and Fall of the Roman Empire,* vol. 1 (New York: Modern Library, 1995), 8.
28. Robert Lopez, *The Birth of Europe* (New York: M. Evans and Company, 1967), 15.
29. Charles Ludwig, *Cities in New Testament Times* (Denver: Accent Books, 1976), 12.
30. J.P.V.D. Balsdon, *Life and Leisure in Ancient Rome* (New York: McGraw-Hill, 1969), 224–25.
31. Childe, *The Dawn of European Civilization,* 267–73; Grant, *The Ancient Mediterranean,* 293; Curtin, *op. cit.,* 99–100.
32. Gibbon, *op. cit.,* 33.
33. G. W. Bowerstock, "The Dissolution of the Roman Empire," in *The Collapse of Ancient States and Civilizations,* 169; Grant, *The Ancient Mediterranean,* 297–99; Richard P. Saller, "Roman Class Structures and Relations," in *Civilization of the Ancient Mediterranean,* 569.
34. Muller, *op. cit.,* 218.
35. Michael Grant, *The Antonines: The Roman Empire in Transition* (London: Routledge, 1994), 55–56; Muller, *op. cit.,* 221.

Chapter Six: The Eclipse of the Classical City

1. Karl Marx, *Das Kapital,* trans. David Fernbach (New York: Vintage, 1977), vol. 1, 232; vol. 2, 730; Michael Grant, *The Fall of the Roman Empire* (London: Weidenfeld and Nicholson, 1997), 103, 126–29.
2. Balsdon, *op. cit.,* 203.
3. Grant, *The Fall of the Roman Empire,* 103, 139.

4. McNeill, *op. cit.,* 115–19.

5. Muller, *op. cit.,* 228.

6. Ludwig, *op. cit.,* 79–81, 85; Wayne A. Meeks, "Saint Paul of the Cities," in Peter S. Hawkins, *Civitas: Religious Interpretations of the City* (Atlanta: Scholars Press, 1986), 17–23; Sandmel, *op. cit.,* 337, 405.

7. Matthew 10:23.

8. Owens, *op. cit.,* 47.

9. Grant, *The Fall of the Roman Empire,* 291.

10. Jacob Burckhardt, *The Age of Constantine the Great* (New York: Doubleday, 1956), 207; McNeill, *op. cit.,* 122; Lopez, *op. cit.,* 25.

11. Saint Augustine, *The City of God,* trans. Marcus Dods (New York: Modern Library, 1993), 476–77.

12. Joseph A. Tainter, *The Collapse of Complex Societies* (Cambridge, Eng.: Cambridge University Press, 1990), 127–50; Childe, *What Happened in History,* 275.

13. Morris, *op. cit.,* 44.

14. Dunbar von Kalckreuth, *Three Thousand Years of Rome,* trans. Caroline Fredrick (New York: Knopf, 1930), 141–43; Cyril Mango, *Byzantium: The Empire of New Rome* (New York: Scribner's, 1980), 21.

15. George L. Cowgill, "Onward and Upward with Collapse," in *The Collapse of Ancient States and Civilizations,* 270.

16. Chandler and Fox, *op. cit.,* 304.

17. Craig Fisher, "The Medieval City," in *Cities in Transition: From the Ancient World to Urban America,* ed. Frank J. Coppa and Philip C. Dolce (Chicago: Nelson Hall, 1974), 22.

18. Vito Fumagalli, *Landscapes of Fear: Perceptions of Nature and the City in the Middle Ages,* trans. Shayne Mitchell (Cambridge, Eng.: Polity Press, 1994), 68.

19. Mango, *op. cit.,* 75.

20. July, *op. cit.,* 46; Michael Grant, *From Rome to Byzantium: The Fifth Century* (London: Routledge, 1998), 11–13: Mango, *op. cit.,* 74; Chandler and Fox, *op. cit.,* 304–6.

21. *The Chronographia of Michael Psellus,* trans. E.R.A. Stewart (New Haven: Yale University Press, 1953), 130.

22. Pirenne, *op. cit.,* 2–3; Childe, *What Happened in History,* 279; Steven Runciman, "Christian Constantinople," in *Golden Ages of the Great Cities,* ed. C.M. Bowra (London: Thames and Hudson, 1952), 64, 70–72; 77–78.

23. Muller, *op. cit.,* 17.

24. Mango, *op. cit.,* 68, 92.

25. Burckhardt, *op. cit.,* 334; Morris, *op. cit.,* 62; Dimitri Obolensky, *The Byzantine Commonwealth: Eastern Europe, 500–1453* (New York: Praeger, 1971), 48.

CHAPTER SEVEN: THE ISLAMIC ARCHIPELAGO

1. Chandler and Fox, *op. cit.,* 270.

2. Geoffrey Barraclough, *The Crucible of Europe: The Ninth and Tenth Centuries in European History* (Berkeley: University of California Press, 1976), 61.

3. Henri Pirenne, *Mohammed and Charlemagne,* trans. Bernard Miall (Cleveland: Meridian Books, 1957), 166.

4. Richard Hodges, *Dark Age Economics: The Origins of Towns and Trade* (New York: St. Martin's Press, 1982), 31, 181; David C. Douglas, *The Norman Achievement, 1050–1100* (Berkeley: University of California Press, 1969), 189.

5. Paul Wheatley, *The Places Where Men Pray Together: Cities in Islamic Lands, Seventh Through the Tenth Centuries* (Chicago: University of Chicago Press, 2001), 41.

6. Philip K. Hitti, *Capital Cities of Arab Islam* (Minneapolis: University of Minnesota Press, 1973), 4–8.

7. Wheatley, *The Places Where Men Pray Together,* 12, 18.

8. Ibn Khaldun, *The Muqaddimah: An Introduction to History,* trans. Franz Rosenthal (Princeton, N.J.: Princeton University Press, 1969), 97.

9. Hitti, *op. cit.,* 14; Albert Hourani, *A History of the Arab Peoples* (Cambridge, Mass.: Harvard University Press, 2002), 120.

10. Hitti, *op. cit.,* 18–19.

11. Ibn Khaldun, *op. cit.,* 74.

12. Grant, *The Ancient Mediterranean,* 192.

13. Stefano Bianca, *Urban Form in the Arab World: Past and Present* (New York: Thames and Hudson, 2000), 25–36.

14. Hitti, *op. cit.,* 61.

15. Pirenne, *Mohammed and Charlemagne,* 154–55; Mango, 91–97.

16. Wheatley, *The Places Where Men Pray Together,* 35–38.

17. Hourani, *op. cit.,* 124–25.

18. Wheatley, *The Places Where Men Pray Together,* 39.

19. Hitti, *op. cit.,* 154–55; Maria Rosa Menocal, *The Ornament of the World: How Muslims, Jews and Christians Created a Culture of Tolerance in Medieval Spain* (Boston: Little, Brown, 2002), 66.

20. Wheatley, *The Places Where Men Pray Together,* 54–57.

21. Hourani, *op. cit.,* 110–11; Chandler and Fox, *op. cit.,* 270.

22. Hourani, *op. cit.,* 49–50.

23. Janet Abu-Lughod, *Cairo: 1,001 Years of the City Victorious* (Princeton, N.J.: Princeton University Press, 1971), 6–21.

24. Ibid., 41; André Raymond, *Cairo,* trans. Willard Wood (Cambridge, Mass.: Harvard University Press, 2000), 36, 47; Ross E. Dunn, *The Adventures of Ibn Battuta: A Muslim Traveler of the 14th Century* (Berkeley: University of California Press, 1986), 41.

25. Raymond, *op. cit.*, 120.
26. Ibid., 123.
27. Dunn, *op. cit.*, 45.
28. Wheatley, *The Places Where Men Pray Together*, 337.
29. Curtin, *op. cit.*, 114–16.
30. July, *op. cit.*, 58–59; Dunn, *op. cit.*, 122–28; Curtin, *op. cit.*, 121–22.
31. Ghirshman, *op. cit.*, 336–41.
32. Masoud Kheirabadi, *Iranian Cities: Formation and Development* (Austin: University of Texas Press, 1991), 45–65.
33. Thapar, *op. cit.*, 52; Chandler and Fox, *op. cit.*, 301.
34. Stephen P. Blake, *Shahjahanabad: The Sovereign City in Mughal India, 1639–1739* (Cambridge, Eng.: Cambridge University Press, 1991), 1–5.
35. Thapar, *op. cit.*, 239.
36. Dunn, *op. cit.*, 136; Tapan Raychaudhuri and Irfan Habib, *The Cambridge Economic History of India, vol. 1, 1200–1750* (Delhi: Orient Longman, 1982), 82–83.
37. Raychaudhuri and Habib, *op. cit.*, 37–42; Curtin, *op. cit.*, 123–25.

CHAPTER EIGHT: CITIES OF THE MIDDLE KINGDOM
1. *The Travels of Marco Polo*, ed. Manuel Komroff (New York: The Modern Library, 1926), 50–71.
2. René Grousset, *The Empire of the Steppes*, trans. Naomi Walford (New Brunswick, N.J.: Rutgers University Press, 1970), 41–50, 90–95, 117–20; Kenneth Scott Latourette, *The Chinese: Their History and Culture* (New York: Macmillan, 1962), 80.
3. Bernard Lewis, *What Went Wrong? The Clash Between Islam and Modernity in the Middle East* (New York: Perennial, 2002), 6.
4. Wheatley, *The Pivot of the Four Quarters*, 176–78; Ray Huang, *1587, A Year of No Significance: The Ming Dynasty in Decline* (New Haven: Yale University Press, 1981), 4.
5. Latourette, *op. cit.*, 216; Chandler and Fox, *op. cit.*, 270.
6. Gilbert Rozman, "East Asian Urbanization in the Nineteenth Century: Comparisons with Europe," in *Urbanization in History: A Process of Dynamic Interactions*, ed. Advan der Woude, Akira Hayami, and Jan de Vries (Oxford, Eng.: Clarendon Press, 1990), 65–66.
7. Sit, *op. cit.*, 22–23.
8. Ma, *op. cit.*, 119–20.
9. Sit, *op. cit.*, 39.
10. Heng Chye Kiang, *Cities of Aristocrats and Bureaucrats: The Development of Medieval Chinese Cityscapes* (Honolulu: University of Hawaii Press, 1999), 19–25.
11. Ibid., 1–3.
12. Ma, *op. cit.*, 109–10; Sit, *op. cit.*, 25.

13. Latourette, *op. cit.,* 140–41; Chandler and Fox, *op. cit.,* 270.

14. L. Carrington Goodrich, *A Short History of the Chinese People* (New York: Harper Torchbooks, 1943), 116–17; Latourette, *op. cit.,* 67–68; Ma, *op. cit.,* 117; Sen-Dou Chang, *op. cit.,* 116.

15. Heng Chye Kiang, *op. cit.,* 3.

16. Latourette, *op. cit.,* 186.

17. Ma, *op. cit.,* 30–31; Goodrich, *op. cit.,* 151; Raychaudhuri and Habib, *op. cit.,* 128–31.

18. Ma, *op. cit.,* 34–35; Chandler and Fox, *op. cit.,* 270.

19. *The Travels of Marco Polo, op. cit.,* 153, 159–63, 254–56.

20. Goodrich, *op. cit.,* 154–59.

21. Ma, *op. cit.,* 5–6, 160; Heng Chye Kiang, *op. cit.,* 135, 150, 170, 192.

22. Grousset, *op. cit.,* 252.

23. Dunn, *op. cit.,* 250; *The Travels of Marco Polo,* xvi; Latourette, *op. cit.,* 215; Raychaudhuri and Habib, *op. cit.,* 135–38.

24. *The Travels of Marco Polo,* 153, 159–63, 254–56; Curtin, *op. cit.,* 125.

CHAPTER NINE: OPPORTUNITY LOST

1. Ma, *op. cit.,* 11–13; Percival Spear, *India: A Modern History* (Ann Arbor: University of Michigan Press, 1961), 153; Raychaudhuri and Habib, *op. cit.,* 141, 170–71; Blake, *op. cit.,* 30; Fernand Braudel, *The Perspective of the World: Civilization and Capitalism:15th–18th Century,* vol. 3, trans. Sian Reynolds (New York: Harper & Row, 1984), 534; Hourani, *op. cit.,* 232. Note: Not only were these cities large, but their economies were, for the most part, more affluent than those of Europe. Indeed, as late as 1700, per capita incomes in China and India equaled or excelled those of Britain or France, not to mention the poorer nations of Europe. Given its larger population, Asia's economies, in aggregate, accounted for a far bigger share of the global economy.

2. Schinz, *op. cit.,* 1–2.

3. Bernard Lewis, *The Muslim Discovery of Europe* (New York: W. W. Norton, 1982), 60–68, 185–87.

4. Blake, *op. cit.,* 183, 192–94.

5. Saggs, *op. cit.,* 49; ibn Khaldun, *op. cit.,* 135–37, 247; Grousset, *op. cit.,* 323–25.

6. Ma, *op. cit.,* 122.

7. Spear, *op. cit.,* 156–57.

8. Ma, *op. cit.,* 43, 134–37, 162; Ira Marvin Lapidus, *Muslim Cities in the Later Middle Ages* (Cambridge, Mass.: Harvard University Press, 1967), 96, 101; Raychaudhuri and Habib, *op. cit.,* 185–87, 277–78.

9. Ibn Khaldun, *op. cit.,* 238.

10. Curtin, *op. cit.,* 127; Latourette, *op. cit.,* 234.

11. Immanuel Wallerstein, *The Modern World-System: Capitalist Agriculture and the*

Origins of the European World-Economy in the Sixteenth Century (New York: Academic Press, 1974), 55–56.

12. Lapidus, *op. cit.,* 50–65, 78–80, 185–91.

13. Abu-Lughod, *op. cit.,* 48–51; Lewis, *What Went Wrong?* 13.

14. Lewis, *The Muslim Discovery,* 195.

CHAPTER TEN: EUROPE'S URBAN RENAISSANCE

1. Pirenne, *Mohammed and Charlemagne,* 277.

2. Lauro Martines, *Power and Imagination: City-States in Renaissance Italy* (New York: Knopf, 1979), 13; Dougerty, *op. cit.,* 44; Pirenne, *Medieval Cities,* 61–64.

3. Fumagalli, *op. cit.,* 81, 92; William H. McNeill, *The Pursuit of Power: Technology, Armed Force and Society Since A.D. 1000* (Chicago: University of Chicago Press, 1982), 86.

4. John Hale, *The Civilization of Europe in the Renaissance* (New York: Touchstone, 1993), 20.

5. Nathan Rosenberg and L. E. Birdzell Jr., *How the West Grew Rich: The Economic Transformation of the Industrial World* (New York: Basic Books, 1986), 59–60, 68; John Langton and Goran Hoppe, "Town and County in the Development of Early Modern Europe," in *Historical Geography Research Series,* no. 11 (1983): 7.

6. Pirenne, *Mohammed and Charlemagne,* 218–19.

7. Jan de Vries, *European Urbanization, 1500–1800* (Cambridge, Mass.: Harvard University Press, 1984), 28–29, 41.

8. Lewis, *The Muslim Discovery,* 26.

9. Brian Pullan, *A History of Early Renaissance Italy: From the Mid-Thirteenth to the Mid-Fifteenth Century* (New York: St. Martin's Press, 1973), 104–7.

10. Chandler and Fox, *op. cit.,* 313.

11. Morris, *op. cit.,* 113–14; Paul Zucker, *Town and Square, from the Agora to the Village Green* (Cambridge, Mass.: MIT Press, 1970), 99–102.

12. Jacob Burckhardt, *The Civilization of the Renaissance in Italy: An Essay,* trans. S.G.C. Middlemore, ed. Irene Gordon (New York: New American Library, 1961), 79; Morris, *op. cit.,* 112–17.

13. Pullan, *op. cit.,* 103.

14. Frederic C. Lane, *Venice: A Maritime Republic* (Baltimore: Johns Hopkins University Press, 1973), 93.

15. Mumford, *op. cit.,* 321–23; Braudel, *op. cit.,* 135–36; Lane, *op. cit.,* 165.

16. Braudel, *op. cit.,* 120, 124–27; Alberto Ades and Edward L. Glaeser, "Trade and Circuses: Explaining Urban Giants," *Quarterly Journal of Economics* 110, no. 1 (1995): 220.

17. Braudel, *op. cit.,* 132.

18. Ibid., 30, 132.

19. Harold Acton, "Medicean Florence," in *Golden Ages of the Great Cities,* 105–8; Fumagalli, *op. cit.,* 91.

20. Frank J. Coppa, "The Preindustrial City," in *Cities in Transition,* 40–41.

21. Karl Polanyi, *The Great Transformation: The Political and Economic Origins of Our Times* (Boston: Beacon Press, 1944), 45; Cecil Fairfield Lavell, *Italian Cities* (Chautauqua, N.Y.: Chautauqua, 1905), 115.

22. Martines, *op. cit.,* 83.

23. Dante, *The Divine Comedy: Inferno,* trans. John D. Sinclair (New York: Oxford University Press, 1939), 209 (Canto XVI).

24. Martines, *op. cit.,* 169–72.

25. Coppa, *op. cit.,* 42.

26. Étienne François, "The German Urban Network Between the Sixteenth and Eighteenth Centuries: Cultural and Demographic Indicators," in *Urbanization in History,* 84–100; Alexandra Richie, *Faust's Metropolis: A History of Berlin* (New York: Carroll and Graf, 1998), 3, 22–24; Giles MacDonogh, *Berlin: A Portrait of Its History, Architecture and Society* (New York: St. Martin's Press, 1998), 40.

27. Mumford, *op. cit.,* 355.

28. Machiavelli, *The Prince,* trans. Luigi Ricci (New York: Mentor, 1952), 119.

29. Lane, *op. cit.,* 177.

30. Martines, *op. cit.,* 169; McNeill, *Plagues and Peoples,* 170–71; Fernand Braudel, *The Mediterranean and the Mediterranean World in the Age of Philip II,* vol. 1, trans. Sian Reynolds (New York: Harper & Row, 1972), 334–36.

31. Braudel, *The Mediterranean,* 388–89.

32. Louis B. Wright, *Gold, Glory and the Gospel: The Adventurous Lives and Times of the Renaissance Explorers* (New York: Atheneum, 1970), 117; Harold Burdett, "Toward the 21st Century," Population Institute 2 (1996).

33. Chandler and Fox, *op. cit.,* 313; de Vries, *op. cit.,* 30.

34. *Prescott's Histories: The Rise and Decline of the Spanish Empire,* ed. Irwin Blacker (New York: Viking Press, 1963), 258–63.

35. Lopez, *op. cit.,* 322–25; Alfred Fierro, *Historical Dictionary of Paris,* trans. Jon Woronoff (Lanham, Md.: Scarecrow Press, 1998), 2–3.

36. Fumagalli, *op. cit.,* 91.

37. Yves Lenguin, *La mosaïque France: Histoire des étrangers et de l'immigration en France* (Paris: Larousse, 1988), 130, 142; Braudel, *The Perspective of the World,* 329–30.

38. James L. McClain and John M. Merriman, "Edo and Paris: Cities and Power," in James L. McClain, John M. Merriman, and Ugawa Kaoru, *Edo and Paris: Urban Life and the State in the Early Modern Era* (Ithaca, N.Y.: Cornell University Press, 1994), 4, 12–13.

39. Ibid., 23, 77.

40. Zucker, *op. cit.*, 195.
41. David Hamer, *New Towns in the New World: Images and Perceptions of the Nineteenth Century Urban Frontier* (New York: Columbia University Press, 1990), 36–37.
42. Michel Carmona, *Haussmann: His Life and Times, and the Making of Modern Paris*, trans. Patrick Camiller (Chicago: Ivan R. Dee, 2002), 10, 113–22, 139, 154–56; Georges Lefebvre, *The Coming of the French Revolution*, trans. R. R. Palmer (Princeton, N.J.: Princeton University Press, 1967), 98–99.

CHAPTER ELEVEN: CITIES OF MAMMON
 1. Nicholas V. Riasanovsky, *A History of Russia* (New York: Oxford University Press, 1963), 92–117.
 2. Rozman, 71–72.
 3. Morris, *op. cit.*, 104–5; de Vries, *op. cit.*, 29, 50.
 4. Hale, *op. cit.*, 456.
 5. *Prescott's Histories*, 155.
 6. Hale, *op. cit.*, 168.
 7. Henry Kamen, *Spain 1469–1714: A Society of Conflict* (London: Longman, 1991), 39–42; Barnet Litvinoff, *1492: The Decline of Medievalism and the Rise of the Modern Age* (New York: Avon, 1991), 34, 58.
 8. Kamen, *op. cit.*, 246–48.
 9. Ibid., 170–71; Litvinoff, *op. cit.*, 66; Wallerstein, *op. cit.*, 195; J. H. Parry, *The Age of Reconnaissance* (New York: Mentor, 1963), 66.
10. Braudel, *The Mediterranean*, 146–52; Kamen, *op. cit.*, 98–99, 224–25; de Vries, *op. cit.*, 30.
11. Edith Ennen, *The Medieval Town*, trans. Natalie Fryde (Amsterdam: North Holland Publishing Company, 1979), 187; de Vries, *op. cit.*, 30.
12. Braudel, *Perspective of the World*, 31.
13. Rosenberg and Birdzell, *op. cit.*, 70, n. 30.
14. Hale, *op. cit.*, 170; de Vries, *op. cit.*, 30.
15. Simon Schama, *The Embarrassment of Riches: An Interpretation of Dutch Culture in the Golden Age* (New York: Knopf, 1987), 261; J. M. Bos, "A 14th Century Industrial Complex at Monnickendam and the Preceding Events," in *Medemblik and Monnickendam: Aspects of Medieval Urbanization in Northern Holland*, ed. H. A. Heidinga and H. H. van Regteren (Amsterdam: Amsterdam University Press, 1989), 21.
16. Morris, *op. cit.*, 164; Simon Groenveld, "For Benefit of the Poor: Social Assistance in Amsterdam," in *Rome & Amsterdam: Two Growing Cities in Seventeenth Century Europe*, ed. Peter van Kessel and Elisja Schulte (Amsterdam: Amsterdam University Press, 1997), 206–8.
17. Braudel, *Perspective of the World*, 184–85; Jonathan Israel, *The Dutch Republic: Its Rise, Greatness and Fall* (Oxford, Eng.: Oxford University Press, 1995), 113–15.

18. Schama, *op. cit.,* 15, 253, 294, 311.

19. Ibid., 44–46, 300.

20. Braudel, *Perspective of the World,* 30.

21. Kamen, *op. cit.,* 116–17.

22. Braudel, *Perspective of the World,* 185–88; Israel, *op. cit.,* 116–17.

23. Israel, *op. cit.,* 350–51.

24. Hale, *op. cit.,* 274–76.

25. Ibid., 78–79, 137; A. R. Meyers, *England in the Late Middle Ages* (London: Pelican, 1951), 211.

26. Henri and Barbara van der Zee, *A Sweet and Alien Land: The Story of Dutch New York* (New York: Viking, 1978), 2–3; "New Amsterdam, Frontier Trading Post," from Nicholas van Wassenaer, *Historisch Verhael,* in *Empire City: New York Through the Centuries,* ed. Kenneth T. Jackson and David S. Dunbar (New York: Columbia University Press, 2002), 26.

27. Peter Burke, *Venice and Amsterdam: A Study of Seventeenth-century Elites* (Cambridge, Eng.: Polity Press, 1994), 135–39; van der Zee and van der Zee, *op. cit.,* 492–94; Edwin G. Burrows, and Mike Wallace, *Gotham: A History of New York City to 1898* (New York: Oxford University Press, 1999) 73–74.

28. Oliver A. Rink, *Holland on the Hudson: An Economic and Social History of Dutch New York* (Ithaca, N.Y.: Cornell University Press; Cooperstown, N.Y.: New York State Historical Association, 1986), 248–50.

29. F.R.H. Du Boulay, *An Age of Ambition: English Society in the Late Middle Ages* (New York: Viking, 1970), 66.

30. Meyers, *op. cit.,* 37; Du Boulay, *op. cit.,* 30.

31. Spear, *op. cit.,* 231.

32. McNeill, *The Pursuit of Power,* 151; Rhoads Murphey, "The City as a Centre of Change: Western Europe and China," in *The City in the Third World,* ed. D. J. Dwyer (New York: Barnes and Noble Books, 1974), 65.

33. Hale, *op. cit.,* 143.

34. Israel, *op. cit.,* 1011; Braudel, *Perspective of the World,* 365; Hall, *op. cit.,* 116.

35. Meyers, *op. cit.,* 161–63, 225, 232–33.

36. Hamish McRae and Frances Cairncross, *Capital City: London as a Financial Centre* (London: Eyre Methuen, 1973), 9.

37. Emrys Jones, *Metropolis,* (Oxford, Eng.: Oxford University Press, 1990), 93; Zucker, *op. cit.,* 196–98.

CHAPTER TWELVE: THE ANGLO-AMERICAN URBAN REVOLUTION

1. Hale, *op. cit.,* 355; Braudel, *Perspective of the World,* 548.

2. Braudel, *Perspective of the World,* 575–81; Karl Marx, *Das Kapital, op. cit.,* 914–30.

3. Jones, *op. cit.,* 94.

4. Du Boulay, *op. cit.,* 41; de Vries, *op. cit.,* 101.

5. John L. and Barbara Hammond, "The Industrial Revolution: The Rulers and the Masters," in *The Industrial Revolution in Britain: Triumph or Disaster?* ed. Philip A. M. Taylor (Boston: D. C. Heath & Company, 1958), 40; Mark Giroud, *Cities and People: A Social and Architectural History* (New Haven: Yale University Press, 1985), 265; Theodore Koditschek, *Class Formation and Urban-Industrial Society, Bradford, 1750–1850* (Cambridge, Eng.: Cambridge University Press, 1990), 79.

6. Arnold J. Toynbee, *The Industrial Revolution* (Boston: Beacon Press, 1956), 10–11.

7. Koditschek, *op. cit.*, 107.

8. Friedrich Engels, *The Condition of the Working Class in England*, trans. W. O. Henderson and W. H. Chaloner (Stanford, Calif.: Stanford University Press, 1968), 57–61.

9. Hammond and Hammond, *op. cit.*, 41; Koditschek, *op. cit.*, 100; de Vries, *op. cit.*, 179.

10. Alexis de Tocqueville, "Memoir on Pauperism," in *Tocqueville and Beaumont on Social Reform*, ed. Seymour Drescher (New York: Harper Torchbooks, 1968), 2, 13.

11. Hammond and Hammond, *op. cit.*, 36.

12. Koditschek, *op. cit.*, 133–37, 144.

13. Andrew Lees, *Cities Perceived: Urban Society in European and American Thought: 1820–1940* (New York: Columbia University Press, 1985), 29.

14. *The Complete Poetry and Prose of William Blake*, ed. David V. Erdman (New York: Anchor Books, 1988), 329.

15. Tocqueville, *op. cit.*, 2.

16. Lees, *op. cit.*, 40–41.

17. Hartmut Kaelble, *Historical Research on Social Mobility: Western Europe and the U.S.A. in the Nineteenth and Twentieth Centuries*, trans. Ingrid Noakes (New York: Columbia University Press, 1981), 42–43, 62–65, 96–97; Reuven Brenner, *Rivalry: In Business, Science, Among Nations* (Cambridge, Eng.: Cambridge University Press, 1987), 43.

18. Gertrude Himmelfarb, *The De-moralization of Society: From Victorian Virtues to Modern Values* (New York: Knopf, 1995), 39; McNeill, *Plagues and Peoples*, 275; Thomas S. Ashton, "Workers Living Standards: A Modern Revision," in *The Industrial Revolution in Britain*, 481; Lees, *op. cit.*, 40–41.

19. Lees, *op. cit.*, 53–54.

20. Ibid., 44–55.

21. Fierro, *op. cit.*, 18.

22. Henry Nash Smith, *Virgin Land: The American West as Symbol and Myth* (Cambridge, Mass.: Harvard University Press, 1950), 32, 127–78.

23. Jonathan Hughes, *American Economic History* (New York: HarperCollins, 1990), 334.

24. Arthur M. Schlesinger, Jr. *The Age of Jackson* (New York: Book Find Club, 1945), 315.

25. Bernard Bailyn, *Voyagers to the West: A Passage in the Peopling of America on the Eve of the Revolution* (New York: Knopf, 1986), 152–54; Brinley Thomas, *Economics of International Migration* (New York: Macmillan, 1958), 65–66, 575.

26. Joseph Salvo and Arun Peter Lobo, "Immigration and the Changing Demographic Profile of New York," in *The City and the World: New York's Global Future*, ed. Margaret Crahan and Alberto Vourvoulias-Bush (New York: Council on Foreign Relations, 1997), 88–89.

27. Mumford, *op. cit.*, 467–68.

28. Sven Beckert, *The Monied Metropolis: New York City and the Consolidation of the American Bourgeoisie, 1850–1896* (Cambridge, Eng.: Cambridge University Press, 2001), 47.

29. Kaelble, *op. cit.*, 36–37; Paul H. Wilken, *Entrepreneurship: A Complete and Historical Study* (Norwood, N.J.: Ablex Publishing, 1979), 207.

30. Beckert, *op. cit.*, 51.

31. Jon C. Teaford, *Cities of the Heartland: The Rise and Fall of the Industrial Midwest* (Bloomington: Indiana University Press, 1994), 1–4; Lawrence R. Larsen, "Chicago's Midwest Rivals: Cincinnati, St. Louis and Milwaukee," in *Chicago History* (Fall 1976): 144.

32. Teaford, *op. cit.*, 66.

33. Charles and Mary Beard, *The Rise of American Civilization*, vol. 2 (New York: Macmillan, 1950), 176–206; Teaford, *op. cit.*, 4, 49, 52–54; Hughes, *op. cit.*, 268–69.

34. Larsen, *op. cit.*, 141–47; Bessie Louise Pierce, *A History of Chicago: 1848–1871*, vol. 2 (New York: Knopf, 1940), 117.

35. Teaford, *op. cit.*, 11, 19.

36. J. A. Dacus and James M. Buel, *A Tour of St. Louis, or the Inside Life of a Great City* (St. Louis: Western Publishing Company, 1878), 406–13.

37. Teaford, *op. cit.*, 68.

38. Lees, *op. cit.*, 166–69; Teaford, *op. cit.*, 113–17; Samuel Hays, *The Response to Industrialism* (Chicago: University of Chicago Press, 1957), 22–24, 71–72.

39. Beard and Beard, *op. cit.*, 748; Beckert, *op. cit.*, 297.

40. Jane Allen Shikoh, "The Higher Life in the American City of the 1900s: A Study of Leaders and Their Activities in New York, Chicago, Philadelphia, St. Louis, Boston and Buffalo," PhD dissertation in Department of History, Graduate School of Arts and Science, New York University, October 1972, 5–8, 81–85.

41. Lees, *op. cit.*, 1.

42. Frederick Law Olmsted, "Selected Writings on Central Park," in *Empire City: New York City Through the Centuries*, 278–79.

43. C.A.E. Goodhart, *The New York Money Market and the Finance of Trade: 1900–1913* (Oxford, Eng.: Oxford University Press, 1969), 9–10.

44. Robert Bruegmann, "The Paradoxes of Anti-Sprawl Reform," uncorrected draft for *The Twentieth Century Planning Experience*, ed. Robert Freestone (London: Routledge, 1999).

45. Max Page, *The Creative Destruction of Manhattan: 1900–1940* (Chicago: University of Chicago Press, 1999), 5; *Empire City: New York City Through the Centuries*, 404.

46. Emanuel Tobier, "Manhattan's Business District in the Industrial Age," in *Power, Culture, and Place: Essays on New York*, ed. John Mollenkopf (New York: Russell Sage Foundation, 1988), 85–87.

47. Beard and Beard, *op. cit.*, 787.

48. Tyler Cowen, *In Praise of Commercial Culture* (Cambridge, Mass.: Harvard University Press, 1998), 120.

49. Hall, *op. cit.*, 522; Fred A. McKenzie, *The American Invaders* (New York: reprinted by Arno Press, 1976), 9; William R. Taylor, *In Pursuit of Gotham: Culture and Commerce in New York* (New York: Oxford University Press, 1992), 74–76.

50. Anton C. Zijderveld, *A Theory of Urbanity: The Economic and Civic Culture of Cities* (New Brunswick, N.J.: Transaction Publishers, 1998), 2.

51. Beard and Beard, *op. cit.*, 780–82.

52. John Dos Passos, *Manhattan Transfer* (Boston: Houghton Mifflin, 1925), 305.

53. Paul Crowell and A. H. Raskin, "New York: The Greatest City in the World," in *Our Fair City*, ed. Robert S. Allen (New York: Vanguard, 1947), 58.

54. Teaford, *op. cit.*, 76; John G. Clark, David M. Katzman, Richard D. McKinzie, and Theodore Watson, *Three Generations in Twentieth Century America: Family, Community, and Nation* (Homewood, Ill.: Dorsey Press, 1977), 403.

55. Robert M. Fogelson, *Downtown: Its Rise and Fall, 1880–1950* (New Haven: Yale University Press, 2001), 112–66.

56. Crowell and Raskin, *op. cit.*, 37.

57. Fogelson, *op. cit.*, 2.

CHAPTER THIRTEEN: INDUSTRIALISM AND ITS DISCONTENTS

1. G. C. Allen, *Appointment in Japan: Memories of Sixty Years* (London: Athlone Press, 1983), 2–5.

2. Ibid., 37.

3. C. E. Elias, Jr., James Gillies, and Svend Riemer, eds., *Metropolis: Values in Conflict* (Belmont, Calif.: Wadsworth Publishing, 1965), 11–12.

4. Dhamar Kumar, *The Cambridge Economic History of India, vol. 2, 1757–1970* (Hyderabad: Orient Longman, 1982), 568–69.

5. Sigmund Freud, *Civilization and Its Discontents,* trans. James Strachey (New York: W. W. Norton, 1962), 59.

6. Carl Mosk, *Japanese Industrial History* (Armonk, N.Y.: M. E. Sharpe, 2001), 50.

7. Thomas O. Wilkinson, *The Urbanization of Japanese Labor: 1868–1955* (Amherst: University of Massachusetts Press, 1965), 22–23.

8. Mosk, *op. cit.,* 55, 201–2; Richard Child Hill and Kuniko Fujita, "Japanese Cities in the World Economy," and Hachiro Nakamura, "Urban Growth in Prewar Japan," in *Japanese Cities in the World Economy,* ed. Kuniko Fujita and Richard Child Hill (Philadelphia: Temple University Press, 1993), 5, 30; Glenn T. Trewartha, *Japan: A Geography* (Madison: University of Wisconsin Press, 1965), 161.

9. Marius B. Jansen, *The Cambridge History of Japan, vol. 5: The Nineteenth Century* (Cambridge, Eng.: Cambridge University Press, 1988), 731; Hachiro Nakamura, *op. cit.,* 30.

10. Mosk, *op. cit.,* 174–75; Wilkinson, *op. cit.,* 45.

11. Allen, *op. cit.,* 124–25.

12. Nishiyama Matsunosuke, *Edo Culture: Daily Life and Diversions in Urban Japan, 1600–1868,* trans. and ed. Gerald Groemer (Honolulu: University of Hawaii Press, 1997), 9.

13. Mosk, *op. cit.,* 217.

14. Beatrice M. Bodart-Bailey, "Urbanisation and the Nature of the Tokugawa Hegemony," in *Japanese Capitals in Historic Perspective,* 175, 199.

15. Wilkinson, *op. cit.,* 77–78.

16. Ibid., 122–23.

17. John W. Dower, *War Without Mercy: Race and Power in the Pacific War* (New York: Pantheon, 1986), 31.

18. Evelyn S. Colbert, *The Left Wing in Japanese Politics* (New York: Institute of Pacific Relations, 1952), 33; George Oakley Totten III, *The Social Democratic Movement in Prewar Japan* (New Haven: Yale University Press, 1966), 106–7, 259.

19. Robert J. C. Butow, *Tojo and the Coming of the War* (Stanford, Calif.: Stanford University Press, 1969), 146–48; Dower, *op. cit.,* 228–29; Sheldon Garon, *Molding Japanese Minds: The State in Everyday Life* (Princeton, N.J.: Princeton University Press, 1997), 82–83.

20. Carola Hein, "Visionary Plans and Planners: Japanese Traditions and Western Influences," in *Japanese Capitals in Historic Perspective,* 309–42.

21. Jeffry M. Diefendorf, "The West German Debate on Urban Planning," "The American Impact on Western Europe: Americanization and Westernization in Transatlantic Perspective," Conference of the German Historical Institute,

Washington, D.C., March 25–27, 1999; Klaus P. Fischer, *Nazi Germany: A New History* (New York: Continuum, 1995), 116–17; Gottfried Feder, "Das Program der N.S.D.A.P.," in Joachim Remak, *The Nazi Years: A Documentary History* (Englewood Cliffs, N.J.: Prentice Hall, 1969), 30.

22. Philipp Oswald, "Berlin: A City Without Form," *Tas Skorupa*, http://www.urban-os.com/think-pool/one?think_id=3164; Engels, *op. cit.*, 333; Helen Meller, *European Cities 1890–1930s: History, Culture and The Built Environment* (New York: John Wiley, 2001), 10; Morris, *op. cit.*, 166–67; Richie, *op. cit.*, 141, 144.

23. Lees, *op. cit.*, 119–21; Richie, *op. cit.*, 163, 167.

24. Georg Simmel, "The Metropolis and Mental Life," in *The Sociology of Georg Simmel*, trans. Kurt H. Wolff (New York: Free Press, 1950), 410–13.

25. Heinrich Class, "Wenn ich der Kaiser war," in Remak, *op. cit.*, 8–9; William Appleman Williams, *The Roots of the Modern American Empire: A Study of the Growth and Shaping of Social Consciousness in a Marketplace Society* (New York: Random House, 1969), 204.

26. Karl Dietrich Bracher, *The German Dictatorship: The Origins, Structure and Effects of National Socialism*, trans. Jean Steinberg (New York: Praeger, 1970), 45; Carl E. Schorske, *Fin de Siècle Vienna: Politics and Culture* (New York: Knopf, 1979), 5–6.

27. Program of the National Socialist German Workers Party, in Remak, *op. cit.*, 27–29.

28. Michael Burleigh and Wolfgang Wippermann, *The Racial State: Germany, 1933–1945* (Cambridge, Eng.: Cambridge University Press, 1991), 220–22.

29. Roger Eatwell, "Fascism: A Three Dimensional Approach," final draft, for inclusion in *Il fascismo e I suoi unterpreti*, ed. Alessandro Campi (Rome: Antonio Pellicani, 2000).

30. Klaus Fischer, *op. cit.*, 367; Richie, *op. cit.*, 407, 432, 437.

31. W. Bruce Lincoln, *Sunlight at Midnight: St. Petersburg and the Rise of Modern Russia* (New York: Basic Books, 2002), 1–3.

32. Roger P. Bartlett, *Human Capital: The Settlement of Foreigners in Russia 1762–1804* (Cambridge, Eng.: Cambridge University Press, 1979), 1–2; 94–95.

33. Reginald E. Zelnik, *Labor and Society in Tsarist Russia: The Factory Workers of St. Petersburg, 1855–1970* (Stanford, Calif.: Stanford University Press, 1971), 221.

34. Ibid., 23, 27; Riasanovsky, *op. cit.*, 309.

35. Daniel R. Brower, *The Russian City Between Tradition and Modernity, 1850–1900* (Berkeley: University of California Press, 1990), 9, 13–14, 23, 202, 221; Nicholas Riasanovsky, *Nicholas I and Official Nationality in Russia, 1825–1855* (Berkeley: University of California Press, 1959), 134–35.

36. Anatole G. Mazour, *The First Russian Revolution, 1825: The Decembrist Movement,*

Its Origins, Development, and Significance (Stanford, Calif.: Stanford University Press, 1961), 261–72; Zelnik, *op. cit.,* 17.

37. Laura Engelstein, *Moscow 1905: Working-Class Organization and Political Conflict* (Stanford, Calif.: Stanford University Press, 1982), 13, 27; Lincoln, *op. cit.,* 9; Zelnik, *op. cit.,* 240–41; Riasanovsky, *History of Russia,* 470–74.

38. Lincoln, *op. cit.,* 242.

39. William J. Chase, *Workers, Society, and the Soviet State: Labor and Life in Moscow, 1918–1929* (Urbana: University of Illinois Press, 1987), 6–7; Paul E. Lydolph, *Geography of the U.S.S.R.,* (New York: John Wiley, 1964), 275.

40. Chase, *op. cit.,* 24–25.

41. Ibid., 73.

42. Lincoln, *op. cit.,* 231–33.

43. Ibid., 260–61; William Henry Chamberlin, *Russia's Iron Age* (Boston: Little, Brown, 1935), 5.

44. Dmitri Volkogonov, *Stalin: Triumph and Tragedy,* trans. Harold Shukman (New York: Grove Weidenfeld, 1991), 234.

45. Dmitri Volkogonov, *Autopsy for an Empire: The Seven Leaders Who Built the Soviet Regime,* trans. Harold Shukman (New York: Free Press, 1998), 184–85.

46. Chamberlin, *op. cit.,* 51–53.

47. Lyndolph, *op. cit.,* 275.

48. N. S. Khrushchev, *Socialism and Communism: Selected Passages 1956–63* (Moscow: Foreign Languages Press, 1963), 18, 43.

49. Volkogonov, *Autopsy for Empire,* 280; "The Environmental Outlook in Russia," National Intelligence Council, January 1999.

50. Nicolas Berdyaev, *The Origin of Russian Communism* (Ann Arbor: University of Michigan Press, 1960), 182.

CHAPTER FOURTEEN: THE SEARCH FOR A "BETTER CITY"

1. Dana W. Bartlett, *The Better City: A Sociological Study of a Modern City* (Los Angeles: Neuner Company Press, 1907), 1.

2. Carey McWilliams, *Southern California Country: An Island on the Land* (New York: Duell, Sloan and Pearce, 1946), 213.

3. Dana W. Bartlett, *op. cit.,* 37, 211.

4. Ibid., 191.

5. David Gebhard and Harriette von Breton, *Los Angeles in the Thirties: 1931–1941* (Los Angeles: Peregrine Smith, 1975), 28; Rybczynski, *op. cit.,* 143.

6. John D. Weaver, *El Pueblo Grande: Los Angeles from the Brush Huts of Yangna to the Skyscrapers of the Modern Megalopolis* (Los Angeles: Ward Ritchie Press, 1973), 38–39.

7. Greg Hise, *Magnetic Los Angeles: Planning the Twentieth-Century Metropolis* (Baltimore: Johns Hopkins University Press, 1997), 10–11.

8. Weaver, *op. cit.*, 48–51.

9. Gebhard and von Breton, *op. cit.*, 26; Richard Longstreth, *City Center to Regional Mall: Architecture, the Automobile, and Retailing in Los Angeles, 1920–1950* (Cambridge, Mass.: MIT Press, 1997), 13.

10. Greg Hise and William Deverell, *Eden by Design: The 1930 Olmsted-Bartholomew Plan for the Los Angeles Region* (Berkeley: University of California Press, 2000), 6–8, 22, 39–51.

11. Hildy Median, "L.A. Job Growth Beats Most Major Cities," *Los Angeles Business Journal*, May 26, 1997.

12. Tobier, *op. cit.*, 78.

13. Rudolf Hartog, "Growth Without Limits: Some Case Studies of 20th Century Urbanization," *International Planning Studies* 4, no. 1 (1999): 98.

14. Kenneth Jackson, *Crabgrass Frontier: The Suburbanization of the United States* (New York: Oxford University Press, 1985), 16–191.

15. Klaus Fischer, *op. cit.*, 25; Frank J. Poppa, "The Pre-Industrial City," in *Cities in Transition*, 43–45; Hale, *op. cit.*, 143; Robert Fishman, *Bourgeois Utopias: The Rise and Fall of Suburbia* (New York: Basic Books, 1987), 20–21.

16. Meller, *op. cit.*, 1, 8.

17. Morris, *op. cit.*, 110.

18. Girouard, *op. cit.*, 268–83.

19. Ibid., 280–83; D. A. Reeder, "A Theater of Suburbs: Some Patterns of Development in West London, 1801–1911," in *The Study of Urban History*, ed. H. J. Dyos (New York: St. Martin's Press, 1968), 253.

20. Girouard, *op. cit.*, 268–69, 282–83; Fishman, *op. cit.*, 75.

21. H. G. Wells, *Anticipations of the Reaction of Mechanical and Scientific Progress upon Human Life and Thought* (London: Chapman and Hall, 1902), 33–62.

22. Carl E. Schorske, "The Idea of the City in European Thought," in *The Historian and the City*, ed. Oscar Handlin and John Burchard (Cambridge, Mass.: MIT Press, 1963), 105–6.

23. Thomas Carlyle, *Selected Writings*, ed. Alan Shelston (Middlesex, Eng.: Penguin, 1971), 64–65; Fishman, *op. cit.*, 34–61.

24. William Peterson, "The Ideological Origins of Britain's New Towns," in *New Towns and the Suburban Dream*, ed. Irving Lewis Allen (Port Washington, N.Y.: University Publications, 1977), 62–65; Schorske, *op. cit.*, 108.

25. A. Digby Baltzell, *Philadelphia Gentlemen: The Making of a National Upper Class* (New Brunswick, N.J.: Transaction Press, 1989), 196–209; John Modell, "An Ecology of Family Decisions: Suburbanization, Schooling and Fertility in Philadelphia, 1880–1920," *Journal of Urban History* 6, no. 4 (August 1980): 397–417.

26. Teaford, *op. cit.*, 238–42.

27. Jackson, *op. cit.*, 176.

28. Scott Donaldson, *The Suburban Myth* (New York: Columbia University Press, 1969), 3.

29. Jackson, *op. cit.,* 172.

CHAPTER FIFTEEN: SUBURBIA TRIUMPHANT

1. Jackson, *op. cit.,* 7; Donaldson, *op. cit.,* 4.

2. Fred Siegel, *The Future Once Happened Here: New York, D.C., L.A., and the Fate of America's Big Cities* (New York: Free Press, 1997; uncorrected proof), x.

3. Robert Moses, "Are Cities Dead?," in *Metropolis: Values in Conflict,* 53.

4. Jon C. Teaford, *Post-Suburbia: Government and Politics in the Edge Cities* (Baltimore: Johns Hopkins University Press, 1997), 10.

5. Ralph G. Martin, "A New Life Style," in Louis H. Masotti and Jeffrey K. Hadden, *Suburbia in Transition* (New York: New Viewpoints, 1974), 14–21; William H. Whyte, *The Organization Man* (Garden City, N.Y.: Doubleday, 1957), 331.

6. Andres Duany, Elizabeth Plater-Zybeck, and Jeff Sperk, *Suburban Nation: The Rise of Sprawl and the Decline of the American Dream* (New York: North Point Press, 2000), xii, 59.

7. Lewis Mumford, *The Urban Prospect* (New York: Harcourt Brace, 1968), 221; Donaldson, *op. cit.,* 202.

8. William M. Dobriner, *Class in Suburbia* (Englewood Cliffs, N.J.: Prentice Hall, 1963), 140.

9. Jackson, *op. cit.,* 42; William H. Whyte, "The Anti-City," in *Metropolis: Values in Conflict,* 69; Clark et al., *op. cit.,* 469; Hise, *op. cit.,* 7.

10. Teaford, *Cities of the Heartland,* 232–44; Clark et al., *op. cit.,* 418.

11. John J. Harrigan, *Political Change in the Metropolis* (Boston: Little, Brown, 1976), 36–37.

12. Mumford, *The Urban Prospect,* 207.

13. Himmelfarb, *op. cit.,* 225–33.

14. Louis M. Hacker, *The Course of American Economic Growth and Development* (New York: John Wiley, 1970), 351.

15. Meller, *op. cit.,* 16, 51; Le Corbusier, *The City of Tomorrow and Its Planning,* trans. Frederick Etchells (Cambridge, Mass.: MIT Press, 1971), 1–7; Rybczynski, *op. cit.,* 158–59; Le Corbusier, "The Fairy Catastrophe," in *Empire City: New York City Through the Centuries,* 611–13.

16. Jones, *op. cit.,* 99.

17. Mariana Mogilevich, "Big Bad Buildings," *The Next American City* 3 (2003); Robert W. Gilmer, "The Urban Consolidation of American Oil: The Case of Houston," Federal Reserve Bank of Dallas, Houston branch, June 6, 1998.

18. Robert Fitch, *The Assassination of New York* (London: Verso, 1993), xi–xiv.

19. Witold Rybczynski and Peter Linneman, "Shrinking Cities," *Wharton Real Es-*

tate Review (Fall 1997); William Kornblum, "New York Under Siege," in *The Other City: People and Politics in New York and London,* ed. Susanne Macgregor and Arthur Lipow (Atlantic Highlands, N.J.: Humanities Press, 1995), 37; Jack Newfield and Paul Du Brul, *The Abuse of Power: The Permanent Government and the Fall of New York* (New York: Viking, 1977), 18–24.

20. Kate Stohr, "Shrinking Cities Syndrome," *The New York Times,* February 5, 2004; "London Comes Back to Life," *The Economist,* November 9, 1996.

21. Eric Sandweiss, introduction, in *Where We Live: A Guide to St. Louis Communities,* ed. Tim Fox (St. Louis: Missouri Historical Society Press, 1995), 2.

22. Teaford, *Cities of the Heartland,* 244, 255.

23. Anna Segre, "Turin in the 1980s," in *Europe's Cities in the Late 20th Century,* ed. Hugh Clout (Utrecht: Royal Dutch Geographical Society, 1994), 106; Gunter Glebe, "Düsseldorf: Economic Restructuring and Demographic Transformation," in *Europe's Cities in the Late 20th Century,* 127.

24. Jack Rosenthal, "The Outer City: An Overview of Suburban Turmoil in the United States," in Masotti and Hadden, *op. cit.,* 269.

25. James R. Scobie, *Buenos Aires: Plaza to Suburb, 1870–1910* (New York: Oxford University Press, 1974), 191; Charles S. Sargent, *The Spatial Evolution of Greater Buenos Aires, Argentina 1870–1930* (Tempe: Center for Latin American Studies, Arizona State University, 1974), 123–25.

26. Geoffrey Bolton, *The Oxford History of Australia: The Middle Way, 1842–1968* (Melbourne: Oxford University Press, 1990), 121–24.

27. Mumford, *The Urban Prospect,* 236; Hartog, *op. cit.,* 103.

28. Richard Rogers and Richard Burdett, "Let's Cram More into the City," *New Statesman,* May 22, 2000.

29. Patrick Collinson, "Property: A Slowdown Will Mean a Steadier Market," *The Guardian,* October 28, 2000; "The Music of the Metropolis," *The Economist,* August 2, 1997.

30. Emrys Jones, "London," in *The Metropolis Era, vol. 2, The Megacities,* ed. Mattei Dogan and John D. Kasarda (Newbury Park, Calif.: Sage Publications, 1988), 105.

31. Hartog, *op. cit.,* 121.

32. Henry Tricks, "Escape from the City," *The Financial Times,* October 12, 2003.

33. Pietro S. Nivola, *Laws of the Landscape: How Politics Shape Cities in Europe and America* (Washington, D.C.: Brookings, 1999), 27–28; Peter Marcuse and Ronald van Kempen, "Conclusion: A Changed Spatial Order," in *Globalizing Cities: A New Spatial Order?,* ed. Peter Marcuse and Ronald van Kempen (London: Blackwell Publishers, 2000), 260.

34. Manuel Valenzuela and Ana Olivera, "Madrid Capital City and Metropolitan Region," in *Europe's Cities in the Late 20th Century,* 57–59; Glebe, *op. cit.,* 126–32.

35. Jeffry M. Diefendorf, "The American Impact on Western Europe: American-

ization and Westernization in Transatlantic Perspective," Conference of the German Historical Institute, Washington, D.C., March 25–27, 1999.

36. Hartog, *op. cit.*, 110–16.

37. "Discussion," in *The Study of Urban History, op. cit.*, 278.

38. Eli Lehrer, "Crime Without Punishment," *Weekly Standard*, May 27, 2002.

39. Jan Rath, "A Game of Ethnic Musical Chairs? Immigrant Businesses and the Alleged Formation and Succession of Niches in the Amsterdam Economy," in Sophie Body-Gendrot and Marco Martiniello, *Minorities in European Cities: The Dynamics of Social Integration and Social Exclusion at the Neighborhood Level* (Houndmills, Basingstoke, Hampshire: Macmillan Press, 2000); "E.U. Needs Foreign Workers but Resents Their Success," *The Hindu*, August 3, 2001; "Crime and Politics," *Business Week*, March 18, 2002.

40. Research provided by Eduourd Bomhoff, Nyber, Netherlands; Jennifer Ehrlich, "Liberal Netherlands Becomes Less So on Immigration," *Christian Science Monitor*, December 19, 2003; Phillip Rees, Evert van Imhoff, Helen Durham, Marek Kupiszewski, and Darren Smith, "Internal Migration and Regional Population Dynamics in Europe: Netherlands Case Study," Council of Europe, August 1998.

41. Jane Holtz Kay, "In Holland, the Pressures of American Style Urban Sprawl," *Christian Science Monitor*, October 3, 2002.

42. Christian Kestletoot, "Brussels: Post Fordist Polarization in a Fordist Spatial Canvas," in *Globalizing Cities, op. cit.*, 186–210.

43. Martine Berger, "Trajectories in Living Space, Employment and Housing Stock: The Example of the Parisian Metropolis in the 1980s and 1990s" *International Journal for Urban and Regional Research* 20.2 (1996), 240–54; Fierro, *op. cit.*, 19; Jean Robert, "Paris and the Ile de France: National Capital, World City," in *Europe's Cities in the Late 20th Century*, 17–22.

44. Andre Sorensen, "Subcentres and Satellite Cities: Tokyo's 20th Century Experience of Planned Polycentrism," *International Planning Studies* 6, no. 1 (September 2001); Mosk, *op. cit.*, 263–64.

45. Edward Seidensticker, *Tokyo Rising: The City Since the Great Earthquake* (New York: Knopf, 1990), 290–303.

46. Carola Hein, *op. cit.*, 309–42.

47. Sorensen, *op. cit.;* Hill and Fujita, *op. cit.*, 11; Seidensticker, *op. cit.*, 336–37.

CHAPTER SIXTEEN: THE POSTCOLONIAL DILEMMA

1. "Urban Agglomerations 2003," United Nations, Department of Economic and Social Affairs, Population Division.

2. Carlos Fuentes, *Where the Air Is Clear*, trans. Sam Hileman (New York: Farrar, Straus and Giroux, 1971), 7.

3. Kamen, *op. cit.*, 13; Chandler and Fox, *op. cit.*, 15.

4. Litvinoff, *op. cit.*, 5, 11.

5. Valliant, *op. cit.*, 127, 138.

6. Díaz, *op. cit*, 215–19.

7. From Nahuatl codices, composed circa 1523–1528, cited in Fehrenbach, *op. cit.*, 146.

8. Hardoy, *op. cit.*, 21; Fehrenbach, *op. cit.*, 189; Wright, *op. cit.*, 199–200.

9. Díaz, *op. cit.*, 200; Valliant, *op. cit.*, 172, 257; W. W. Collins, *Cathedral Cities of Spain* (New York: Dodd, Mead and Company, 1909), 19.

10. Hardoy, *op. cit.*, 22–25; Fehrenbach, *op. cit.*, 147, 159; Kamen, *op. cit.*, 95; Mark D. Szuchman, "The City as Vision—The Development of Urban Culture in Latin America," in *I Saw a City Invincible: Urban Portraits of Latin America*, ed. Gilbert M. Joseph and Mark D. Szuchman (Wilmington, Del.: SR Books, 1996), 5.

11. Hardoy, *op. cit.*, 46–53; Lesley Byrd Simpson, *Many Mexicos* (Berkeley: University of California Press, 1974), 362–63; "Cities: A Survey," *The Economist*, July 19, 1995; Alejandro Portes, "Urban Latin America: The Political Condition from Above and Below," in *Third World Urbanization*, ed. Janet Abu-Lughod and Richard Hay, Jr. (Chicago: Maaroufa Press, 1977), 67–69.

12. "Regions at Risk: Comparisons of Threatened Environments," ed. Jeanne X. Kasperson, Roger E. Kasperson, and B. L. Turner II (New York: United Nations University Press, 1995); Jonathan Kandell, "Mexico's Megalopolis," in *I Saw a City Invincible*, 189; Josef Gugler, "Overurbanization Reconsidered," in *Cities in the Developing World: Issues, Theory and Policy*, ed. Josef Gugler (London: Oxford University Press, 1977), 120.

13. Procuraduría General de la República, Inciodencia Delictiva del Fuero Federal, www.pgr.gob.mx; *The World Almanac and Book of Facts, 2003*, 166.

14. Fuentes, *op. cit.*, 4.

15. "The State of the World's Population, 1996," United Nations Population Fund.

16. Richard Hay, Jr., "Patterns of Urbanization and Socio-Economic Development," in *Third World Urbanization*, 71. "The State of the World's Population, 1996"; "The State of the World's Population, 2001," United Nations Population Fund.

17. Alan Gilbert and Josef Gugler, *Cities, Poverty and Development: Urbanization in the Third World* (London: Oxford University Press, 1991), 13; Edward W. Said, *Orientalism* (New York: Vintage, 1979), 153.

18. McNeill, *Plagues and Peoples*, 151; Murphey, *op. cit.*, 65.

19. Curtin, *op. cit.*, 170–78; Murphey, *op. cit.*, 55; July, *op. cit.*, 57–60, 275–76, 347–48; Curtin, *op. cit.*, 212.

20. Kumar, *op. cit.*, 492–93.

21. Girouard, *op. cit.,* 238–42; Raychaudhuri and Habib, *op. cit.,* 437–39; Parry, *op. cit.,* 272–74; Rhoads Murphey, "The History of the City in Monsoon Asia," in *The Urban Transformation of the Developing World,* ed. Josef Gugler (London: Oxford University Press, 1996), 23.

22. Hourani, *op. cit.,* 295–98, 439–42; Raymond, *op. cit.,* 210; Janet Abu-Lughod, "Urbanization in the Arab World and the International System," in *The Urban Transformation of the Developing World,* 25.

23. Bianca, *op. cit.,* 170–71; Raymond, *op. cit.,* 318; Abu-Lughod, *Cairo,* 98–99.

24. Mattei Dogan and John Kasarda, "Introduction: Comparing Giant Cities," in *The Metropolis Era, vol. 2, Megacities,* 23.

25. Alfred Crofts and Percy Buchanan, *A History of the Far East* (New York: Longmans, Green and Company, 1958), 142–52; Schinz, *op. cit.,* 18; Xiangming Chen, "Giant Cities and the Urban Hierarchy of China," in Mattei Dogan and John Kasarda, *A World of Giant Cities: The Metropolis Era, vol. 1* (Newbury Park: Sage, 1989), 230–32.

26. Murphey, "The City as a Centre of Change," 55–61; Stella Dong, *Shanghai: The Rise and Fall of a Decadent City* (New York: William Morrow, 2000), 1.

27. Abu-Lughod, "Urbanization in the Arab World," 190.

28. "The State of the World's Population, 1996"; Alain R. A. Jacquemin, *Urban Development and New Towns in the Third World: Lessons from the New Bombay Experience* (Aldershot, Eng.: Ashgate, 1999), 5.

29. Robert B. Potter, "Cities, Convergence, Divergence and Third World Development," in *Cities and Development in the Third World,* ed. Robert B. Potter and Ademola T. Salau (London: Mansell, 1990), 1–2.

30. Janice E. Perlman, *The Myth of Marginality: Urban Poverty and Politics in Rio de Janeiro* (Berkeley: University of California Press, 1976), 12; John Vidal, "Disease Stalks New Megacities," *The Guardian,* March 23, 2002; "State of the World Population, 1996"; "Air Pollution for 40 Selected World Cities," World Health Organization; Jorge E. Hardoy, "Building and Managing Cities in a State of Permanent Crisis," Wilson Center, Latin America Program, no. 187, 16; Kalpana Sharma, "Governing Our Cities: Will People Power Work," Panos Institute, London, 2000.

31. David Drakakis-Smith, *The Third World City* (New York: Methuen, 1987), 8, 38; Michael F. Lofchie, "The Rise and Demise of Urban Based Development Policies in Africa," in *Cities in the Developing World,* 23; Ronald McGill, *Institutional Development: A Third World City Management Perspective* (London: I. B. Tauris & Co., 1996), 21; Gilbert and Gugler, *op. cit.,* 25.

32. John M. Shandra, Bruce London, and John B. Williamson, "Environmental Degradation, Environmental Sustainability and Overurbanization in the Developing World," *Sociological Perspectives* 46, no. 3, 309–29; Aprodicio A.

Laquian, "The Asian City and the Political Process," in *The City as a Centre of Change in Asia,* ed. D. J. Dwyer (Hong Kong: Hong Kong University Press, 1972), 50.

33. Gilbert and Gugler, *op. cit.,* 85; Allen C. Kelley and Jeffrey G. Williamson, *What Drives Third World City Growth?: A Dynamic General Equilibrium Approach* (Princeton, N.J.: Princeton University Press, 1984), 5.

34. Rollie E. Poppino, *Brazil: The Land and People* (New York: Oxford University Press, 1968), 113–17; "World Urbanization Prospects: The 2003 Revision," United Nations Population Division; "A World of Cities," *The Economist,* July 29, 1995.

35. "State of the World's Population, 2001."

36. S. I. Abumere, "Nigeria," in *Urbanization in Africa: A Handbook,* ed. James D. Tarver (Westport, Conn.: Greenwood Press, 1994), 262–77; Pauline H. Baker, *Urbanization and Political Change: The Politics of Lagos, 1917–1967* (Berkeley: University of California Press, 1974), 32–34.

37. Drakakis-Smith, *op. cit.,* 8, 38; Lofchie, *op. cit.,* 23; McGill, *op. cit.,* 21; Gilbert and Gugler, *op. cit.,* 25; Alan Mabin, "Suburbs and Segregation in the Urbanizing Cities of the South: A Challenge for Metropolitan Government in the Early 21st Century," Lincoln Institute of Land Policy, 2001; "Black Flight," *The Economist,* February 24, 1996.

38. Lewis, *What Went Wrong?,* 34; Ali Madanipour, *Tehran: The Making of a Metropolis* (New York: John Wiley, 1998), 5, 9.

39. Hourani, *op. cit.,* 373–74; Abu-Lughod, "Urbanization in the Arab World," 189; Salah S. El-Shakhs and Hooshang Amirahmadi, "Population Dynamics, Urbanization, and the Planning of Large Cities in the Arab World," in *Urban Development in the Muslim World,* ed. Salah S. El-Shakhs and Hooshang Amirahmadi (New Brunswick, N.J.: Rutgers University Press, 1993), 21–23; Hooshang Amirahmadi and Ali Kiafar, "The Transformation of Tehran from Garrison Town to a Primate City: A Tale of Rapid Growth and Uneven Development," in *Urban Development in the Muslim World,* 120–21.

40. Manuel Castells, *The Information Age: Economy, Society and Culture, Vol. 3: End of Millennium* (Oxford, Eng.: Blackwell Publishers, 1998), 78–83; John D. Kasarda and Allan M. Parnell, "Introduction: Third World Urban Development Issues," in *Third World Cities: Problems, Policies and Prospects,* ed. John D. Kasarda and Allan M. Parnell (Newbury Park, Calif.: Sage Publications, 1993), xi.

41. Grey E. Burkhart and Susan Older, *The Information Revolution in the Middle East and North Africa,* report prepared for the National Intelligence Council (Santa Monica, Calif.: RAND, 2003), ix, 2, 53.

42. Bianca, *op. cit.,* 170–71; Raymond, *op. cit.,* 318; Abu-Lughod, *Cairo,* 98–99.

43. El-Shakhs and Amirahmadi, *op. cit.,* 234; Burdett, "Toward the 21st Century"; Hourani, *op. cit.,* 374; Jonathan Eric Lewis, "Iraq's Christians," *The Wall Street*

Journal, December 19, 2002; Rachel Pomerance, "Iraq's Glorious Past," Jewish Telegraphic Service, February 9, 2003; Amir Taheri, "Saddam Hussein's Delusion," *The New York Times,* November 14, 2002.

44. Hourani, *op. cit.,* 438; El-Shakhs and Amirahmadi, *op. cit.,* 240; Jacquemin, *op. cit.,* 35.
45. Madanipour, *op. cit.,* 21, 95.
46. Burdett, "Toward the 21st Century"; Amirahmadi and Kiafar, *op. cit.,* 130–31; Masoud Kheirabadi, *Iranian Cities: Formation and Development* (Austin: University of Texas Press, 1991), 60; Madanipour, *op. cit.,* 23; Masserat Amir-Ebrahimi, "L'image socio-géographique de Téhéran en 1986," in *Téhéran: Capitale Bicentenaire,* ed. Chahryar Adle and Bernard Hourcade (Paris: Institut Français de Recherche en Iran, 1992), 268.

CHAPTER SEVENTEEN: "QUEENS OF THE FURTHER EAST"

1. "State of the World's Population, 2001."
2. C. M. Turnbull, *A History of Singapore: 1819–1875* (Kuala Lumpur: Oxford University Press, 1977), 1–45.
3. Sharma, "Governing Our Cities"; Donald N. Wilber, *Pakistan: Its People, Its Society and Its Culture* (New Haven: HRAF Press, 1980), 373; Anthony King, *Colonial Urban Development: Culture, Social Power and Environment* (London: Routledge and Kegan Paul, 1976), 273; Kumar, *op. cit.,* 520.
4. Nigel Harris, *City, Class, and Trade: Social and Economic Change in the Third World* (London: I. B. Tauris & Co., 1991), 30; Barnett E. Rubin, "Journey to the East: Industrialization in India and the Chinese Experience," in *Social and Economic Development in India: A Reassessment,* ed. Dilip K. Basu and Richard Sisson (New Delhi: Sage Publications, 1986), 69.
5. "Plenty of Space, Few Takers," *Businessline,* May 24, 1999; Jacquemin, *op. cit.,* 275–77.
6. Sharma, "Governing Our Cities"; "Orillion India Thriving in Hyderabad," *Orillion Source,* August 2000; Isher Judge Ahluwalia, *Industrial Growth in India: Stagnation Since the Mid-Sixties* (Delhi: Oxford University Press, 1985), 161–87.
7. Ali Sharaf and Leslie Green, "Calcutta," in *Great Cities of the World: Their Government, Politics, and Planning,* ed. William A. Robson and D. E. Regan (Beverly Hills, Calif.: Sage Publications, 1972), 299; Tim McDonald, "U.S. Tech Bust a Boon for Asia," *NewsFactor Network,* June 7, 2001; Arvind Singhal and Everett M. Rogers, *India's Information Revolution* (New Delhi: Sage Publications, 1989), 163–65.
8. Kyle Eischen, "India's High-Tech Marvel Makes Abstract Real," *San Jose Mercury News,* March 19, 2000; Joanna Slater, "Influx of Tech Jobs Ushers in Malls, Modernity to Calcutta," *The Wall Street Journal,* April 28, 2004.
9. Castells, *op. cit.,* 151–55; Amy Waldman, "Low-Tech or High, Jobs Are Scarce in India's Boom," *The New York Times,* May 6, 2004.

10. Peter John Marcotullio, "Globalisation, Urban Form and Environmental Conditions in Asia-Pacific Cities," *Urban Studies* 40, no. 2 (2003).

11. Joochul Kim and Sang-Chuel Choe, *Seoul: The Making of a Metropolis* (West Sussex, Eng.: John Wiley, 1997), 3, 8–11.

12. Jacquemin, *op. cit.*, 35; A.S. Oberoi, *Population Growth, Employment and Poverty in Third-World Mega-Cities: Analytical and Policy Issues* (New York: St. Martin's Press, 1993), 11; Kim and Choe, *op. cit.*, 11–12, 26–29, 191–92.

13. Hardoy, "Building and Managing Cities in a State of Permanent Crisis," 21.

14. El-Shakhs and Amirahmadi, *op. cit.*, 240; Jacquemin, *op. cit.*, 35.

15. Richard Child Hill and June Woo Kim, "Global Cities and Development States: New York, Tokyo and Seoul," *Urban Studies* 37, no. 12 (2000).

16. John Rennie Short and Yeong-Hyun Kim, *Globalization and the City* (London: Longman, 1999), 26, 57.

17. Barbara Demick, "South Korea Proposes a Capital Change," *Los Angeles Times,* July 9, 2004.

18. Gerald Segal, *The Fate of Hong Kong* (New York: St. Martin's Press, 1993), 1–27; Roy Hofheinz, Jr. and Kent E. Calder, *The EastAsia Edge* (New York: Basic Books, 1982), 103.

19. Turnbull, *op. cit.*, 1–45; Lynn Pan, *Sons of the Yellow Emperor: A History of the Chinese Diaspora* (Boston: Little, Brown, 1990), 110.

20. Janet W. Salaff, *State and Family in Singapore: Restructuring a Developing Society* (Ithaca, N.Y.: Cornell University Press, 1988), 3, 226–27; Lim Chong-Yah, "The Transformation of Singapore in Twenty-five Years: A Glimpse," in *Singapore: Twenty-five Years of Development,* ed. You Poh Seng and Lim Chong Yah (Singapore: Nan Yang Xing Zhou Lianhe Zaobao, 1984), 6–7; Giok-Ling Ooi, "The Role of the State in Nature Conservation in Singapore," *Society and Natural Resources* 15 (2002): 445–60.

21. T.J.S. George, *Lee Kuan Yew's Singapore* (Singapore: Eastern Universities Press, 1984), 109.

22. Pan, *op. cit.*, 264–65; George, *op. cit.*, 16.

23. George, *op. cit.*, 16, 109.

24. Ibid., 28; David S. G. Goodman, *Deng Xiaoping and the Chinese Revolution: A Political Biography* (London: Routledge, 1994), 120; Hoiman Chan and Rance P. L. Lee, "Hong Kong Families: At the Crossroads of Modernism and Traditionalism," *Journal of Comparative Family Studies* (Spring 1995); Marcotullio, "Globalisation"; Castells, *op. cit.*, 292; Weiming Tu, "Beyond Enlightenment Mentality: A Confucian Perspective on Ethics, Migration and Global Stewardship," *International Migration Review* (Spring 1996).

25. Rhoads Murphey, "The City as a Centre of Change: Western Europe and China," in D. J. Dwyer, ed., *The City in the Third World* (New York: Barnes and Noble Books, 1974), 62–63.

26. Gilbert and Gugler, *op cit.*, 187; Weiming Tu, "Beyond Enlightenment Mentality"; Yue-Man Yeung, "Great Cities of Eastern Asia," in *The Metropolis Era, vol. 1, A World of Giant Cities,* 158; Martin King Whyte, "Social Control and Rehabilitation in Urban China," *Third World Urbanization,* 264–70; Sidney Goldstein, "Levels of Urbanization in China," in *The Metropolis Era: vol. 1, A World of Giant Cities,* 200–221; Chen, *op. cit.,* 230–32; Deborah Davis, "Social Transformation of Metropolitan China Since 1949," in *Cities in the Developing World,* 247–52.

27. James Kynge, "An Industrial Powerhouse Emerges by the Waterfront," *Financial Times,* January 23, 2003.

28. Davis, *op. cit.,* 249–54; "China: Can the Centre Hold?," *The Economist,* November 6, 1993; Lin You Su, "Introduction," in *Urbanization in Large Developing Countries: China, Indonesia, Brazil and India,* ed. Gavin W. Jones and Pravin Visaria (Oxford, Eng.: Clarendon Press, 1997), 26–44; Ben Dolven, "Economic Lure of China's Cities Grows," *The Wall Street Journal,* February 26, 2003.

29. "The Decline of Hong Kong," *The Wall Street Journal,* July 1, 2003; "Shanghai: 2004," *The Economist,* January 15, 2004; Shahid Yusuf and Weiping Wu, "Pathways to a World City: Shanghai Rising in an Era of Globalization," *Urban Studies* 39, no. 7 (2002); Zhao Bin, Nobukazu Nakahoshi, Chen Jia-kuan, and Kong Ling-yi, "The Impact of Urban Planning on Land Use and Land Cover in Pudong of Shanghai, China," *Journal of Environmental Sciences* 15, no. 2 (2003).

30. David Lague, "China's Most Critical Mass Movement," *The Wall Street Journal,* January 8, 2003; David Murphy, "Outcasts from China's Feast: Millions of Laid Off Workers Are Getting Angry," *The Wall Street Journal,* November 6, 2002; "Sex of a Cultural Sort in Shanghai, China," *The Economist,* July 13, 2002; Eugene Linden, "The Exploding Cities of the Developing World," *Foreign Affairs,* January 1996; David Clark, *Urban World/Global City* (London: Routledge, 1996), 175.

31. Harris, *op. cit.,* 73; Mabin, "Suburbs and Segregation in the Urbanizing Cities of the South"; Yeung, *op. cit.,* 158, 181; Marcotullio, "Globalisation," 219–47.

32. Elisbeth Rosenthal, "North of Beijing, California Dreams Come True," *The New York Times,* February 3, 2003; "Shanghai Plans Massive Surburban Development," *People's Daily,* May 18, 2003.

33. Thomas Campenella, "Let a Hundred Subdivisions Bloom," *Metropolis,* May 1998; Mabin, "Suburbs and Segregation in the Urbanizing Cities of the South"; Norton Ginsburg, "Planning the Future of the Asian City," *The City as a Centre of Change in Asia,* 277.

CONCLUSION: THE URBAN FUTURE

1. "World Population Prospects: The 2000 Revision," United Nations Population Division.

2. "World Population Prospects, Population Data Base," United Nations Population Division, 2000; "World Urbanization Prospects: The 2003 Revision," United Nations Population Division.

3. El-Shakhs and Amirahmadi, *op. cit.*, 237; Sally E. Findley, "The Third World City: Development Policy and Issues," in *Third World Cities*, 7, 11; "*The* State of the World's Population, 2001"; Harris, *op. cit.*, 49.

4. Ali Parsa, Ramin Keivani, Loo Lee Sin, Seow Eng Ong, Asheed Agarwai, and Bassem Younes, "Emerging Global Cities: Comparisons of Singapore and the Cities of the United Arab Emirates" (London: Rics Foundation, 2003); Sulong Mohamad, "The New Town as an Urbanization Strategy in Malaysia's Regional Development Planning," in Robert B. Putter and Adenola T. Salau, *Cities and the Development in the Third World* (London: Mansell, 1970), 127–28.

5. Kandell, *op. cit.*, 187.

6. Fehrenbach, *op. cit.*, 627; Sergio Aguayo Quezada, *Mexico in Cifras: El Almanaque Mexicano* (Mexico City: Editorial Hechos Confirables, 2002), 58–59, 66–68; INEGI, *Conteo de Poblaciation y Vivienda* 1995 (Mexico, 1995); INEGI, *Conteo de Poblaciation y Vivienda* 1 (Mexico, 2001); Szuchman, *op. cit.*, 5; George Martine and Clelio Campolina Diniz, in *Urbanization in Large Developing Countries,* "Economic and Demographic Concentration in Brazil: Recent Inversion of Historical Patterns," 205–27; Teresa P. R. Caldeira, *City of Walls: Crime, Segregation and Citizenship in São Paulo* (Berkeley: University of California Press, 2000), 233; "World Urbanization Prospects: The 2003 Revision"; Findley, *op. cit.*, 27; Harry W. Richardson, "Efficiency and Welfare in LDC Megacities," in *Third World Cities*, 37; Larry Rohter, "Model for Research Rises in a Third World City," *The New York Times*, May 1, 2001; "Chilango Heaven," *The Economist*, May 1, 2004.

7. Parsa et al., "Emerging Global Cities"; Tüzin Naycan-Levent, "Globalization and Development Strategies for Istanbul: Regional Policies and Great Urban Transportation Projects," 39th IsoCa Congress, 2003.

8. Josef W. Konvitz, "Global Cities and Economic Growth," *OECD Observer* (Paris: Organization for Economic Cooperation and Development, 1994).

9. Susan S. Fainstein and Michael Harloe, "Introduction: New York and London in the Contemporary World," in *Divided Cities: New York and London in the Contemporary World,* ed. Susan S. Fainstein, Ian Gordon, and Michael Harloe (London: Blackwell Publishers, 1992), 7.

10. Manuel Castells, *The Informational City* (Oxford, Eng.: Blackwell Publishers, 1989), 146–52; Hall, *op. cit.*, 7, 23; Eli Lehrer, "Crime Without Punishment," *Weekly Standard,* May 27, 2002.

11. Saskia Sassen, *Cities in a World Economy* (Thousand Oaks, Calif.: Pine Forge Press, 2000), 5, 21.

12. Susanne MacGregor and Arthur Lipow, "Bringing the People Back In: Economy and Society in New York and London," in *The Other City,* 5; Peter Hall, "Urban Growth and Decline in Western Europe," in *The Metropolis Era, vol. 1, A World of Giant Cities,* 113; Segre, *op. cit.,* 99–107; John R. Logan, "Still a Global City: The Racial and Ethnic Segmentation of New York," in *Globalizing Cities,* 158–61.

13. Robert McC. Adams, "Contexts of Civilizational Collapse," in *The Collapse of Ancient States and Civilizations,* 20.

14. Thomas Klier and William Testa, "Location Trends of Large Company Headquarters During the 1990s," *Economic Perspectives,* Federal Reserve Bank of Chicago, 2002; Ron Martin and Peter Sunley, "Deconstructing Clusters: Creative Concept or Policy Panacea," *Journal of Economic Geography,* June 6, 2002.

15. Peter Muller, "The Suburban Transformation of the Globalizing American City," *Annals of the American Academy of Political and Social Science* (May 1997); John Friedmann, *The Prospect of Cities* (Minneapolis: University of Minnesota Press, 2002), 41.

16. Lee Burdet, "The Unthinkable Move Not Any Longer," Southern Business and Development, February 6, 2004.

17. Peter Muller, *op. cit.;* Short and Kim, *op. cit.;* "Engine Failure," Center for an Urban Future, September 2003; Burdet, *op. cit.;* Tom Shachtman, *Around the Block: The Business of a Neighborhood* (New York: Harcourt Brace, 1997), 5.

18. *Inc.* "Best Places" survey, March 2004, research by economist David Friedman; "Leeds: Cities Paved with Brass," *The Economist,* August 29, 1998; Paul Fox and Rachael Unsworth, "City Living in Leeds—2003," University of Leeds, 2003; Jonathan Tilove, "2000 Census Finds America's New Mayberry Is Exurban and Overwhelmingly White," *Newhouse News Service,* November 26, 2001.

19. "Will Asian Crisis Spare the Suburbs," *Real Estate Forum,* November 1998, 101.

20. Castells, *The Informational City,* 151; Peter Muller, *op. cit.;* "Engine Failure"; *Inc.* "Best Places" survey, May 2004, research by economist David Friedman.

21. National Retail Federation, 2003, from Web site.

22. Charles V. Bagli, "Office Shortage in Manhattan Imperils Growth," *The New York Times,* September 9, 2000; Siegel, *op. cit.,* 253; "Engine Failure"; Jackson, *op. cit.,* 185; John Norquist, *The Wealth of Cities: Revitalizing the Centers of American Life* (New York: Perseus Books, 1999), 60; Andy Newman, "Recession Seen as Gentler for New York City's Outer Boroughs," *The New York Times,* February 6, 2004.

23. Joseph N. Pelton, "The Rise of Telecities: Decentralizing the Global Society," *The Futurist,* January–February 2004; William J. Mitchell, *City of Bits: Space, Place, and the Infobahn* (Cambridge, Mass.: MIT Press, 1995), 94–98; Doug

Bartholomew, "Your Place or Mine?," *CFO* magazine, March 15, 2004; Sheridan Tatsuno, *The Technopolis Strategy: Japan, High Technology and the Control of the 21st Century* (New York: Prentice Hall, 1986), xv–xvi; Bruce Stokes, "Square One," *National Journal,* May 24, 1997; Alvin Toffler, *The Third Wave* (New York: William Morrow, 1980), 204–7.

24. Fishman, *op. cit.,* 187; U.S. Census analysis by William Frey, Brookings Institution; *Technological Reshaping of America,* 93; Sara B. Miller, "Big Cities Struggle to Hold On to New Immigrants as Costs Rise," *Christian Science Monitor,* October 9, 2003; "U.S. Cities Have Fewer Kids, More Singles," News Max.com, June 13, 2001; William H. Frey, "Metropolitan Magnets for International and Domestic Migrants," Brookings Institution, October 2003; Berger, *op. cit.;* Friedmann, *op. cit.,* 40–41.

25. Fogelson, *op. cit.,* 42; Wells, *op. cit.,* 32.

26. Jacques Ellul, *The Technological Society,* trans. John Wilkinson (New York: Vintage, 1967), 113–15; Norman Birnbaum, *The Crisis of Industrial Society* (New York: Oxford University Press, 1969), 113–14.

27. B. Joseph Pine II and James H. Gilmore, *The Experience Economy: Work Is Theatre and Every Business a Stage* (Cambridge, Mass.: Harvard Business School Press, 1999), 1–3; a good discussion of Las Vegas as modern urban paradigm can be found in Robert Venturi, Denise Scott Brown, and Steven Izenour, *Learning from Las Vegas* (Cambridge, Mass.: MIT Press, 1977).

28. Keith Schneider and Charlene Crowell, "Granholm's Urban Theory," Great Lakes News Service, May 6, 2004; Richard Florida, "The Rise of the Creative Class," *The Washington Monthly,* May 2002; Larry Solomon, "Canada's Outsourcing," *Financial Post,* March 31, 2004; Peggy Curan, "Montreal's Bright Side," *The Gazette,* September 25, 2000.

29. Alan Cowell, "Manchester Rising," *The New York Times,* June 24, 2001; Bruce Weber, "Arts Sapling Bears Fruit in Downtown U.S.," *The New York Times,* November 19, 1997; Ben Craft, "City of Brotherly Love Bets on the Arts," *The Wall Street Journal,* June 24, 1998; "In London's Shadow," *The Economist,* August 1, 1998; Yusuf and Wu, "Pathways to a World City."

30. Richard Bernstein, "Vienna's Grandeur Fails to Mask a Sense of Loss," *The New York Times,* August 3, 2003; Akin Ojumu, "Escape: Berlin," *The Observer,* July 15, 2001; John Burgess, "A Renaissance of Counterculture," *The Washington Post,* March 9, 2004; David Wessel, "If a City Isn't Sunny—and Air Conditioned—It Should Be Smart," *The Wall Street Journal,* February 26, 2004.

31. Peter Hall, "Changing Geographies: Technology and Income," in *High Technology and Low-Income Communities: Prospects for the Positive Use of Advanced Information Technology,* ed. Donald A. Schon, Bish Sanyal, and William J. Mitchell (Cambridge, Mass.: MIT Press, 1999), 51–53; "Engine Failure."

32. Jean Gottmann, *The Coming of the Transactional City* (College Park: University of Maryland Press, 1983), 28–43.

33. Robert Bruegmann, "The American City: Urban Aberration or Glimpse of the Future," in *Preparing for the Urban Future: Global Pressures and Local Forces,* ed. Michael A. Cohen, Blair A. Ruble, Joseph S. Tulchin, and Allison Garland (Baltimore: Johns Hopkins University Press, 1996), 59.

34. Tyler Cowen, *In Praise of Commercial Culture* (Cambridge, Mass.: Harvard University Press, 1998), 31, 83–96, 108–10, 120.

35. David Clark, *op. cit.,* 161–63; Taichi Sakaiya, *The Knowledge-Value Revolution, or, A History of the Future,* trans. George Fields and William Marsh (Tokyo: Kodansha, 1985), 348; "Population Drop to Affect Tokyo Policy," *Daily Yomiuri,* January 31, 1997; Yusuf and Wu, "Pathways to a World City,"; "Falling Birth Rates Revive E. E. Debate on Immigration," *The Hindu,* May 31, 2001; "State of the World's Population, 1999."

36. Tamara Theissen, "Marriages, Mussolini Losing Their Grip in Italy," *The Gazette* (Montreal), August 6, 2000; Susan H. Greenberg, "The Rise of the Only Child," *Newsweek,* April 23, 2001; David Holley, "Italy's Aging Bambini," *Los Angeles Times,* September 14, 2002; "Population Drop to Affect Tokyo Policy"; "Global Baby Bust," *The Wall Street Journal,* January 24, 2003.

37. "Uptown, Downtown," advertising supplement to the *Dallas Morning News,* April 14, 1999; Yusuf and Wu, "Pathways to a World City"; Weber, "Arts Sapling Bears Fruit in Downtown US."

38. Julian Wolpert, "Center Cities as Havens or Traps for Low Income Communities: The Potential Impact of Advanced Information Technology," in *High Technology and Low-Income Communities,* 78–94; Hill and Kim, "Global Cities and Development States"; Logan, *op. cit.,* 158–59; Castells, *The Informational City,* 172–228.

39. Eli Lehrer, "Broken Windows Reconsidered," *Public Interest* (Summer 2002); Friedmann, *op. cit.,* 40–41.

40. Fred Siegel, "The Death and Life of American Cities," *The Public Interest* (Summer 2002).

41. Burdett, "Toward the 21st Century."

42. Larry Rohter, "As Crime and Politics Collide in Rio, City Cowers in Fear," *The Wall Street Journal,* May 8, 2003; Jonathan Friedlan, "Living a Cut Above Mexico: Offices, Shops and Restaurants Cash In Need for 'Safer Ground,'" *The Wall Street Journal,* June 24, 1998.

43. Linden, "The Exploding Cities of the Developing World"; Vidal, "Disease Stalks New Megacities"; Thomas H. Maugh, "Plunder of Earth Began with Man," *Los Angeles Times,* June 12, 1994.

44. Drakakis-Smith, *op. cit.,* 8, 38; Lofchie, *op. cit.,* 23; McGill, *op. cit.,* 21; Gilbert

and Gugler, *op. cit.*, 25; Mabin, "Suburbs and Segregation in the Urbanizing Cities of the South"; "Black Flight," *The Economist,* Feburary 24, 1996.

45. Bianca, *op. cit.*, 329–30.

46. Ali Parsa et al., "Emerging Global Cities"; Robert Looney, "Beirut: Reviving Lebanon's Past," *Journal of Third World Studies* (Fall 2001).

47. Frantz Fanon, *The Wretched of the Earth*, trans. Constance Farrington (New York: Grove Press, 1965), 315.

48. Fouad Ajami, "Arabs Have Nobody to Blame but Themselves," *The Wall Street Journal*, October 16, 2001; Daniel Benjamin and Steven Simon, *The Age of Sacred Terror* (New York: Random House, 2002), 79.

49. Yossi Klein Halevi, "Islam's Outdated Domination Theology," *Los Angeles Times*, December 4, 2002; Benjamin and Simon, *op. cit.*, 5.

50. "One Year Later: New Yorkers More Troubled, Washingtonians More on Edge," Pew Research Center for the People and the Press, September 2003; "The Impact of 9/11 on Workplace Security and Business Continuity Planning," *Business Continuity Planning*, October 2002; Daniel Benjamin, "The 1,776 Foot Target," *The New York Times*, March 23, 2004; Jonathan D. Glater, "Travel Fears Cause Some to Commute Online," *The New York Times*, April 7, 2003; *Innovation Briefs*, Urban Mobility Corporation, July–August 2002.

51. Benjamin, "The 1,776 Foot Target"; Pelton, "The Rise of Telecities: Decentralizing the Global Society"; Jason Singer, "Tokyo Braces for Tsunami of New High-Rises," *The Wall Street Journal*, December 11, 2002; Charles V. Bagli, "$3.7 Billion Plan to Alter Far West Side Is Revealed," *The New York Times*, February 12, 2004; Margaret Ryan, "Skyscrapers Transforming City Skyline," *BBC News Online*, March 24, 2004.

52. Jane Jacobs, *The Economy of Cities* (New York: Random House, 1969), 141.

53. H. J. Dyos, "Agenda for Urban History," in *The Study of Urban History*, 1; Ryan, "Skyscrapers Transforming City Skyline."

54. Coulanges, *op. cit.*, 310.

55. Mike Biddulph, "Villages Don't Make a City," *Journal of Urban Design* 5, no. 1 (2000); William J. Stern, "How Dagger John Saved New York's Irish," *City Journal* (Spring 1997).

56. Eli Lehrer, "Broken Windows Reconsidered"; Charles Zwingmann and Maria Pfister-Ammende, *Uprooting and After* (New York: Springer-Verlag, 1973), 25; Schorske, *op. cit.*, 109–11.

57. Daniel Bell, *The Coming of Post-Industrial Society: A Venture in Social Forecasting* (New York: Basic Books, 1973), 367, 433; Arthur Herman, *The Idea of Decline in Western History* (New York: Free Press, 1997), 312, 348–57.

58. Lenn Chow, Des Verma, Martin Callacott, and Steve Kaufmann, "Ethno-Politics Threaten Canadian Democracy," *National Post*, March 31, 2004;

Stephen Toulmin, *Cosmopolis: The Hidden Agenda of Modernity* (Chicago: University of Chicago Press, 1992), 26.

59. Hill and Kim, "Global Cities and Development States"; Weiming Tu, "Beyond Enlightenment Mentality"; David Bonavia, *The Chinese: A Portrait* (London: Penguin, 1980), 18–19; "Shanghai Tries to Stay Original," *China Daily*, August 6, 2002; Lily Kong and Brenda S. A. Yeoh, "Urban Conservation in Singapore: A Survey of State Policies and Popular Attitudes," *Urban Studies* (March 1994).

60. Bianca, *op. cit.*, 324–41; Wilfred Cabtwell Smith, *Islam in Modern History* (New York: Mentor, 1959), 204–7; Naycan-Levent, "Globalization and Development Strategies for Istanbul"; Bruce Stanley, "Going Global and Wannabe World Cities: (Re)conceptualizing Regionalism in the Middle East," Globalization and World Cities Study Group, 2003; David Lamb, "In Egypt, a Bastion of Learning Rises from the Ashes of History," *Los Angeles Times*, December 5, 2002.

SUGGESTED READING

Although writing is a largely solitary art, in the process of completing this work I found good companions in literally hundreds of books. Following is a list of the volumes that readers might find most useful as they continue their exploration of urban history.

In trying to write history, one experiences few greater pleasures than those first-person accounts that bring the reader closer to the daily life and times of cities in their contemporary context. I have started the text with one—Bernal Díaz del Castillo's *The Discovery and Conquest of Mexico, 1517–1521,* an almost magical work that transports the reader to the first encounter of Europeans with the great urban civilization of central Mexico.

Other books that have given me this first-person insight include the work of the Greek historian Herodotus, writings of the Roman satirist Petronius, the poetry of Dante, the diaries of the Arab traveler ibn Battuta, the memoirs of Marco Polo, the reminiscences of the British historian and longtime Japan resident G. C. Allen, the poetry of William Blake, and the novels of John Dos Passos. All of these are cited in the text.

Perhaps the hardest thing to find are books that take in the broad sweep of urban history. Without question, the classic work remains Lewis Mumford's *The City in History* (Harcourt Brace, 1961). I have assigned this book to my classes on the history of cities, and despite its weight and complexity, it inevitably inspires, stimulates, and at time infuriates them.

I would also recommend the series of essays collected in Mumford's *The Urban Prospect* (Harcourt Brace, 1968).

Other works have value in understanding the evolution of cities. A.E.J. Morris's *History of Urban Form: Before the Industrial Revolution* (Longman, 1994); *Cities in Civilization* (Pantheon Books, 1998) by Peter Hall; and Mark Girouard's *Cities and People: A Social and Architectural History* (Yale University Press, 1985) provide many interesting insights.

In terms of understanding the demography of cities, I have relied heavily on Tertius Chandler and Gerald Fox's *Three Thousand Years of Urban Growth* (Academic Press, 1974) and essays in *Urbanization in History: A Process of Dynamic Interactions* (Clarendon Press, 1990). This reliance was tempered by the recognition that demographic estimates, particularly in the further past, are notoriously speculative. In most cases, I have tried to err toward the most conservative estimates or to give readers the widest range of possible truths.

The work of William H. McNeill was particularly useful in two areas. His *Plagues and Peoples* (Anchor Press, 1976), with its emphasis on the impact of disease on the development of cities, let me look at urban evolution from a distinctly biological point of view. Similarly, his *The Pursuit of Power: Technology, Armed Force and Society Since A.D. 1000* (University of Chicago Press, 1982) provided a focus on the often unappreciated role of military technology. Along with these works, I frequently consulted a longtime favorite, *Cross-Cultural Trade in World History,* by Philip D. Curtin (Cambridge University Press, 1984), on matters relating to transnational commerce, one of the prime shapers of great cities.

In this book, I have made particular reference to the issue of religion, moral order, and sacred place. This is a notion that, while clear to secular scholars such as Mumford, has all too often been lost among modern historians. Mircea Eliade's *The Myth of the Eternal Return,* translated by Willard R. Trask (Princeton University Press, 1971), was especially inspirational in discussing the religious roots of the urban experience, as was Jacques Ellul's *The Meaning of the City* (Vintage, 1967).

Historians of ancient cities almost universally acknowledge the role of religion and sacred space. Good places to start include Grahame Clark, *World Prehistory: An Outline* (Cambridge University Press, 1961); Mason Hammond, *The City in the Ancient World* (Harvard University Press, 1972); Gordon Childe, *What Happened in History* (Penguin, 1957); Numa Denis Fustel de Coulanges, *The Ancient City* (Johns Hopkins University Press,

1980); Herbert Muller, *The Uses of the Past* (Oxford University Press, 1952); and my personal favorite, Werner Keller, *The Bible as History* (William Morrow, 1981). If the writer wants to approach this topic more intimately, I would also recommend *The Epic of Gilgamesh,* translated by Andrew George (Penguin, 1999), which brings the reader in touch with the spiritual life of the earliest urban dwellers.

Outside the Western tradition, I would strongly recommend Paul Wheatley, *The Pivot of the Four Quarters: A Preliminary Enquiry into the Origins and Character of the Ancient Chinese City* (Aldine Publishing Company, 1971). Wheatley's work on religion and cities across cultures provides a valuable means of exploring this critical topic. G. C. Valliant, *Aztecs of Mexico* (Doubleday, 1944), and Jeremy A. Sabloff, *The Cities of Ancient Mexico: Reconstructing a Lost World* (Thames and Hudson, 1989), both helped to inform me on similar processes in early Mesoamerica. T. R. Fehrenbach's *Fire and Blood: A History of Mexico* (Macmillan, 1979) deals evocatively with both the earliest period and the subsequent scope of the Mexican experience.

Mesopotamia and the ancient Near East are generally considered the critical crucible of urban history. A. Bernard Knapp, *The History and Culture of Ancient Western Asia and Egypt* (Wadsworth Press, 1988), H.W.F. Saggs, *The Greatness That Was Babylon: A Sketch of the Ancient Civilization of the Tigris-Euphrates Valley* (Hawthorn Publishers, 1962), and Michael Grant, *The Ancient Mediterranean* (Scribner's, 1969), are all excellent places to start an exploration of this fascinating region.

The Phoenicians held a particular allure for me, in large part because they seemed such apt precursors of the modern commercial city. To learn more about these fascinating people, I would recommend Gerhard Herm, *The Phoenicians: The Purple Empire of the Ancient World* (William Morrow, 1975), and Sabatino Moscati, *The World of the Phoenicians,* translated by Alastair Hamilton (Praeger, 1968).

The classical Greek and Roman civilizations produced many fine chroniclers, perhaps none greater than Herodotus, whom I could recommend not only as a fine ancient historian, but as a philosopher of history and thus of cities. I made *The Histories,* translated by Aubrey de Sélincourt (Penguin Books, 1954), required reading in my history of cities class. I also heartily recommend the diverse essays in *Civilization of the Ancient Mediterranean,* edited by Michael Grant and Rachel Kitzinger (Scribner's, 1988), as an excellent starting point.

I would like to express my particular debt to Michael Grant, the British classical historian. To understand the classical mind, one can gain much from his many works on Greek and Roman history. His production is prodigious, his writing clear and concise, his insights almost uniformly rich. Grant's *From Alexander to Cleopatra* (Scribner's, 1982) covers a critical period between the rise of the Macedonian Empire with a singular flair and revealing analysis.

For the Roman period, the foremost work remains Edward Gibbon's magisterial *The Decline and Fall of the Roman Empire* (Modern Library, 1995). Two works that give an especially intimate view of urban life in Rome are Jérôme Carcopino's *Daily Life in Ancient Rome* (Yale University Press, 1940) and J.P.V.D. Balsdon's *Life and Leisure in Ancient Rome* (McGraw-Hill, 1969). For a look at the end of the Roman Empire and its enduring legacy, Robert Lopez, *The Birth of Europe* (M. Evans and Company, 1967), and Cyril Mango, *Byzantium: The Empire of New Rome* (Scribner's, 1980), make compelling reading.

The Islamic city, so relevant in our time, should be of interest to contemporary readers and followers of current events. If there is an equivalent to Herodotus in the Islamic world, it would be ibn Khaldun, a writer I was delighted to be reacquainted with after an earlier encounter during the writing of my book *Tribes*. His *The Muqaddimah: An Introduction to History*, translated by Franz Rosenthal (Princeton University Press, 1969), ranks among the most insightful books not only on the Islamic world, but on the forces that drive the creation of great cities.

In addition to ibn Khaldun, there are many excellent, more modern histories. The prime texts for me included Albert Hourani, *A History of the Arab Peoples* (Harvard University Press, 2002); Philip K. Hitti, *Capital Cities of Arab Islam* (University of Minnesota Press, 1973); Stefano Bianca, *Urban Form in the Arab World: Past and Present* (Thames and Hudson, 2000); and *The Places Where Men Pray Together: Cities in Islamic Lands, Seventh Through the Tenth Centuries* (University of Chicago Press, 2001) by the remarkable Paul Wheatley.

Janet Abu-Lughod's *Cairo: 1,001 Years of the City Victorious* (Princeton University Press, 1971) and André Raymond's *Cairo* (Harvard University Press, 2000) greatly enhanced my appreciation of Islam's greatest city. The evolution of India's cities was well covered in the magisterial *Cambridge Economic History of India, Volume One, 1200–1750* (Orient Longman,

1982) by Tapan Raychaudhuri and Irfan Habib, as well as in Romila Thapar's *History of India* (Penguin, 1990).

The history of early and medieval China was a particular challenge, despite my numerous trips to that country and long acquaintance with its culture, both there and in California. In addition to Wheatley's *Four Pivots,* I benefited greatly from Kenneth Scott Latourette's *The Chinese: Their History and Culture* (Macmillan, 1962), Laurence J. C. Ma's *Commercial Development and Urban Change in Sung China* (Michigan Geographical Society, 1971), Victor F. S. Sit's *Beijing: The Nature and Planning of a Chinese Capital City* (John Wiley, 1995), and Alfred Schinz's *Cities in China* (Gebruder Borntraeger, 1989).

The rise of Western cities in the Renaissance and early modern period has generated many excellent works. Fernand Braudel and Henri Pirenne most shaped my views of this exciting period. Pirenne's *Medieval Cities: Their Origins and the Revival of Trade* (Princeton University Press, 1925) and *Mohammed and Charlemagne* (Meridian Books, 1957) are extremely useful in understanding the early reemergence of European cities. Braudel's *The Perspective of the World: Civilization and Capitalism:15th–18th Century* (Harper & Row, 1984) and *The Mediterranean and the Mediterranean World of Philip II* (Harper & Row, 1972) are full of illustrative detail and knowing insight about sweeping global changes following the Middle Ages.

In the early modern period this history of cities focuses largely on two cities in particular, London and Amsterdam. In addition to Braudel, the text benefited greatly from such works as Simon Schama's *The Embarrassment of Riches: An Interpretation of Dutch Culture in the Golden Age* (Vintage, 1987); Jonathan Israel's *The Dutch Republic: Its Rise, Greatness and Fall* (Oxford University Press, 1995); and F.R.H. Du Boulay's *An Age of Ambition: English Society in the Late Middle Ages* (Viking, 1970).

The shift into the industrial age, and the growing domination of the Anglo-American powers, cannot be adequately understood without looking into three classic texts—Karl Marx's *Das Kapital,* translated by Ben Fowkes (Vintage, 1976); Friedrich Engels's *The Condition of the Working Class in England,* translated by W. O. Hennderson and W. H. Chaloner (Stanford University Press, 1968); and Arnold Toynbee's *The Industrial Revolution* (Beacon Press, 1956).

There are many excellent histories on the impact of industrialism in specific parts of the world. In Japan, I drew heavily on Carl Mosk, *Japa-*

nese Industrial History (M. E. Sharpe, 2001); Thomas O. Wilkinson, The Urbanization of Japanese Labor: 1868–1955 (University of Massachusetts Press, 1965); and several essays collected by Kuniko Fujita and Richard Child Hill, in Japanese Cities in the World Economy (Temple University Press, 1993).

Jon C. Teaford, Cities of the Heartland: The Rise and Fall of the Industrial Midwest (Indiana University Press, 1994), and Andrew Lees, Cities Perceived: Urban Society in European and American Thought: 1820–1940 (Columbia University Press, 1985), as well as Charles and Mary Beard, The Rise of American Civilization (Macmillan, 1950), provide excellent resources to understand the impact of industrial growth on American cities.

In studying the German experience, Carl E. Schorske's Fin de Siècle Vienna: Politics and Culture (Knopf, 1979), remains among the great classic studies. The book also drew on the work of both Alexandra Richie, Faust's Metropolis: A History of Berlin (Carroll and Graf, 1998), and Klaus P. Fischer, Nazi Germany: A New History (Continuum, 1995).

For insight into Russian industrial urbanization, I looked to W. Bruce Lincoln, Sunlight at Midnight: St. Petersburg and the Rise of Modern Russia (Basic Books, 2002); Reginald E. Zelnik, Labor and Society in Tsarist Russia: The Factory Workers of St. Petersburg, 1855–1970 (Stanford University Press, 1971); and the more recently published, revealing work by Dmitri Volkogonov, Stalin: Triumph and Tragedy, translated by Harold Shukman (Grove Weidenfeld, 1991).

Rather than dismiss suburbia as the "anticity," I have chosen to treat it more as its predominant modern expression. Southern California served as my model for this analysis. Greg Hise and William Deverell's Eden by Design: The 1930 Olmsted-Bartholomew Plan for the Los Angeles Region (University of California Press, 2000) and William Fulton's The Reluctant Metropolis: The Politics of Urban Growth in Los Angeles (Solano Books Press, 1997) proved an excellent starting point for an understanding of Southern California. Anyone delving into things Californian must also linger with the magnificent series of California histories written by Kevin Starr (all available from Oxford University Press).

Excellent general histories of suburbia include Kenneth Jackson's Crabgrass Frontier: The Suburbanization of the United States (Oxford University Press, 1985), Robert Fishman's Bourgeois Utopias: The Rise and Fall of Suburbia (Basic Books, 1987), and Joel Garreau's Edge City: Life on the New Frontier (Doubleday, 1991). The parallel decline of traditional cities is well chronicled in such worthy books as Witold Rybczynski's *City Life: Urban Expectations in the New World* (Scribner's, 1995), Robert M. Fogelson's *Downtown: Its Rise and Fall, 1880–1950* (Yale University Press, 2001), and Fred Siegel's *The Future Once Happened Here: New York, D.C., L.A., and the Fate of America's Big Cities* (Free Press, 1997).

The definitive account of the contemporary third world city may still not have been written. David Drakakis-Smith's *The Third World City* (Methuen, 1987) does provide an excellent start. Several books of essays collected in separate volumes by Josef Gugler and by John D. Kasarda—particularly *Third World Cities: Problems, Policies and Prospect,* edited by Kasarda and Allan M. Parrell, (Sage Publications, 1993)—are must-reads in this topic area. I would also recommend A. S. Oberoi, *Population Growth, Employment and Poverty in Third-World Mega-Cities* (St. Martin's Press, 1993).

The rise of East Asia as the focal point for twenty-first-century urbanism also is perhaps only now being chronicled. Valuable insights into this evolution can be gleaned from D. J. Dwyer, editor, *The City as a Centre of Change in Asia* (Hong Kong University Press, 1972), as well as from Joochul Kim and Sang-Chuel Choe, *Seoul: The Making of a Metropolis* (John Wiley, 1997).

Finally, as we contemplate the contemporary city and the future, several works stand out. Perhaps most impressive in my mind is a century-old work, H. G. Wells's *Anticipations of the Reaction of Mechanical and Scientific Progress upon Human Life and Thought* (Chapman and Hall, 1902), which contains some of the most piercing insights into the role of technology in cities. Of somewhat more recent vintage but also quite prophetic are Manuel Castells's *The Information Age: Economy, Society and Culture, Volume III: End of Millennium* (Blackwell Publishers, 1998); Jacques Ellul's *The Technological Society,* translated by John Wilkinson (Vintage, 1967); Taichi Sakaiya's *The Knowledge-Value Revolution, or, A History of the Future,* translated by George Fields and William Marsh (Kodansha, 1985); Daniel Bell's *The Coming of Post-Industrial Society: A Venture in Social Forecasting* (Basic Books, 1973); and works by Alvin and Heidi Toffler, and most particularly Alvin Toffler's *The Third Wave* (William Morrow, 1980).

INDEX

Abercrombie Plan, 123
Abu Dhabi, 148
Abu-Lughod, Janet, 48, 131
Adcock, F. E., 29
Addams, Jane, 92
Afghanistan, 52
Africa, xx, 14, 25, 48, 49, 57, 61, 71, 98, 124, 128, 137; modern, 133–34. *See also specific cities*
African Americans, 119
Agade, xx, 10
agora, 22, 25, 54
agriculture, 25, 71, 86, 102, 104, 105; Chinese, 53, 58; early, 4, 5, 6, 10, 25, 44; modern, 133, 138
Alba, Duke of, 77
Alberuni, 50
Alexander the Great, 24–26, 33
Alexandria, xxi, 9, 24–26, 33, 39, 48, 56, 129, 130, 135, 159
Allen, G. C., 97, 98
alphabet, 15
America, 81, 98; colonies, 80, 81; early, 8, 11; industrialism, 89–96; modern city, 111–14; New York, 93–95; suburbia, 111–14, 116, 117–22. *See also specific cities*
Amman, 134
Amsterdam, 14, 77, 78–79, 80, 124, 148
Andhra Pradesh State, 138–39
Antioch, 24, 36, 39, 56, 129
anti-Semitism, 103
Antwerp, 77–78
Arabs, 43–51, 59–60, 68, 120, 131, 134–35, 148, 156. *See also* Islam; Muslims; *specific countries and cities*
architecture: American, 93, 94, 95–96, 112, 120–21; early, 4–5, 6–7; Egyptian, 6–7; European, 67, 73, 74, 103, 107, 120; future, 151–52, 154, 157, 158; Greek, 19, 21, 24, 25; Islamic, 46, 47, 58; Japanese, 99, 101–2, 122, 125; modern, 119–21, 151; Nazi, 103–4; Renaissance, 67; Roman, 27, 30, 31. *See also specific cities*
Argentina, 122
aristocracy, 13, 16, 29, 60, 76, 77, 81, 85, 104

Aristotle, 21, 24
Arkwright, Richard, 85
art, xx, xxii; American, 94–95;
    European, 67, 70, 79, 80, 106;
    Greek, 20; Japanese, 101
artisan class, xxii, 5, 11, 13, 14, 15, 35,
    60, 66, 81, 90, 99, 100
Asia. *See specific countries*
Assyria, 5, 11, 16
Athens, xxi, 20, 21, 22, 23, 24, 31, 33,
    36
Atlanta, 149
Augustine, St., *The City of God,* 37
Augustus, 30
Aurelius, Marcus, 34, 35
Australia, xx, 98, 116, 122–23;
    suburbia, 122–23. *See also specific
    cities*
autocracy, limits of, 59–60
automobiles, 112, 116, 123
Azores, 71
Aztecs, 4, 126, 127

Babylon, xx, xxi, 5, 6, 10–11, 14, 16,
    22, 25, 27, 47
Baghdad, xx, 47–48, 59–60, 134, 135;
    early, 47–48
Bangalore, 138, 154
Bangkok, 137, 146
Bartlett, Dana, 111–12, 113, 114; *The
    Better City,* 111
Basra, 47
bedouins, 44–45
Beijing, 53, 54, 58, 128, 130, 144,
    154
Beirut, 156
Belgium, 150
Bell, Daniel, 159
Berdyaev, Nicolas, 108
Berlin, 70, 95, 98, 102–3, 152
Bianca, Stefano, 156
Bible, 80; Hebrew, 26
Blake, William, 88

Bologna, 67, 69
Bombay, 129, 131, 132, 138, 144, 147,
    152
books, 47–48, 65, 80, 94, 100
Boston, 91, 93, 95, 113, 120, 149
Bradford, 86, 87, 88, 89
Braudel, Fernand, 79
Brazil, 120, 133
Bruegmann, Robert, 153
Brussels, 124
Budapest, 32
Buddhism, 4, 57, 159
Buenos Aires, 122
Burckhardt, Jacob, 40, 67
Burnham, Daniel H., 94
Bylbos, 14, 15
Byzantium, 22, 38–40, 46, 59, 68

Cabot, John, 72
Caesar, Julius, 30, 31, 33
Cairo, 48–49, 58, 61, 130, 131, 134,
    135, 139, 140, 147, 148, 156
Calcutta, 129–30, 131, 138, 139, 147
Caldeira, Teresa, 133
Calvinism, 78–79
Cambay, 50
canal systems, 4, 10, 58, 76, 78, 100
Canton, 141, 144
Capetian dynasty, 72–73
Cape Town, 129, 134
capitalism, xxii, 81–82, 86, 87, 90, 115,
    143
Carlyle, Thomas, 115
Carthage, 15–16, 29, 31, 37, 38, 46,
    113
Catholics, 4, 38, 65, 73, 77, 79, 85
Central America, 8, 11, 126–28, 137;
    early, 8, 11. *See also specific
    countries and cities*
Chang'an, xx, 12, 54, 59
Charles V, King of Spain, 77
Charnock, Job, 129
Chelyabinsk, 107

Chicago, 91, 92, 93, 95, 112, 113, 116, 120, 148, 149
Chilango, 148
Child, Lydia, 90
China, xx, 7, 8, 33, 44, 48, 49, 51, 58, 68, 81, 120, 129, 130, 131, 159; Communist, 141, 143–45; early, 7, 11–12, 13; "Four Modernizations," 144–45; imperial city, 11–12; Middle Kingdom, 52–57; modern, 139, 141–46, 150, 153, 159; opportunity lost, 58–61. *See also specific cities*
Christianity, 36–37, 39, 44, 46, 47, 57, 65, 66, 85, 135
Cicero, 29, 37
Cincinnati, 91, 92
cities: classical European, 17–40; first commercial capitals, 13–16; future of, 147–60; imperial, rise of, 9–12; industrial, 83–108; modern, 109–60; Oriental epoch, 41–61; postcolonial, 126–46; religious origins, 3–8; universality of, xx–xxi; Western primacy reasserted, 63–82. *See also specific countries and cities*
civic identity, 121; early, 4–5, 6, 15; Greek, 20–21; modern erosion of, 121–22; Renaissance, 67–69, 70; Roman, 29, 33–34
Clark, Grahame, 6
classical cities, 17–40; eclipse of, 35–40; Greek, 19–26; Rome, 27–38
Claudius, 33
Cleopatra VII, 25, 30
Cleveland, 92, 93, 95, 119, 121
Clive, Robert, 131
coffee, 61
coinage, 24
colonialism, 80, 81, 129–32, 139,

141–42; British, 81, 129–30, 141–42; end of, 131–32; postcolonial dilemma, 126–36
Columbus, Christopher, 72, 76
commerce and trade, xx, xxi, xxii, 13–16; American, 90–96; Chinese, 13, 52–59, 60, 61, 141–46; early, 5, 6, 7, 10, 11, 13–16; Egyptian, 6–7, 13, 48–49; European, 61, 65, 66–74, 75–76, 78–82, 85–90, 102–8; first commercial capitals, 13–16; future, 147–60; Greek, 19, 20, 22–23, 25; home-centered, 149–51; Indian, 50–51, 61, 130, 138–39; industrialism and, 83–108; Japanese, 99–102, 139; modern, 129–46; Muslim, 43–45, 47, 48–51, 58, 59, 61; Phoenician, 14–16; Renaissance, 65–74; role of, xxii, 13–16; Roman, 28, 32, 33, 35; Singapore, 141–43; suburbia and, 113–25. *See also specific countries and cities*
Communism, 105–8, 140, 141, 143–45
Confucianism, 12, 55, 60, 159; revitalization of, 143, 159
Conrad, Joseph, 142
Constantine, 38
Constantinople, 22, 38–40, 43, 47, 54, 59, 66–67
Contini, Edgardo, 122
Copenhagen, 70
Córdoba, 44, 47, 59
Cornwall, 123
Cortés, Hernán, 76, 127
"cosmic pattern," 7
Coulanges, Fustel de, 158
Crete, 19–20
crime, xxii, 10, 89, 92, 113, 115, 119, 124, 131, 135, 144, 145, 148; security and urban future, 154–57

Crusades, 66, 68
Cultural Revolution, 144
Cuzco, 8
Cyprian, 37
Cyprus, 14, 20
Cyrus the Great, 22, 23, 33

da Gama, Vasco, 71
Dallas, 154
Damascus, 46–47
Dante, 70
Dar al-Islam, 43, 49, 58, 59, 159
Delhi, 44, 50, 58, 128, 130, 131
Deng Xiaoping, 143, 144
Des Moines, 150
Detroit, 91, 92, 93, 95, 119, 121, 149, 152
developing countries, 129, 140;
    "European microcosms," 129–31;
    postcolonial dilemma, 126–36;
    "social time bombs," 134–36;
    squatter cities, 132–33, 137, 140.
    See also specific countries and cities
Díaz del Castillo, Bernal, xix–xx
Dionysius I, 22
disease and epidemics, 21, 36, 39, 71,
    77, 87, 90, 105, 115, 133, 155
Diu, 71
Dos Passos, John, 95
Dubai, 148
Du Boulay, F.R.H., 81
Düsseldorf, 122, 124

Earth Mother, 7, 19
Egypt, 3, 4, 5–7, 13, 14, 15, 19, 24, 25,
    26, 31, 36, 48–49, 60, 130; Cairo,
    48–49; early, 6–7, 48–49;
    modern, 129, 130, 131, 134, 135,
    148, 156. See also specific cities
Eliade, Mircea, 5
Ellul, Jacques, 151
Engels, Friedrich, 87, 115
Enlightenment, 159

entertainment industry, 151–54
entrepreneurial class, 13, 99; early,
    13–16; modern, 135, 138, 148,
    150–51; suppression of, 60, 138
ephemeral city, rise of, 151–54
Epic of Gilgamesh, The, 5
Etruscans, 16, 28, 29
Europe, 43, 44, 58, 59, 60, 63–82, 113,
    120; classical cities in, 17–40;
    colonialism, 80, 81, 127–32, 139,
    141; deurbanization, 37–38, 43;
    exploration, 71–72, 76, 127;
    ghettoization of cities, 124;
    Iberian empires, 71–72, 76–77;
    modern, 128, 151, 152, 153;
    Northern, 77–82; reemergence,
    60–61, 63–82; Renaissance,
    65–74, 75–76; return of city-
    states, 66–69; suburbanization,
    114–16, 122–25. See also specific
    countries and cities
"European microcosms," 129–31
exploration, European, 71–72, 76, 127

Fanon, Frantz, 156
Fargo, 150
Feder, Gottfried, Die nue Stadt, 102–4
Fehrenbach, T. R., 8
Fertile Crescent, 3, 7
fertility cults, 7
First Crusade, 66
Florence, 66, 67, 69, 70, 71, 72, 148
France, 22, 70, 71, 72, 85, 130, 150;
    Paris, 72–74, 114; suburbia,
    124–25. See also specific cities
Frankfurt, 124, 141, 149
Freud, Sigmund, Civilization and Its
    Discontents, 98, 99
Fuentes, Carlos, Where the Air Is Clear,
    126, 128
Fujiwara, 12
Fukuoka, 99
future city, 147–60; crisis of the

megacity, 147–48; ephemeral, 151–54; gentrification and, 152–54; limits of urban renaissance, 148–49; sacred place, 157–60; security issues, 154–57; technology and globalization, 148–52
Fuzhou, 56

Gandhi, Mahatma, 138
"garden city" model, 116, 123, 125
Gaul, 33
Gdansk, 75
gender issues, 80, 94; Greek, 21, 25; Muslim, 45
Genoa, 66, 67, 69, 70, 71
gentrification, future of, 152–54
Germantown, 116
Germany, 33, 116, 152; industrialization, 98, 102–4; Nazi, 102–4; suburbia, 124. *See also specific cities*
ghettoization of European cities, 124
Gibbon, Edward, 32, 33, 36
globalization, 148–54, 159–60
Goebbels, Joseph, 103
Gogol, Nikolay, 105
gold, 49, 61, 77
Gorky, 106, 107
government and politics, 13; Carthaginian, 16; Chinese, 53–55, 59, 60, 141–46; early, 12, 16; emergence of modern urban politics, 69; European, 61, 67, 68, 69, 70–71, 73, 74, 102, 105; Greek, 23, 25; modern upheavals, 134–36, 137, 140, 155–57; Muslim, 49, 59–60, 135, 156; Roman, 29, 33. *See also specific countries and cities*
Grant, Michael, 25
Great Britain, 14, 16, 33, 60, 80–82, 85, 98; colonialism, 81, 129–30, 141–42; industrialism, 85–89; London, 80–82, 85–86, 115–16; suburbia, 114–16, 123. *See also specific cities*
Great Depression, 116
Great Revolt of 1572, 77
Greece, 19–26, 28, 29, 30, 31, 54, 70, 71, 159; classical, 15, 16, 20–26; decline of city-states, 23; diaspora, 22–23; Hellenistic, 24–26, 30; polis, 20–21. *See also specific cities*
Gregory, Pope, 37
Guadalajara, 128, 148
Guangzhou, 53, 56, 57, 141, 144

Hall, Peter, 149
Hamburg, 124, 156
Hammarabi, 10
Han dynasty, 11, 52
Hangzhou, 53
Harappa, xx, 7, 11
Haussmann, Georges Eugène, 74, 89, 114
health care, 155
Hebrew Bible, 26
Hellenistic cities, 24–26, 30
Henry, O., 94
Henry IV, King of France, 73
Henry VIII, King of England, 81
Herodotus, xxi, 10, 11
Hideaki, Ishikawa, 125
Hinduism, 4, 50, 159
Hitler, Adolf, 103, 107
Hittites, 14
Holland, 77–79, 80
home commuting, 149–51
home ownership, 117, 123, 125
Homer, *The Iliad,* 15, 20
Hong Kong, 129, 139, 141, 142, 143, 144, 145, 146, 149, 150, 152
Hoover, Herbert, 116
Houston, 120, 149, 154

Howard, Ebenezer, 115–16
Huns, 46
Huntington, Henry, 111, 112
Hyderabad, 138–39

Iberian empires, 71–72; ascendancy
    of, 71–72; failure of, 76–77. *See
    also specific countries and cities*
ibn Battuta, 43, 48, 49, 50, 58
ibn Khaldun, 43, 44, 59, 60
Ikebukuro, 125
immigration, 90, 113, 124, 145, 151
imperial cities: Renaissance, 70–71;
    rise of, 9–12
Incas, 8
India, xx, 7, 24, 25, 33, 43, 44, 48, 49,
    50–51, 57, 68, 71, 159; colonial,
    81, 129–30; early, 7, 11; Islam,
    50–51; opportunity lost, 58–61;
    postcolonial, 130–32, 138–39. *See
    also specific cities*
industrialism, 83–108, 113–14, 115,
    121–22, 125; American, 89–96;
    British, 85–89; German, 98,
    102–4; global implications, 98,
    121–22; Japanese, 97, 98, 99–102,
    104, 122; Russian, 98, 104–8
Industrial Revolution, 85–108, 113
Inquisition, 76
Internet, 153
Iran, 3, 47, 135, 148, 156; Tehran, 135,
    148, 156
Iraq, 4, 47–48, 134; Baghdad, 47–48,
    59–60
Ireland, 87
irrigation and canal systems, 4, 10, 58,
    67, 78, 100
Isfahan, 49
Islam, 39, 43–51, 52, 55, 57, 65, 66,
    130; anti-modernist movements,
    134–36, 137, 155–57, 159;
    Baghdad, 47–48; Cairo, 48–49;
    early, 43–45; fundamentalism,

135; future of, 159–60; India,
    50–51; Muhammad's urban
    vision, 44–45; nature of the city,
    45–46; opportunity lost, 58–61;
    terrorism, 155–57. *See also specific
    countries and cities*
Israel, 134, 156
Istanbul, 58–59, 61, 128, 159
Italy, 15, 22, 37, 60, 85; Renaissance
    city-states, 65–72, 77; Rome,
    27–38. *See also specific cities*

Jackson, Kenneth, 114
Jacobs, Jane, 121
Jakarta, 129, 137, 146, 147
Japan, 12, 52, 53, 55, 60, 99, 107, 116,
    120; early, 12; industrialism, 97,
    98, 99–102, 104, 122; modern,
    125, 139–40, 142, 146, 150,
    153–54; suburbia, 125, 146. *See
    also specific cities*
jazz, 94, 103
Jericho, 3
Jerusalem, 15, 33, 46, 55
Jews, 25, 26, 36, 39, 44, 46, 47, 56, 68,
    76, 80, 103, 135; persecution of,
    76, 103
Jiddah, 156
Johannesburg, 129, 134
Johnson, James Weldon, 94
Jones, Emrys, 120
Judea, 26
Justinian, 39
Jutland, 20
Juvenal, 31

Kaifeng, 12, 54, 56
Karachi, 137, 156
Kawasaki, 99
Keller, Werner, 3
Kent, 123
Khiyami, Sami, 134
Khrushchev, Nikita, 107, 108

Knossos, xx, 19
Koran, 45, 46
Korea, 12, 52, 55, 60, 101, 139–41, 150.
    See also specific cities
Korean War, 140
Kuala Lumpur, 146, 147
Kublai Khan, 57
Kuomintang, 143
Kuwait, 134, 156
Kyoto, 12, 99

Labé, Louise, 80
Lagos, 129, 130, 131, 133, 139, 147
Lahore, 131
Lancashire, 86–87, 114
landownership, 10, 104, 117, 123, 125;
    early, 9, 10
Las Vegas, 152
law, 15, 45; Babylonian, 10; European,
    69; Islamic, 46, 49; Roman, 29
Lebanon, 46
Le Corbusier, 119–20
Leeds, 88, 89
Lee Kuan Yew, 142–43
Leipzig, 121, 149
Leningrad, 106, 107
Letchworth, 116
Levittown, 117–18
Lewis, Bernard, 52
Lisbon, 70, 72, 76
Litvinoff, Barnet, 76
Liverpool, 89, 115, 139, 149
Livy, 29
London, 32, 70, 77, 80–82, 95, 98, 101,
    114–15, 122, 128–29, 139, 141,
    148, 150, 152, 156, 157;
    emergence of, 80–82, 85;
    industrialism, 85–89; suburbs,
    114–15, 123
Lopez, Robert, 33
Los Angeles, 101, 111–14, 120, 121,
    125, 146, 149, 152, 155
Louis XIV, King of France, 73

Louis Napoleon, 74
Loyang, xx, 12, 54
Lueger, Karl, 103
Luxembourg, 148
Lynch, Kevin, xxii
Lyon, 73

Macedonia, 24, 25
Machiavelli, Niccolò, 71
Madras, 129
Madrid, 70, 71, 76, 82, 124
Magnitogorsk, 107
Malaysia, 120, 142
Mamluks, 48
Manchester, 86–89, 98, 115, 121, 122,
    149, 152
Manila, 131, 137, 146, 147
manufacturing, 85–108
Mao Zedong, 143–44, 159
marketplace. *See* commerce and trade
marketplace economy, development
    of, 6
Marrakesh, 47
Marseilles, 22, 33, 129
Martin, Ralph G., 118
Marx, Karl, 86, 88, 129
mass telecommunications, xx,
    149–54
Mauryan Empire, 50–51
Maya, 8, 11
Mecca, 43, 44, 45, 46, 55
media, mass, 151–52
Medicis, 69, 72
Medina, 45, 46, 55
Meiji Restoration, 99
Melbourne, 122
Melos, 20
Memphis, xx, 6
merchant class, 13–16, 47, 49, 60, 66,
    73, 77, 81, 130
Mesopotamia, xx, 3–5, 6, 7, 8, 9–11,
    19, 36, 45, 49, 85. *See also specific
    cities*

Mexico, xix–xx, 8, 126–28, 148; conquest of, 127; early, 8, 11, 126–27; modern, 127–28. *See also specific cities*
Mexico City, 8, 126–28, 133, 144, 147, 148, 155
Miami, 149, 152
Middle East. *See specific countries and cities*
Middle Kingdom, 52–57
Milan, 37, 38, 47, 67, 71
military, 13; Chinese, 53, 54, 55, 60; European, 66, 71–72, 77; Greek, 21, 22; Roman, 28, 29, 30, 32–34
Milwaukee, 93
Ming dynasty, 53, 60
modern art, 94
modern city, 109–60; Asian, 137–46; future of, 147–60; postcolonial dilemma, 126–36; suburbia, 113–25
Mogadishu, 49
Moguls, 58
Mohenjo-daro, xx, 7
Mombasa, 49
Monaco, 22
Mongols, 50, 56–57, 58, 59
Montreal, 152
Moors, 71
Moscow, 57, 104, 105, 106–8, 120
Moses, Robert, 117
mosques, 46, 49
Mother Goddess, 7, 19
Muhammad, 43, 44–45, 52
Mumbai, 138, 147, 154
Mumford, Lewis, 7, 27, 118, 119
Muslims, 4, 39, 40, 43–51, 52, 55, 56–57, 58–61, 66, 68, 71, 130, 131, 134–35, 142, 159–60. *See also* Islam
Mycenae, 20

Nagoya, 97, 98, 99, 101, 122
Naniwa, 12

Nanjing, 54
Naples, 77
Napoleon I, 74
Napoleon III, 89, 114
Nara, 12
natural disasters, 39, 99
Nazism, 102–4
Netherlands, 60, 61, 72, 77–79, 80, 81, 124; Amsterdam, 78–79
New Amsterdam, 80, 81
New York, 80, 81, 90, 93–95, 98, 101, 113, 115, 119, 120, 121, 128–29, 146, 148, 149, 150, 152, 153, 154, 156, 157; 2001 terrorist attack, 157
Nezahualcoyotl, 128
Nicholas II, Czar of Russia, 106
Nile River, 3, 28, 49
Nineveh, xx, xxi, 11
Nishiyama, Uzo, 101–2
nomadic invasions. *See specific groups*
North Africa, 15, 33, 38, 46, 47, 49, 61, 136
Novgorod, 57, 106

Oakland, 119
Odoacer, 37
oil, 134, 135
Olmecs, 11
Olmsted, Frederick Law, 93, 113, 125
Oriental epoch, 41–61; decline, 58–61; Islamic archipelago, 43–51; Middle Kingdom, 52–57
Orlando, 152
Osaka, 14, 99, 100, 101, 122, 125, 139, 141, 149, 150

Pacific Electric Railway, 112
Padua, 66
pagan worship, 45, 159
Pakistan, 7, 136, 137
Palestine, 3

Paris, 32, 47, 70, 72–74, 75, 76, 82, 89, 95, 114, 124, 149, 152, 153; suburbs, 124–25
Park, Robert Ezra, 157
Parthians, 26
Paul, 36
Pearl River Delta, 144
peasant class, 70, 106, 144; early, 6, 7
Pericles, 22
Perry, Commodore William, 99
Persia, 5, 9, 16, 22, 23, 24, 25, 26, 39, 46, 48, 49
Peru, xx, 8
Peter, Czar of Russia, 104, 105
Petronius, 27, 28, 29, 31; *Satyricon,* 32
Philadelphia, 93, 95, 115, 116
Philip, King, 24
Phoenicia, 14–16, 21, 22, 23, 25, 28, 67, 70; decline of, 15–16; rise of, 14
Phoenix, 154
Pirenne, Henri, xxii, 39, 66
Pisa, 66
Plato, 20, 21
politics. *See* government and politics
Pollio, Marcus Vitruvius, 67
pollution, 100, 108, 132, 155
Polo, Marco, 56, 57
Polos, 52, 57
Pope, Alexander, 81
population, 98, 113; American, 89–93, 117, 119, 121; Chinese, 56, 58, 144; declines, 38; early, 4–8, 16; European, 70–71, 72, 73, 75–77, 81–82, 86–87, 102, 104, 106, 107, 114, 123–24; future, 147–60; Greek, 21, 22, 26; Japanese, 99, 101, 122, 125; Mexican, 127–28; modern, 128–46; Muslim, 47; Rome, 27, 30, 31–32, 37, 38. *See also specific countries and cities*
Portugal, 61, 71–72, 76–77;

ascendancy of, 71–72. *See also specific cities*
postcolonial city, 126–46; Africa, 133–34; Asia, 137–46; "European microcosms," 129–31; Middle East, 134–36; "urbanization of the countryside," 128–29
priesthood, 4, 158; early, 4–5, 6, 7, 10, 13, 16
Procopius, 39
Protestantism, 77, 78, 81
"proto-cities," 3–8
Psellus, Michael, *Chronographica,* 39
Ptolemies, 25, 30
Pudong New Area, 145
Punjab, 7
Pyramids, 6–7

Quat-Hadasht, 15

racism, 119
Raffles, Sir Stamford, 141
railroads, 94, 112; suburban, 115, 116; subways, 94, 107, 142
Ravenna, 37
reform, social, 89, 92–93
religion, xx, xxi–xxii, 4; American, 92; Chinese, 52, 55, 57, 60, 143, 159; early, 4–8, 10, 19; European, 65, 71, 73, 75, 77, 78–79, 81, 85; future city and, 157–60; Islam, 44–50; modern, 134–36, 143; pagan, 45, 159; Roman, 28, 29, 36–37; sacredness of place, xxi–xxii, 157–60; sacred origins of cities, 3–8. *See also specific religions*
Rembrandt van Rijn, 79
Renaissance, 15, 65–74; city-states, 66–69; imperial cities, 70–71
Rhodes, 20, 22–23, 24, 33
Riga, 75
Rio de Janeiro, 155

Riyadh, 134
Rome, xxi, 9, 27–38, 39, 43, 46, 54, 67, 69, 72, 76, 113, 129, 151, 152, 153, 157; as archetypal megacity, 30–32; collapse, 35–38, 39, 65; power and victory, 28–34; security, 32–34, 35
Romulus and Remus, 28
Rossi, Niccolò de, 69
Rotterdam, 78, 124
Russia, 75, 104–8; Bolshevik regime, 105–6; industrialism, 98, 104–8; Soviet, 105–8, 120. See also specific cities

sacredness. See religion
St. Louis, 91, 92, 93, 95, 111, 119, 121
St. Petersburg, 82, 98, 104, 105
Salamis, 23
San Francisco, 120, 148, 149, 152, 153
San Jose, 146
San Salvador, 155
São Paulo, 133, 147, 155
Sapporo, 99
Sardinia, 14
Sargon, 9–10, 11, 49
Sassen, Saskia, 149
Seattle, 95, 149
security, xxi, xxii, 113, 154–57; early, 5, 11; need for, xxii; Roman, 32–34, 35; terrorist threat, 155–57; urban collapse and, 11; urban future and, 154–57
Seleucid Empire, 24, 26, 30
Seoul, 12, 142, 146; emergence of, 139–41
Seville, 72, 76
Shang dynasty, 7
Shanghai, 129, 130, 131, 141, 144, 146, 154, 157; resurgence of, 145
Shenzen, 144
Shibuya, 125

Shih Huang-ti, 55
Shinjuku, 125
Shiraz, 47, 49
shopping centers, 32; early, 5, 32
Sicily, 22
Sidon, 14, 15, 16
silk, 56, 66, 130
Silk Road, 43
Simmel, George, 102
Sind, 7
Singapore, 120, 129, 130, 139, 141–43, 145, 147, 148
Sioux Falls, 150
skyscrapers, 94, 95–96, 119–21
slavery, xxii, 48, 49, 86; African, 61; early, 6, 10, 16, 23, 24; Egyptian, 6, 48; Roman, 30, 35
Smith, Adam, 90
Socialism, 102–8
society: American, 90–91, 112; Chinese, 7, 13, 53, 59, 60, 141–46; early, 4–8, 10, 13; Egyptian, 6, 13, 60; European, 65, 66, 70, 76–77, 78, 79, 81, 85, 87–89, 102, 103, 104–8, 114, 115; Greek, 21, 25; Indian, 138–39; industrial, 87–108; Japanese, 99–102; Mesopotamian, 4–5; Mexican, 127–28; modern, 128–46; Muslim, 44, 45, 49, 59, 60, 155–57; Phoenician, 14–16; reform movements, 89, 92–93; Roman, 29, 30, 31, 32, 35–36; suburban, 115–25. See also specific countries, cities, and social classes
Socrates, 21, 46
Solomon's Temple, Jerusalem, 15
Soseki, Natsume, 100
South America, 8, 98, 122–23, 128, 137; early, 8. See also specific countries and cities
Southeast Asia, 52, 55, 61
South Korea, 120, 139–41

Spain, 14, 15, 16, 44, 46, 48, 61, 70, 71, 127; ascendancy of, 71–72; decline of, 76–78. *See also specific cities*
Sparta, 23
Speer, Albert, 103
spice trade, 61, 66
squatter cities, 132–33, 137, 140
Stalin, Joseph, 106–7
Stalingrad, 106, 107
suburbia, 113–25, 128, 150; American, 111–14, 116, 117–22; Argentina and Australia, 122–23; Asian, 125, 145–46; British, 114–16, 123; French, 124–25; future of, 150; German, 124; history of, 113–16; racism, 119
subways, 94, 107, 142
sugar, 80
Sui dynasty, 54
Sui Wen-ti, 54
Sumer, xx, 3–5, 6–7, 9, 10, 15, 70
Sung dynasty, 55, 56, 60
Suriname, 80
Sverdlovsk, 106, 107
Sydney, 122, 149
Syracuse, xxi, 22, 24
Syria, 33, 44, 134

Tabriz, 49, 57
Taipei, 139, 145
Taiwan, 143
Tang dynasty, 11, 54, 55
Taoism, 57
Teaford, Jon C., 118, 121
technology, xx; industrialism, 85–108; modern, 119, 134–35, 138–39, 149–54; Roman, 33
Tehran, 135, 148, 156
Tel Aviv, 148
television, 151
temples, 100; early, 5–8, 10, 15
Tenochtitlán, 8, 71, 76, 126–27

Teotihuacán, 8, 11
terrorism, 136, 155–57
Tertullian, 37
textile industry, 14–15, 48, 66, 69, 79
Thebes, 6, 20, 24
Thrace, 33
Thucydides, 21
Tiber river, 28
Tigris and Euphrates rivers, xx, 3, 4, 28, 47
Tijuana, 155
Timbuktu, 49, 130
Tocqueville, Alexis de, 87, 88
Tokyo, 98, 99–101, 122, 125, 139, 140, 146, 148, 150, 152, 157
Toledo, 44
Tolstoi, Aleksey, 205
tourism, 152, 154, 155
trade. *See* commerce and trade
Trajan, 33
Trier, 32, 33, 38, 129
Trollope, Frances, 92
Troy, 20
Turin, 122, 149
Turkey, 3, 22, 58, 134, 159
Turks, 50, 59
Tyre, xx, 14, 15, 16, 25, 113, 148

Ugarit, 14
United Arab Emirates, 156
United Nations, 129, 133
universality of urban experience, xx–xxi
Ur, xx, xxi, 4, 5, 10
usury, 66

Valladolid, 72
Venice, 14, 47, 52, 56, 153; Renaissance, 66, 67–69, 70, 71, 80
Verona, 66
Verrazano, Giovanni da, 72
Versailles, 73

Vespucci, Amerigo, 72
Vienna, 32, 70, 82, 99, 103, 107, 152
Vikings, 65
Visigoths, 37

walled towns: early, 11, 12;
    Renaissance, 67
Warsaw, 70
Washington, D.C., 95, 113, 115
Wells, H. G., 115, 123, 151
Welwyn, 116
Whyte, William H., 119
Wilbur, Richard, 118

Winchester, 81
working class, 88–89, 90, 101, 114, 115
World Trade Center, 121; 2001
    terrorist attack, 157
World War II, 104, 108, 117, 123, 125,
    142
writing, 15, 65; early, 5, 15

Yamasaki, Minoru, 120–21
York, 32

Zhangzhou, 53, 56, 57, 58
Zhou dynasty, 11–12, 53

About the Author

JOEL KOTKIN is an Irvine senior fellow with the New America Foundation, which is based in Washington, D.C. He is the author of five books, including *Tribes* and *The New Geography*, both published by Random House.

Kotkin is a frequent contributor to *The Washington Post, The Wall Street Journal, Inc.* magazine, the *American Enterprise,* and the *Los Angeles Times* "Opinion" section. He also serves as a senior fellow of the Newman Institute at Baruch College of the City University of New York and lectures at the Southern California Institute of Architecture.

He lives in Valley Village, Los Angeles, with his wife, Mandy, and two daughters, Ariel and Hannah.